Shadows
In the Desert

Brian W. Larson

True To His Word Publishing

Truckee, California

Unless otherwise noted, all Scripture is taken from the NEW AMERICAN STANDARD BIBLE®, Copyright © 1960, 1962, 1963, 1968, 1971, 1972, 1973, 1975, 1977, 1995 by the Lockman Foundation. Used by permission.

Scripture quotations marked "KJV" are taken from the Holy Bible, King James Version, Cambridge, 1769.

Shadows In the Desert
Christ's Tabernacle Blueprint for Living the Abundant Life

Copyright © 2004 by Brian W. Larson
First printing, 2004

Published by True To His Word, the teaching ministry of Brian Larson and Calvary Chapel of Truckee, P.O. Box 2691, Truckee, CA 96160.

The watercolors on pages 4 and 56 are by Barbera Hyytinen.

All line drawings are by Jodi Kuhnmuench, except the diagram on page 31, which is by Barbera Hyytinen.

ISBN 0-9761300-0-9
Printed in the United States of America

Table of Contents

Introduction 7

Chapter One—Getting To Sinai 13

Chapter Two—An Overview of the Tabernacle 23

Chapter Three—The Wall of Witness 33

Chapter Four—The Gate 49

Chapter Five—The Altar 57

Chapter Six —The Offerings of Non-Sweet Aroma 75

Chapter Seven—The Offerings of Sweet Aroma 91

Chapter Eight—The Priesthood of the Tabernacle 115

Chapter Nine—Consecration Into Service 139

Chapter Ten—The Laver 161

Chapter Eleven—The Tent of Meeting 177

Chapter Twelve—The Golden Lampstand 201

Chapter Thirteen—The Golden Table of the
Bread of the Presence 221

Chapter Fourteen—The Golden Altar of Incense 241

Chapter Fifteen—The Ark of the Covenant 257

Chapter Sixteen—The Day of Atonement 275

"Therefore let no one act as your judge in regard to food or drink or in respect to a festival or a new moon or a Sabbath day, things which are a mere shadow of what is to come; but the substance belongs to Christ."

Colossians 2:16-17

Introduction

Things which are a mere shadow of what is to come; but the substance belongs to Christ.

Colossians 2:17

Have you ever made a New Year's resolution to read completely through the Bible in one year, only to get bogged down by all the "boring" instructions from God to Moses about how he was to construct the tabernacle in the wilderness? If so, you are not alone! Many good intentions have been derailed in that section of the Old Testament that monopolizes the latter part of Exodus and all of Leviticus. Have you ever wondered what spiritual lessons for Christians today could *possibly* be extracted from the nearly endless and seemingly insignificant details recounted about that ancient two-room desert tent?

That question becomes even more compelling when you consider that the God of creation, the One who brought all things great and small, all things seen and unseen, into existence, only chose to write one book to reveal to us Himself and our relationship to Him. Compared to the billions upon billions of pages gathering dust on library shelves around the world, there truly are precious few pages in God's only literary creation. Even though the quantity of words may be few, as a thirty-year-plus teacher of the Bible, I've always proclaimed—and heartily believe—that they are enough to lead us into the abundant life Jesus promised. I believe that every word in God's Word is inspired by

God and is life to us.

Since that is the case, why, oh why, does God spend so much time and space telling us how many cubits wide and how many cubits tall each plank was to be in that tent built some 3,500 years ago? Does it really *matter* that each of those planks rested in sockets of silver? Why did God "waste" all that space in His book giving such excruciatingly minute details about the measurements, layout, and construction of that tent, not to mention instructions about the design and manufacturing of, and use for each piece of furniture in it? Believe it or not, there truly is a wealth of spiritual insight into the person of Jesus Christ contained in God's blueprint for that desert tent!

Because studying and teaching the Bible has been my life's passion and ministry for so long, I have heard every imaginable reaction to God's book. Occasionally I hear people say, "I can relate to the *loving* God of the New Testament, but I can't understand the *wrathful* God of the Old Testament"—as if they are two different Persons! The Old Testament is more than three times the size of the New Testament and it is clear that, for many, it is equally as mysterious. At first glance, all of those details about the measurements, layout, and construction of that wilderness tent only serve to deepen the mystery.

Yet in the New Testament, in Romans 15:4, the Apostle Paul says something very interesting about the Old Testament that should cause us to take another look at the tabernacle section:

> **For whatever was written in earlier times was written for our instruction, so that through perseverance and the encouragement of the Scriptures we might have hope.**

The things that happened to those people in the Old Testament—the instructions God gave to them and the things that were recorded—are actually more important to us today as believers in Christ than they were to the people to whom they happened, to whom the instructions were actually given. Because that is so, those measurements and instructions for the tabernacle actually are more meaningful to you today than they were to the goldsmith who had to pound out an elaborate golden menorah from one piece of gold to God's exacting specifications. The Israelite people went through everything they endured in the Old Testament, including the construction of and service in that tabernacle, for our benefit, for our instruction, and for our encouragement.

Paul said to Corinthian believers in 1 Corinthians 10:11:

> **Now these things happened to them as an example, and they were written for our instruction, upon whom the ends of the ages have come.**

Keep in mind that when the gospel first went out to the ends of the earth via the apostles, the only Scripture those men had to take with them to proclaim Christ was the Old Testament. There was no "New" Testament. The apostles couldn't quote Romans or Galatians, or 1 and 2 Corinthians, for example, until after Paul had written them. They used the Old Testament, exclusively, to proclaim and explain the gospel of Jesus Christ.

Likewise, you can find out a lot about your Lord and Savior, Jesus Christ, in the pages of the Old Testament—that part of the Bible that was written between 1,500 and 500 years before He was even born. In John 5:39, Jesus Himself said to the Pharisees (who intently studied the Old Testament):

> **"You search the Scriptures because you think that in them you have eternal life; it is these that testify about Me ..."**

To paraphrase that, Jesus was saying, "You are searching through that Old Testament because you think you will find eternal life. Guess what? It talks about *Me*."

Do you remember the incident described in Luke 24:13-32 when, on the day of Jesus' resurrection, He suddenly appeared next to a couple of disciples on the Emmaus road? Jesus did not allow them to recognize Him as they walked together and as He asked them all kinds of questions. They were amazed that this stranger did not know about the recent events in Jerusalem, so they started explaining to Jesus about His own life and death by crucifixion. They told Him that things had really gotten weird that very morning when a couple of ladies had come running from the tomb of this Jesus of Nazareth saying His body was gone and He had risen. Obviously, these men were perplexed about what had actually happened. After listening, Jesus gently admonished His clueless disciples in Luke 24:25-27:

> And He said to them, "O foolish men and slow of heart to believe in all that the prophets have spoken! Was it not necessary for the Christ to suffer these things and to enter into His glory?" Then beginning with Moses and with all the prophets, He explained to them the things concerning Himself in all the Scriptures.

Wouldn't you love to have been in on that Bible study?

Do you also remember the story of Philip and the Ethiopian eunuch described in Acts 8:26-39? The Ethiopian was traveling down the road in his chariot reading Isaiah 53, when the Holy Spirit spoke to Philip's heart and told him to go up to the eunuch's chariot. Philip obeyed, approached the chariot, and basically said, "I see you are reading the Word. Do you understand what you are reading?"

The eunuch replied with his own question, "How can I understand unless someone explains it to me?"

After Philip climbed into the chariot to help him understand, the eunuch asked whom Isaiah was talking about in that passage. Was Isaiah talking about himself or about someone else? In reply, starting with that 700-year-old Scripture, Philip shared the good news of Jesus Christ with the Ethiopian. A few miles down the road, that eunuch was baptized in the name of Jesus Christ because of what was written about Jesus in the pages of the Old Testament.

In John 5:46, Jesus said:

> "For if you believed Moses, you would believe Me, for he wrote about Me."

In the books of law, so revered by the Jews, Moses was actually writing about Jesus. I like the way one person put it, "In the Old Testament the New Testament is contained. In the New Testament, the Old Testament is explained."

The Holy Spirit is using all of these superficially mundane details about the tent tabernacle to paint a beautiful picture of Jesus Christ and our relationship with Him as believers. The tabernacle and the system of priesthood and sacrifices established there were only shadows of a greater reality, the reality of who Jesus is as Immanuel, God with us. Every facet of that tent in the wilderness, of each piece of furniture— and even how they were positioned—points to some facet of Jesus,

His relationship with individual believers and His church, and what it means to abide in Him. In this book, we will take a look at the tabernacle through New Testament eyes. What is God really explaining in these lengthy passages?

As you study the tabernacle in the pages ahead, you will see some of the most "boring" Scripture in the Bible come to life. I liken it to two men who stand looking at an ugly brown mountain that, by all outward appearance, seems to hold nothing of value. Only the one who climbs onto that mountain and digs beneath the surface will discover the extraordinary veins of pure gold that await discovery below. Likewise, you will not obtain the spiritual gold that lies covered in that tabernacle section of the Old Testament until you look beneath the surface. As you do, you will discover for yourself that Jesus is the One whom the Old Testament tabernacle is actually all about. My prayer is that, through this study, you will be rewarded by a richer, deeper look at the Person and ministry of your Lord and Savior Jesus Christ, and more fully enjoy the fruits of an intimate, loving relationship with Him in your own life.

Chapter One

Getting to Sinai

Our fathers ... were drinking from a spiritual rock which followed them; and the rock was Christ.

1 Corinthians 10:1, 4

Before getting into the particulars of the tabernacle, let's pause for a moment and look at the context in which God commanded Moses to build this wilderness tent. In approximately 1500 B.C., a series of events unfolded that Jews have always memorialized. Those events are recorded in Scripture. They are remembered in song. They have remembered those events in the celebration of Passover each year since the God of Israel miraculously delivered approximately 1.5 million people—His people—from slavery in Egypt. You know the story of the plagues, the Passover, the parting and crossing of the Red Sea, the miraculous provision of God to more than a million people during forty years of wilderness wanderings, the establishment of the law of God, and the building of that tabernacle in the desert. Each of those provides an incredible picture of our salvation that comes through Jesus Christ.

As we read those stories, like the ones about God's provision of manna and water in the desert, we might be tempted to think, "I wish God would give *us* manna and show us His power that way! Wouldn't it be great to just hit a rock and have water come gushing out of it?"

Do you know how our Father in Heaven would likely respond to that? He might say, "Why do you want that little picture? That is just a shadow of the real thing. You know what the *real* thing is? It is the water of life that is Jesus Christ. It is the bread of life that is Jesus Christ, and Jesus Himself is what you have. You have no need for manna or that water in the desert. Cheer up because you have the spiritual reality of it, which is Jesus. I was drawing a picture there, but you have the real thing."

It is as if somebody came along and drew you a picture of a shiny new car and asked, "Hey, isn't this cool?"

You reply, "Sure is! I want that picture."

Then your dad comes along and says, "Look, here are the keys. The car is now yours. You don't need the picture any longer because I have given you the real thing." Will you take the keys and drive that car home, or will you ignore it in favor of that two-dimensional picture?

The point is: when we read the Old Testament and we put it together with the New Testament, we see that Jesus Christ Himself is the answer and the "meet-er" of the greatest needs in life. He is the One to look to for everything. He is the reality of the picture that the entire Old Testament draws for us.

> **For I do not want you to be unaware, brethren, that our fathers were all under the cloud and all passed through the sea; and all were baptized into Moses in the cloud and in the sea; and all ate the same spiritual food; and all drank the same spiritual drink, for they were drinking from a spiritual rock which followed them; and the rock was Christ.**
> (1 Corinthians 10:1-4)

That was the heart of it. It was all about Jesus Christ. This detailed picture of Jesus becomes clearer to us as we look back on those events of the Old Testament.

Bondage and Deliverance

Exodus opens with the children of Israel in severe and bitter bondage to their Egyptian masters. Oh, how that is like the human spirit in bondage to sin, in bondage to the world, in bondage to Satan! As Jesus said in John 8:34-36:

> "Truly, truly, I say to you, everyone who commits sin is the slave of sin. The slave does not remain in the house forever; the son does remain forever. So if the Son makes you free, you will be free indeed."

Paul said of our spiritual bondage in Romans 7:14:

> For we know that the Law is spiritual, but I am of flesh, sold into bondage to sin.

In the case of the Hebrew slaves, it was God Himself who decided He was going to set these people free and separate them unto Himself as His people in a land chosen by Him. God is the one who decided when and how to make this deliverance. The descendants of Jacob did not vote on it. They were not even asked if they wanted to be set free. God unilaterally decided He was going to do this for them.

Do you realize that in the very same way, your salvation was decided long before you were ever on the scene? God Himself chose to set you free from sin.

> But we should always give thanks to God for you, brethren beloved by the Lord, because God has chosen you from the beginning for salvation through sanctification by the Spirit and faith in the truth. It was for this He called you through our gospel, that you may gain the glory of our Lord Jesus Christ. (2 Thessalonians 2:13-14)

> In this is love, not that we loved God, but that He loved us and sent His Son to be the propitiation for our sins. (1 John 4:10)

Plagues and Passover

We read of the plagues God inflicted on Egypt in Exodus 7:14 through Exodus 12:30. The first nine plagues simply point out the hardness of Pharaoh's heart and the utter impossibility of man to deliver himself. But it was that tenth plague that set the people free. On the night of Passover, the angel of death was going to pass over Egypt. God told Israel, through Moses, to take a lamb, slay it, have a Passover feast, and take the blood of that lamb and put it over the doorpost. Wherever the angel saw the blood, He passed over that household.

What is interesting about that whole scenario is that the Passover was not based on race. God was not saying, "I will be careful to pass over the Israelite homes and I will just slay the firstborn of Egypt." He said in Exodus 12:13, **"when I see the blood I will pass over you."** Their salvation was based on the shed blood—not race or color.

> **For Christ our Passover also has been sacrificed.** (1 Corinthians 5:7)

This first Passover was a picture of Christ sacrificed for us, even to the point of the blood on the lintel of the doorpost. They used the blood, as commanded by God, to make the form of a cross on either side of the door. This is not a coincidence. The connection is made as only God could make it: 1,500 years later Jesus Christ was crucified on the very day of the Passover celebration. When Jesus was crucified, the Lamb of God was sacrificed to set men free.

So our human condition and our salvation through Jesus Christ is all right there, pictured in Israel's bondage to Egypt, and in its deliverance through the Passover.

Salvation Confirmed at the Red Sea

The Israelites' salvation and freedom from bondage was confirmed at the Red Sea when those great waters covered the Egyptian army that was determined to force God's people to return to their old bondage. Once the Hebrews crossed the Red Sea, they would never again live in Egypt, which in the Bible is always a picture of the world. The Red Sea experience separated God's people from their past.

Likewise, our salvation is affirmed and confirmed in water baptism. However, our deliverance, our salvation, is accomplished when we are born again by the sovereign Spirit of God, simply through faith in Jesus Christ.

> **In Him, you also, after listening to the message of truth, the gospel of your salvation—having also believed, you were sealed in Him with the Holy Spirit of promise, who is given as a pledge of our inheritance, with a view to the redemption of God's own possession, to the praise of His glory.** (Ephesians 1:13-14)

Baptism is simply a God-given way to say "amen" to the salvation God Himself effected for each of us. As we are submerged beneath the water, we say goodbye to our old life. Emerging from those baptismal waters demonstrates that we have been raised to a new, abundant life with Christ.

> **Therefore if anyone is in Christ, he is a new creature; the old things passed away; behold, new things have come.** (2 Corinthians 5:17)

We are free. We have absolute confirmation of our salvation in Jesus Christ pictured in water baptism.

Manna and the Bread of Life

We read in Exodus 16 of how God provided manna for the Israelites in the wilderness. In Hebrew "manna" literally means, "What is it?" One morning the Israelites came out of their tents to find a never-before-seen white-frosty substance covering the ground. They walked around asking each other, "Manna? Manna? Manna?" So they called this mysterious food "manna," meaning "what is it?"

What is the New Testament reality of that Old Testament picture? The answer is found in John 6:32-35 where Jesus says:

> **"Truly, truly, I say to you, it is not Moses who has given you the bread out of heaven, but it is My Father who gives you the true bread out of heaven. For the bread of God is that which comes down out of heaven, and gives life to the world."** Then they said to Him, **"Lord, always give us this bread."** Jesus said to them, **"I am the bread of life; he who comes to Me will not hunger, and he who believes in Me will never thirst."**

The manna simply pictures the nourishment and life that come through abiding in Christ. That's the reality. Manna is the picture.

Desert Thirst and Our Living Water

In Exodus 17, we read that God miraculously provided His thirsty people with water from a rock in the middle of a barren desert.

Likewise, in John 4:14, Jesus told the Samaritan woman drawing water from a well:

> "... whoever drinks of the water that I will give him shall never thirst; but the water that I will give him will become in him a well of water springing up to eternal life."

In John 7:37-38, Jesus gets specific about what, or rather, Who that living water is:

> Now on the last day, the great day of the feast, Jesus stood and cried out, saying, "If anyone is thirsty, let him come to Me and drink. He who believes in Me, as the Scripture said, 'From his innermost being will flow rivers of living water.'"

When the Israelites were thirsty and needing water, God directed Moses to take a rock, told him to strike it, and water would come forth. So Moses gathered the people around, hit the rock and water gushed forth. They drank freely (Exodus 17:1-6).

This is just like Jesus Christ. He was smitten on the cross, once and for all, and forever, that we might drink of the water of life in a parched desert land, absolutely free. It is there for us. It does not matter how spiritually dry we are, or how dry the circumstances of our lives may be; if we have Jesus, we have the living water.

The rest of this story is contained in Numbers 20:1-12. Once again, a parched and thirsty Israelite camp complains to Moses. God so often created types and pictures in the Old Testament, and He painted a great one here. In essence, God told Moses, "This time just *speak* to the rock. You will not have to hit it. Just go up and say, 'Water, come forth,' and it will come."

But Moses was so furious with the people that he may have said something like, "What do I have to do, hit the rock again?" In his anger, Moses not only hit the rock instead of just speaking to it, he struck it twice! Even so, God was faithful to provide the water, but He was definitely upset with Moses' failure to follow His instructions. In effect, God said, "Moses, you blew My analogy! You blew My picture."

You see, Christ was crucified one time for you. He was struck once, bringing forth living water; now all you have to do is ask. He does not have to be crucified again for you, and you do not have to be flagellated to get Him. You just ask and He is yours. Moses blew it—he hit the rock again. He ruined God's picture. Realizing what the rock was a picture of, it may be a little easier to understand why God did not let Moses into the Promised Land because of this act of disobedience.

A Divine Conference

After crossing the Red Sea, the Israelites trekked in the wilderness for about three months before coming to the foot of Mt. Sinai, where they were to encamp for about a year. It was there that God chose to introduce Himself to His people. With the children of promise gathered before the foot of that great mountain, God Almighty, the Creator of the universe, manifested an aspect of His glory in their presence. Thunder rolled, lightning flashed, the earth quaked, and smoke covered the mountain as a loud trumpet blared (Exodus 19). That introduction was so overwhelming to God's people that they cried out to their leader, Moses, and asked him to act as their mediator with God, saying essentially, "Moses, *you* talk to Him! Then come back and tell us what He says."

Moses agreed and hiked up Mt. Sinai where he had a divine conference with God for forty days and forty nights. At the end of that time, he descended that mountain ready to share the two things God had given him. Let's take a look at the first of those two things: the Ten Commandments.

God's Law, The Proof We Need a Savior

The Ten Commandments are the perennial, generation-to-generation proof that each and every one of us needs a savior.

When I was a freshman in college, I took a philosophy class from a young professor named Dr. Howard. I will never forget Dr. Howard. He stood up on the first day of class in front of about twenty-five eighteen-year-olds and said, "I feel it is my duty to divest you of any archaic faith you may have in some God so you can be free thinkers."

By the second day there were only eleven people left in the class, and I was one of them. You would think I would have gotten a clue on that one, but I didn't. I stayed—the only believer in a class filled with "free thinkers."

One day I walked into Dr. Howard's class to find that he had written the Ten Commandments on the chalkboard. He announced to the class,

"I want to show you just how stupid this God of the Bible is. Here are the Ten Commandments. Man has never, ever been able to keep any of those commandments. He has failed miserably at all of them. Now, I ask you, what kind of a God would give us commandments that not one of us can keep? It is just ludicrous. It is stupid."

I sat there amazed, thinking, "Man, did he open himself up!" I raised my hand.

Surprised, Dr. Howard asked, "Oh, have you got an answer for us, Mr. Larson?"

I said, "I believe so, Dr. Howard. That's the whole point of the commandments—to show us that we need a savior. Those are good commandments, but we can't keep them—that's the whole reason for Jesus."

The professor stood there with his jaw dropped open and nothing to say. He hated me after that. I remember my grade to this day. We were graded on only two things in that class, the midterm and the final exam. He gave me a B+ for my midterm, taken before this incident. I know I did better on my final; however, I got a D for my semester grade. I want you to know I embraced that D with pride!

Fact is, Dr. Howard was right, in one sense. No one, aside from Jesus that is, has ever been able to keep those ten simple little commandments. But he missed the whole point: consequently, we need a savior.

It is interesting that as Moses was receiving the Ten Commandments, as he was undoubtedly excited about sharing them, the children of Israel were down in the valley already breaking the first two, worshipping the golden calf (Exodus 32).

The Tabernacle, God with Us

Most folks are aware of the fact that Moses came down that mountain holding the stone tablets inscribed with the Ten Commandments by God's own finger. But many Christians are not as familiar with the second thing Moses brought back from his forty-day conference with God. As Chuck Missler has said, "Moses had the stone tablets of the Ten Commandments under one arm, but under his other arm he carried a set of building plans." It was there upon Mt. Sinai that Moses was given instructions from God for the building of the tabernacle. In fact, the largest part of those forty days was probably spent receiving instructions for the building of this tent tabernacle. When Moses hiked back down the mountain, it was time to build the tabernacle that God Himself designed.

> Then the LORD spoke to Moses, saying, "Tell the sons of Israel to raise a contribution for Me; from every man whose heart moves him you shall raise My contribution. This is the contribution which you are to raise from them: gold, silver and bronze, blue, purple and scarlet material, fine linen, goat hair, rams' skins dyed red, porpoise skins, acacia wood, oil for lighting, spices for the anointing oil and for the fragrant incense, onyx stones and setting stones for the ephod and for the breastpiece. Let them construct a sanctuary for Me, that I may dwell among them. According to all that I am going to show you, as the pattern of the tabernacle and the pattern of all its furniture, just so you shall construct it." (Exodus 25:1-9)

In effect God was saying, "Moses, I want you to take a contribution of certain materials from the people and I am going to tell you exactly what I want constructed. I want you to build it *exactly* like I tell you to build it. I do not want any deviation. I do not offer any leniency here for even a few creative juices to flow in your mind about how you might like to do it. You do *exactly* what I say. You build this to My specifications." In the last sixteen chapters of Exodus and throughout the entire book of Leviticus this tabernacle is described and explained.

It is in that context that we come to the Scripture on the tabernacle. God said, in effect, "I am going to dwell amongst My people. I have chosen these people. They are My people and I want to dwell in their midst" (Exodus 29:45-46).

Obviously, God does not need a tent in which to live. He is saying something else with that tabernacle. It is an object lesson about man's relationship with his God. God desires to dwell with His people. Who is Jesus? He is "Immanuel," which means "God with us" (Isaiah 7:14). The tabernacle is an awesome picture of Christ. It is an incredible thing that God desires to be with us because of His love for us. His is not a selfish love. Our fellowship with Him is a blessing to us, just as it is to Him. As we begin to study the tabernacle of the Lord, we will see more clearly the love He has for us.

Not only will we study the historical aspects of the tabernacle, but we will find many interesting and relevant points which apply directly to our lives. We will discover that in the design and structure of the tabernacle, the materials used, the numbers and colors, and the priests and their duties, God has drawn an incredible prophetic picture of our relationship with Jesus Christ.

Please know that this study will simply scratch the surface of what is in the Bible for you on this topic. There is a great deal of information which will not be covered. Even so, this study should give you some clues about what the Lord may have for you as you prayerfully consider what He has given you in these tabernacle pictures: they are "Shadows [of Christ] in the Desert."

Chapter Two

An Overview of the Tabernacle

Do you not know that you are a temple of God and that the Spirit of God dwells in you?

1 Corinthians 3:16

Providing for the Building of the Tabernacle

When Moses walked down Mt. Sinai with the Ten Commandments, he may have been leaning dramatically to one side. As we've said, under one arm he carried the tablets containing the Ten Commandments. Under the other arm must have been God's building plans for the tabernacle, which were probably much bulkier than the tablets of law. The tabernacle instructions certainly take up a lot more space in your Bible than do the Ten Commandments.

Have you ever wondered how the Israelites were able to construct and furnish this impressive, yet portable structure? They had been slaves after all, and slaves who left Egypt quickly once the way was made. Exodus chapter 25 describes the process of preparing to construct the tabernacle. Read verses 1 and 2:

> Then the LORD spoke to Moses, saying, "Tell the sons of Israel to raise a contribution for Me; from every man whose heart moves him you shall raise My contribution."

I love that! Notice that God called for this contribution from "every man whose heart moves him." There were no forced donations, no pressure at all to give. It was not a matter of "you will give so much of what you have for this contribution." It was purely voluntary. As each heart was touched, so he gave. Exodus 25:3-9 says:

> "This is the contribution which you are to raise from them: gold, silver and bronze, blue, purple and scarlet material, fine linen, goat hair, rams' skins dyed red, porpoise skins, acacia wood, oil for lighting, spices for the anointing oil and for the fragrant incense, onyx stones and setting stones for the ephod and for the breastpiece. Let them construct a sanctuary for Me, that I may dwell among them. According to all that I am going to show you, as the pattern of the tabernacle and the pattern of all its furniture, just so you shall construct it."

So where in the world did these former slaves come up with all the gold, silver, bronze, and other precious stones, and the blue, purple, and scarlet material for the construction of the tabernacle? Just before they left Egypt, God had provided that for them. In Exodus 3:21-22 we read:

> "And I will grant this people favor in the sight of the Egyptians; and it shall be that when you go, you will not go empty-handed. But every woman shall ask of her neighbor and the woman who lives in her house, articles of silver and articles of gold, and clothing; and you will put them on your sons and daughters. Thus you will plunder the Egyptians."

And so it was.

Now the sons of Israel had done according to the word of Moses, for they had requested from the Egyptians articles of silver and articles of gold, and clothing; and the LORD had given the people favor in the sight of the Egyptians, so that they let them have their request. Thus they plundered the Egyptians (Exodus 12:35-36).

God never asks anything of His children that He doesn't also provide the means to do it. "Where God guides, God provides." God had seen to it that the Israelites were given the materials for the construction of the tabernacle, but even then, God only asked in return what was in their own hearts to give for His work.

We can see two wonderful spiritual principles in operation right here. First of all, our Heavenly Father will faithfully provide whatever is necessary for us to do that which He calls us to do. All we have to do is be willing. Secondly, our part is always of our own free will. He doesn't demand our giving and serving, He simply gives us the opportunity. The choice is always ours.

> **For God loves a cheerful giver.** (2 Corinthians 9:7)

The Israelites were simply offered the opportunity to contribute to, and be a part of, this work of God's.

> **And everyone whose heart stirred him and everyone whose spirit moved him came and brought the LORD's contribution for the work of the tent of meeting and for all its service and for the holy garments.** (Exodus 35:21)

Just Follow the Instructions!

If you have read Exodus chapters 25 through 40, you realize that God was very specific about wanting every detail of His instructions regarding the tabernacle to be followed precisely. The details are really incredible. For the Israelites, it was an exercise in humble, simple, blind obedience to the God who had delivered them from Egypt. They had no idea what this meant or why they were doing it. They just knew that God said, "Do it this way and do it exactly this way." It was simply their job to do it, and to do it His way.

We, as Christians, can often get a little irked when God comes along and says, "Do this for Me," if we do not get a satisfactory explanation of why He wants it done. With a complete Bible in our hands and the Holy Spirit living within us, we are told much more about the "whys" in our lives than these people ever were, yet they went to incredible effort to build this tabernacle just the way God said. They obeyed without having a clue as to why they were doing it. The result was that God blessed them with the presence of His Shekinah glory hovering over the ark of the covenant in the "Holy of Holies" of the tabernacle.

So when the Lord says, "Here is what I am doing in your life," quit asking why and just trust Him. There is precedence in God's Word for saying, "Yes, Lord," and simply trusting Him that some day the reason will be unveiled, and meanwhile you will be blessed with His presence.

Why this minute detail regarding the tabernacle? Look at what the writer of Hebrews says in chapter 8, verses 1-2, and 5, regarding the tabernacle:

> Now the main point in what has been said is this: we have such a high priest, who has taken His seat at the right hand of the throne of the Majesty in the heavens, a minister in the sanctuary and in the true tabernacle, which the Lord pitched, not man. ... who serve a copy and shadow of the heavenly things, just as Moses was warned by God when he was about to erect the tabernacle; for, "See," He says, "that you make all things according to the pattern which was shown you on the mountain."

One reason for this attention to detail is that the tabernacle was a pattern or a picture of the very throne room of God Himself. It is, in design, a shadow of God's throne room in heaven.

But, as we are going to see, and as the writer of Hebrews points out so vividly, it is also a detailed picture of what it means to be a Christian, and to come to God and enter into fellowship with Him through faith in Jesus Christ. Every little detail lends itself to that picture. What we have in the tabernacle is a picture of Jesus Christ and Him crucified 1,500 years before the event took place.

This tabernacle gives us a richer and fuller understanding of what Christ accomplished for us at the cross and what a privilege we have as believer-priests (1 Peter 2:9), to be daily living in fellowship with the Living God.

Strategic Positioning

This tabernacle sat in the center of the Israelite wilderness camp. The camp was divided with the various tribes on each side of the tabernacle. The huge tribe of Judah, the biggest tribe, faced the door on the east. The smallest tribe was on the opposite side, to the west. The tribes on the north and the south of the tabernacle were nearly equal in size. Consequently, the camp itself formed a giant cross with the tabernacle at the center.

> **Let them construct a sanctuary for Me, that I may dwell among them.** (Exodus 25:8)

God was stating His desire to dwell in fellowship with His people. Here, we see through the tabernacle the way given by God of spiritual restoration to Him. It is the way to live in fellowship with our Creator and Redeemer God. The New Testament tells us these things were actually for our benefit.

> For whatever was written in earlier times was written for our instruction, so that through perseverance and the encouragement of the Scriptures we might have hope. (Romans 15:4)

Tent of Testimony

In Numbers 17:7, Moses calls the tabernacle **"the tent of the testimony."** To Israel, this tent was the center of the camp. The God of Israel was to be the center of Israeli life. God was to be the very hub of family, social, and national life.

This tabernacle was a "testimony" of four things to His people:

1. The tabernacle served as a testimony that God was in the midst of His people.

> He erected the court all around the tabernacle and the altar, and hung up the veil for the gateway of the court. Thus Moses finished the work. Then the cloud covered the tent of meeting, and the glory of the LORD filled the tabernacle. (Exodus 40:33-34)

> For throughout all their journeys, the cloud of the LORD was on the tabernacle by day, and there was fire in it by night, in the sight of all the house of Israel. (Exodus 40: 38)

It was an outward witness that God was in the midst of His people. They could look and see that God was with them. Jesus makes the same guarantee to every believer today. In Matthew 28:20, after His resurrection, Jesus said to His disciples before ascending to heaven:

> "... lo, I am with you always, even to the end of the age."

That means that every single day of your life as a believer, He will not leave you or forsake you (Hebrews 13:5).

2. The tabernacle was a testimony to His purity.

Everything about it conveyed holiness. The altar of sacrifice, the laver, the tent, the unapproachable Holy of Holies, the high priestly garments, and the turban that had the letters which read "Holiness to the Lord,"—all these things conveyed separation, holiness. In the midst of the people, it conveyed separation; the tent was situated in the middle of camp, but was truly separate from it. In it was the Holy Place, the veil, and the Holy of Holies. Jesus Christ is our great High Priest who brings you to Him who is holy.

Our God is a holy God to be reverently feared.

> **The fear of the LORD is the beginning of knowledge…** (Proverbs 1:7a)
>
> **The fear of the LORD is a fountain of life …** (Proverbs 14:27a)
>
> **You shall be holy, for I am holy …** (1 Peter 1:16)

3. The tabernacle is a testimony of the protection of the Lord.

> **"How often I wanted to gather your children together, the way a hen gathers her chicks under her wings, and you were unwilling."** (Jesus in Matthew 23:37b)
>
> **How precious is Your lovingkindness, O God! And the children of men take refuge in the shadow of Your wings.** (Psalm 36:7)

In Exodus 13:21-22 we see that big cloud in the camp hovering overhead by day, and a pillar of fire by night, leading and protecting. The Lord protected them. They were protected at the Red Sea (Exodus 14). There were God's chosen people, at a stand still, with the Red Sea on one side, and Pharaoh and his Egyptian army screaming after them on the opposite side. They accused Moses of bringing them out there to die. If they were going to die, they told him they would rather have died in Egypt. The cloud that was leading them moved around behind them and all night long it gave them fire on their side to give them light so they could see God parting the Red Sea. That must have been the most incredible sight ever. On the Egyptian side, all they could see was a thick black cloud which they could not penetrate. And thus Israel went across the Red Sea on dry ground, protected by God.

It is interesting that some theologians think they have that all figured out. I am sure you have heard this theory. It was supposedly low tide and they just walked through a shallow part of the Red Sea, known as the "Sea of Reeds." Well, if that were the case, that is an even bigger miracle because it means that the entire Egyptian army drowned in a foot of water!

> Behold, He who keeps Israel
> Will neither slumber nor sleep.
> The LORD is your keeper;
> The LORD is your shade on your right hand.
> The sun will not smite you by day,
> Nor the moon by night.
> The LORD will protect you from all evil;
> He will keep your soul.
> The LORD will guard your going out and your coming in
> From this time forth and forever. (Psalm 121:4-8)

Picture yourself in that camp, with that tabernacle in the center, with a cloud by day and a pillar of fire by night. What a testimony of God's protection for His people!

4. The tabernacle was a testimony of His provision.

They saw God provide in awesome ways. He gave them water from a rock. He gave them manna. He gave them meat. He provided for them in battles. The tabernacle was also a picture of God's spiritual provision for His people. He covered every need. By His power He provided for all their physical needs and through the tabernacle He made provision for their every spiritual need so that they might be complete in Him.

> **Do you not know that you are a temple of God and that the Spirit of God dwells in you?** (1 Corinthians 3:16)

What they had in that wilderness tabernacle, we have in its spiritual fullness in our relationship with Jesus Christ. He has redeemed you that He might dwell in the tabernacle of your heart. By invitation He has come (or will come, if you ask Him) into your life. Christ has come to you to dwell in your very being. He is in your midst. He is pure. He protects you. He provides for your every need. What God reveals about Himself through that tent tabernacle, and our coming into and living in a meaningful relationship with Him, Jesus lives out the reality of it in your heart. Not only are we enriched by a picture of Christ our Lord in the details of the tabernacle, but we are invited to partake in the spiritual reality of that which He describes in those Old Testament pages. So let's drink deeply of this water of life.

A Preview of Coming Attractions

This study will approach the tabernacle in the same manner and order as would a person from the outside. In other words, we will walk from the camp up to the tabernacle and examine the tabernacle as a common person coming out of the Israelite camp. Or, in the picture that God is drawing for us, as a natural man, coming to Christ, and how that happens.

If you were to walk around the outside of the tabernacle site, you would see only the exterior linen curtain that would bring you to the only gate, the only entrance, into the tabernacle. There was one gate to the tabernacle, just one. There were no back entrances. There was no other way to get into that structure other than through that one gate. Does that sound familiar? Here's how Jesus put it in John 10:1 and 9:

> "Truly, truly, I say to you, he who does not enter by the door into the fold of the sheep, but climbs up some other way, he is a thief and a robber. ... I am the door; if anyone enters through Me, he will be saved, and will go in and out and find pasture."

Jesus said He is the door and, not coincidentally, there was only one door into that tabernacle. That one gate, and the screen in front of the gate, was held up by four pillars. How many gospels are there in your Bible that tell us about Jesus? There are, of course, four. The screen which was in front of the gate had four colors. When we get into the study of these four colors, we will see that each one tells us something significant about our Lord Jesus Christ.

Just through the gate, in the courtyard outside the tent itself, was the largest piece of furniture in that whole tabernacle: the giant bronze altar, sitting right there at ground level. Everything that happened at that altar was a prophetic picture of Calvary.

An Overview of the Tabernacle — 31

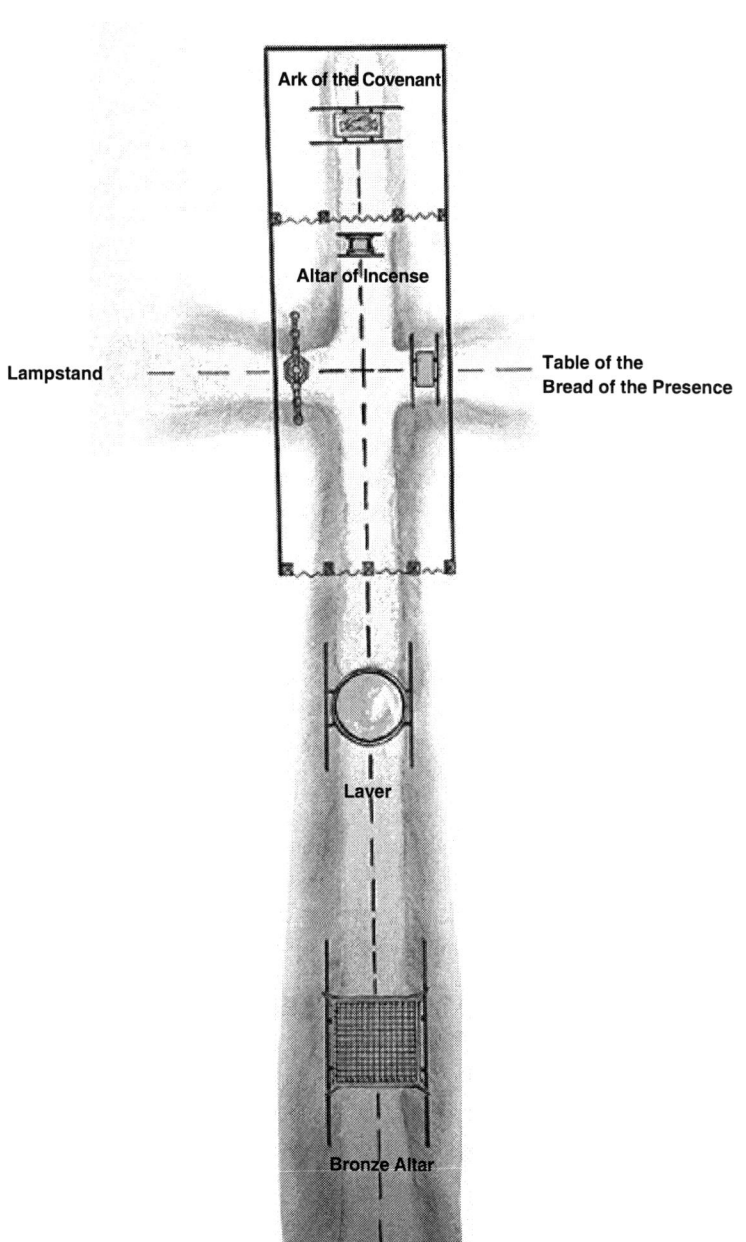

Five different sacrifices were made at that brass altar in the tabernacle. Two sacrifices were referred to as the sacrifices of non-sweet aroma. There were also three sacrifices of sweet aroma. If you could have been there in person and smelled those sacrifices while they burned, you would not have been able to smell much difference between them. But God knew the difference. There were five sacrifices and each one is very significant to us, portraying a different aspect of the one all-encompassing sacrifice of Jesus Christ for our sins.

If you were to diagram the furniture in the tabernacle, a startling truth becomes evident. Just inside the entrance was the bronze altar. Behind that was the bronze laver (the washing basin for the priests). The next item in the courtyard was the tent. Inside the tent, on the left side, was the golden lampstand. On the right side was the golden table of the bread of the Presence. In the center, in front of the veil was the golden altar of incense. Behind the veil was the Holy of Holies where the ark of the covenant was kept. These six pieces of furniture in the tabernacle were literally laid out in the shape of a cross. As a person walked through the gate and stood before the bronze altar of sacrifice, he would literally be standing, as it were, at the foot of the cross.

From that place before the bronze altar, in God's tabernacle picture to New Testament believers, begins the adventure of entering into the fullness of relationship and fellowship with the Living God of all creation, who is our Heavenly Father. Everything in the tabernacle, its furnishings, the materials and metals, where they are laid out and the way they are situated, and how they are used, the priests and their attire and duties, all together draw an amazing picture for everyday Christians of how we have available to us, and can enter into, an intimate relationship and abiding fellowship with our God through our Lord Jesus Christ. It's all there, in a glorious, detailed picture, drawn by the Holy Spirit in the pages of the Old Testament for our benefit, **"upon whom the end of the ages has come"** (1 Corinthians 10:11).

With that in mind, the man or woman in the camp would first see the linen wall that surrounded the courtyard and the tent of the tabernacle. That would be the essence of their daily view of the tabernacle until they would decide to go in through the gate themselves. What does that wall tell us of the witness of Jesus Christ to the world?

Chapter Three

The Wall of Witness

It was given to her to clothe herself in fine linen, bright and clean; for the fine linen is the righteous acts of the saints.

If you were to visit the tabernacle during the time of Moses, the first thing you would come to is that high curtained wall that surrounded the tabernacle and enclosed its courtyard. In Exodus 27:9-15 and 17-18 we read what God said about that wall around the court.

> "You shall make the court of the tabernacle. On the south side there shall be hangings for the court of fine twisted linen one hundred cubits long for one side; and its pillars shall be twenty, with their twenty sockets of bronze; the hooks of the pillars and their bands shall be of silver. Likewise for the north side in length there shall be hangings one hundred cubits long, and its twenty pillars with their twenty sockets of bronze; the hooks of the pillars and their bands shall be of silver. For the width of the court on the west side shall be hangings of fifty cubits with their ten pillars and their ten sockets. The width of the court on the east side shall be fifty cubits. The hangings for the one side of the gate shall be fifteen cubits with their three pillars and their three sockets. And for the other side shall be hangings of fifteen cubits with their three pillars and their three sockets. ... All the pillars around the court shall be furnished with silver bands with their hooks

> of silver and their sockets of bronze. The length of the court shall be one hundred cubits, and the width fifty throughout, and the height five cubits of fine twisted linen, and their sockets of bronze."

What is described here is basically a large wall that was made of fine white twisted linen. To put it in terms that a modern architect can understand, the wall was 7.5 feet high, 150 feet long, and 75 feet wide. To put it in terms that *I* can understand, the wall encompassed a long and narrow area that today would cover about one-fourth of a football field, approximately from the goal line to the 50-yard line, from the side-line to mid-field.

The poles that held the wall up were made of acacia wood and sat in big bronze sockets. The poles were dropped into the sockets so they would stand upright. Silver bands were wrapped around the poles with silver hooks that pulled the linen cloth taut around the tabernacle.

The wall itself formed an outward picture, in a small way, of what the inside of the tabernacle was really all about. It's significant that the wall would have been all one could see from the outside. It was high enough that one could not look over and see inside. To really know what was happening on the other side of that linen wall, a person would have to go through the one and only gate.

The Spiritual Meaning of the Wall

One of the interesting things about the study of the Old Testament is that materials often symbolize something spiritual. The materials of this linen wall and what they represent to us create a picture, in this case, of how a Christian is a witness of Jesus Christ to the world. This wall was all that those in the camp would see of the tabernacle; likewise believers today are the only visible representation of the reality of Jesus Christ—we are all they see. Thus, the tabernacle wall provides a picture of a believer's witness to an unbelieving world.

First of all, just as the tabernacle was situated in the very center of the camp, so believers are in the midst of the world. We are not *of* the world, nor should we be; but we are *in* the world. That is exactly how the tabernacle related to its surroundings—it was in the midst of the camp, but it definitely was not of the camp. It was completely separate. The tabernacle belonged to God. It was God's abode.

Likewise, as believers, we have been purchased by the blood of Jesus Christ, and so we belong to God. Indwelt by the Holy Spirit, the believer himself is God's dwelling place, one that is surrounded by the world and non-believers.

> **Or do you not know that your body is a temple of the Holy Spirit who is in you, whom you have from God, and that you are not your own? For you have been bought with a price: therefore glorify God in your body.**
> (1 Corinthians 6:19-20)

In the Old Testament, the tabernacle was the place God designed for His dwelling place among His people. By Solomon's time, the Israelites had built a stone temple that represented exactly the same thing as the tent tabernacle; it was built with the same concepts in mind. It was simply a stone version of the wilderness tabernacle.

As a believer, your body is the tabernacle of the Holy Spirit who is in you, whom you have from God. You are a flesh and blood tabernacle of the Living God, surrounded by an unbelieving world. You do not belong to yourself. You, believer, belong to God.

So what exactly *is* our testimony to people who are of the world? Our testimony is of Jesus Christ. We are not here to promote ourselves, to represent ourselves, or to put ourselves forward. We are here to reflect Jesus Christ. That is our goal and our job. We are to reflect Him, just as the wall of the tabernacle reflected and represented what the tabernacle inside was all about.

Wooden Poles of Humanity

The tabernacle wall was held up by wooden poles. Wood in the Old Testament symbolizes humanity. Do you know what is exciting about the wood that was used? It was the old desert acacia wood, which is a weathered, gnarled, tough, scrub wood. What a picture of humanity, and an encouragement to us! God chose to use old desert scrub wood for His tabernacle, just as He uses these frail earthen vessels of flesh as the dwelling place of His Spirit today.

The poles of wood supported the fine white linen. Both the linen and the color white symbolize the righteousness and the purity of God. Jesus Christ is the very manifestation of the righteousness and purity of God.

> But now apart from the Law the righteousness of God has been manifested, being witnessed by the Law and the Prophets, even the righteousness of God through faith in Jesus Christ for all those who believe; for there is no distinction ... (Romans 3:21-22)
>
> And the Word became flesh, and dwelt among us, and we beheld His glory, glory as of the only begotten from the Father, full of grace and truth. (John 1:14)

Bronze in the Old Testament always symbolizes judgment. Notice the sockets were made of bronze and sat right down on the earth. The purpose of Jesus Christ being on the earth was to endure the judgment of sin upon Himself, to bear the judgment of sin.

> "... the Son of Man did not come to be served, but to serve, and to give His life a ransom for many." (Jesus in Matthew 20:28)

> But He was pierced through for our transgressions,
> He was crushed for our iniquities;
> The chastening for our well-being fell upon Him,
> And by His scourging we are healed.
> All of us like sheep have gone astray,
> Each of us has turned to his own way;
> But the LORD has caused the iniquity of us all
> To fall on Him. (Isaiah 53:5-6)

The reason Jesus came to earth was to bear the judgment for the sin of the world upon Himself. The Man who was the very purity of God bore the sin of the world. That is why He walked this planet.

Silver Bands and Hooks of Redemption

The more you study the Old Testament and look for the materials used in the tabernacle in other parts of Scripture, the more fully you will realize what God is saying to us through the materials He chose to build His tabernacle. If you take the time to study this symbolism, the Old Testament becomes even more exciting to read.

Notice that the bands on the poles and the hooks which attached the linen to the poles were made of silver. The Old Testament consistently uses silver as a symbol of redemption. Every male adult in that Israeli camp in the wilderness was required to give a half-shekel to the treasury for his own redemption. God had redeemed them from Egyptian slavery. This was the price each was to pay to the tabernacle for his redemption, his freedom. Every male gave his half-shekel, regardless of how poor or how rich he was. That was the non-negotiable price of redemption.

That shekel, that redemption money, was given in silver—it was a silver shekel. The redemption money gathered was actually used in the tabernacle. It's good to note that the redemption money wasn't used to go to the nearest Home Depot or silversmith shop to purchase some standard-brand silver bands and hooks. That redemption money was melted down and fashioned into the very bands and hooks that were used. Those silver bands and those silver hooks were a continual reminder to the people of Israel of their redemption by God. He redeemed them from slavery to life, with Him now dwelling in their midst.

To us, that wall, held together by those silver hooks and bands, represents the witness of the believer to the outside world. Notice, then, that our witness of Christ is held forth by that work of redemption. Just as God delivered the Israelites from Egypt, he redeemed us from death and destruction. We deserve to be judged by God; instead, He has redeemed us to Himself, that we might live in His presence, and point others to Him. So the silver of the tabernacle paints a picture of redemption.

A Reflection of Jesus

What we see in those pillars and in that curtain is an awesome picture of Jesus Christ. He became a man (that old acacia wood pole). He exhibited the very righteousness of God (that white fine linen cloth), and He came to earth to take the judgment and the penalty for our unrighteousness upon Himself (those old bronze sockets). Consequently, He offers redemption of our souls and the righteousness of God as a free gift (silver). Jesus was pictured there in the wall of the tabernacle.

So what is our job? It is to reflect Him. The truth of the Bible is to be manifested through the believer. That is how God has ordained us to be manifested to the world. Jesus told His disciples in Acts 1:8:

> **"... but you will receive power when the Holy Spirit has**

> come upon you; and you shall be My witnesses both in Jerusalem, and in all Judea and Samaria, and even to the remotest part of the earth."

What does that mean? It means, you, as a believer, *will* witness and testify of Jesus. You will represent Him. You will be an ambassador of Jesus Christ in Jerusalem, Judea, Samaria, and to the uttermost ends of the earth. In other words, *wherever* you go, you will be a witness of Jesus Christ.

As you read on in Acts, that is exactly what you find. The church was so human. They were just like those acacia wood poles. After Jesus' resurrection, His followers wanted to cluster together. The early church enjoyed such rich fellowship. Indeed, the church in Jerusalem was where it was happening: Peter was there, James was there, John was there. Saul of Tarsus came to visit for awhile. Jerusalem was the place to be—that is, until persecution broke out. Some of the disciples, the believers, were freaked by the persecution. They had to get out of town, and they had to get out of town right then!

I have a hunch that God allowed that because He wanted these people to go to the uttermost ends of the earth instead of just cocooning there in Jerusalem. He allowed the persecution as an "encouragement" to spread out. They did, too, fleeing to the uttermost parts of the earth.

But what happened when they fled? Everywhere they went, they could not keep their mouths shut about Jesus. The result was that believers started popping up in Judea, even in—can you believe it?—Samaria! That must have really rattled some Jewish believers' cages. They probably chose Samaria as a hiding place because they thought it would be the only place nearby that would be safe, because no good Jew would go there. Instead of just hiding, though, the gospel started breaking out in Samaria. Then Paul and Barnabus and others started spreading out around the empire, causing the gospel to take root in the furthest parts of the earth, just as Jesus said would happen.

"You will be my witnesses," Jesus said. That is not so much a "great commission" as it is the great byproduct of a life that is more ruled by, and overflowing with, the love of God than it is by the fear of men.

As we look at the outside of this wall, consider that we, as believers, are the only Bible that some people are ever going to read. The closest some people will ever get to understanding what the Bible is all about is what they see reflected in us about the truth of Jesus Christ. In the same way, that tabernacle wall was probably the only part of the tabernacle some people ever saw.

How Can a Wall Witness?

You may be picturing that tabernacle wall in your mind, and still be wondering how that pictures a modern-day believer's witness to an unbelieving world. First, look again at those old wooden poles which represent our humanity. God could not have picked a better wood than that common acacia wood to describe us. But, praise the Lord, we, as believers, have been clothed in the righteousness of Jesus Christ, symbolized by the white linen of the wall. It is His righteousness, not ours, that makes us witnesses for Jesus.

The Linen of Righteousness

If that wall were to reflect our own righteousness, it would not be 7.5 feet high; it would probably reach no more than a couple of inches off the ground. The linen of our own righteousness would be tattered, soiled, broken in places, and probably lying on the ground where people could walk all over it. Thankfully, it is the righteousness of Jesus that we show forth, not our own.

> **He made Him who knew no sin to be sin on our behalf, so that we might become the righteousness of God in Him.** (2 Corinthians 5:21)

You see, when Jesus Christ died on the cross for you, He took your sin from you. He took all of it, and He exchanged it for the righteousness of God. It was as though He said, "Give me your sin, so I can give you My righteousness." That was a trade effected in the spiritual realm, in heaven, and you are simply the recipient of it. So, whether you believe it or not, you, as a believer, are robed in the righteousness of Jesus Christ, by the work and declaration of a Living God, and not by your manner or your lifestyle. It is in Jesus that you stand justified before God.

There is a wonderful example of this in the New Testament that illustrates this concept. Remember that this wall was made of fine white twisted linen as you consider what John saw in heaven as he witnessed the marriage feast of the lamb (described for us in Revelation 19).

As background, the marriage feast of the Lamb will occur when born-again Christians are in heaven before God, just before Christ comes back to Planet Earth with all believers accompanying Him. As soon as the rapture takes place, we will be in heaven, and the great marriage feast will proceed. Today, here on earth, we are betrothed to Christ. On that future day in heaven, the bride of Christ, the church, will be married to Him, and made one with Him in a very eternal, physical, and spiritual way.

Look at how John sees that marriage feast, talking about Jesus' bride, the church:

> **It was given to her to clothe herself in fine linen, bright and clean; for the fine linen is the righteous acts of the saints.** (Revelation 19:8)

So there is the church, clothed in the very thing in which the tabernacle was clothed. Linen is the clothing of the bride of Christ.

The righteous acts of the saints are those things that you have done or said which were anointed, directed, and guided by the power of the Holy Spirit, many of which you did not even know were happening. As you wander around like a little sheep, God could very well be working His works. There may have been a time when you had just fought with your spouse, kicked the dog on the way out the door, then walked outside and actually said something kind to your neighbor that touched his heart. Maybe he went on to know Jesus on his own. Meanwhile, you drive your car away, huffing and puffing all the way to work. That kind word could have been a righteous act that took place by His Spirit, without you even being aware of it. That turned out to be a manifestation of "the righteousness of Christ" to the world.

Do you think that God can only use you as you consciously permit? No! He will use you by His grace—and often despite yourself.

> **If we are faithless, He remains faithful, for He cannot deny Himself.** (2 Timothy 2:13)

Obviously we become a lot more usable when we are bowed before Him, totally surrendered. Nonetheless, that is how the white linen cloth reflects the reality of Jesus Christ.

I like the admonition Paul gave the Christians who were in Philippi:

> ... **work out your salvation with fear and trembling; for it is God who is at work in you, both to will and to work for His good pleasure.** (Philippians 2:12b & 13)

It does not say work *for* your salvation. It has been given to you, it is there. It is in your heart, in your life, and in your spirit, in all its glory. Work it out, live it out with fear and trembling.

The Christian life can be so exciting, because you can just lay your life down and say, "Go for it, Lord." It is not your job to determine what God is supposed to do with it. Your only job is to lay that life down, to lay down that will of yours, and say, "Here it is, Lord. However You want to use my life, it's Yours. Go for it." Let Him be sovereign. Let Him guide you in power. Let Him direct you. When we look at that wall, we see wooden poles robed in white linen, manifesting the reality of Jesus Christ in righteousness, His righteous acts through us.

The Silver of Redemption

The silver hooks and the bands held the curtain in its place. That curtain would not stay up without those silver hooks and silver bands. Being robed in His righteousness is not because of, or based upon our good works. But it is because of, and based upon, His redemptive work on the cross. Jesus cried out, "It is finished!" on the cross, and that is what holds the curtain up on those old wooden poles.

> **He saved us, not on the basis of deeds which we have done in righteousness, but according to His mercy, by the washing of regeneration and renewing by the Holy Spirit ...** (Titus 3:5)

Our place, our standing in that wall, and that curtain which is held up as a witness to the world, is held in place by His redemption of us, by His work on the cross. Those bands securely bound around that pole tell us that by His redemption, we have been securely bound in our salvation. Jesus is keeping those bands around that pole, and those hooks hold up my righteous standing before God. My righteous standing before God is held in place by those silver hooks, representing the redemption Christ won on the cross.

You can stand before God, if you know Jesus Christ as your Savior. You stand before Him, robed in His righteousness—not because you have been a "goody-two-shoes" today—but because Jesus accomplished your salvation on the cross, once and for all and forever. Your standing before God is a free gift. It is not a matter of being as pious, religious, and as good as you can be so that you can make Brownie points with God. You simply cannot earn your standing with God. Once you have it, that standing, that gift, is something you possess as much today as you ever will.

As a result, hopefully, each day you will say, "Here I am, Lord. Today, I want to be used by You because You are so awesome. I want to lay this life down because I want You to use me today." When you go forth in that spirit, it is exactly the opposite of your average Jehovah Witness who knocks on doors, trying to earn his standing with God. He does that out of fear, hoping he will earn enough points to help with God. You, however, do it because you know the truth and you just want to honor the God who purchased you for Himself and gave you that standing.

As a believer in Jesus Christ, you represent Him. So let whatever you do be done for the glory of Jesus Christ, and not for any other reason.

The Bronze Sockets

But, alas, those poles are seated in bronze sockets. In the context of a believer, those bronze sockets represent trials and tribulations, the suffering of believers on the earth (and only on the earth). Those are such necessary and real parts of each believer's life that they make up part of that picture drawn by the tabernacle wall. Trials and tribulations are necessary for the Lord to accomplish that perfecting work that He wants to accomplish in your life.

The reality is that there is not going to be any real growth apart from the trials and tribulations of life. That is the crucible of spiritual growth.

After you go to church and soak in the Word, you may leave thinking, "Oh, that sermon was enlightening. This new understanding has caused growth in me." That's probably true, but it is merely the lecture portion of your spiritual college course entitled Christian Life 101A. When you walk out those church doors, you enter the lab session of that course. Living your everyday life is where your faith becomes real to you.

You've probably heard talk about head-knowledge versus heart-understanding. You may have the Word in your head, but you need it in your heart. So, how do you get it to trickle down? *You don't.* It doesn't. The Word does not trickle down; it gets *pressed* firmly into your heart through the trials of life.

The Christians I really feel sorry for are the ones who have been "flee-ers" all their life. Let me explain. In Psalm 55:6, David says:

> **"Oh, that I had wings like a dove! I would fly away and be at rest."**

If God had given us the wings of a dove, we would be flying off every time something goes wrong. A little heat in the kitchen, and we would be gone, flying off somewhere a little cooler. If we were to do that, however, we would never experience God's victory on the battlefield. There are Christians whose entire lives have been spent fleeing, running, and hiding; the result is that they are stunted in their growth. They do not know the riches and the reality of a relationship with the Living God. For them, it has never progressed beyond mere head knowledge. That, to me, is a tragedy.

Those brass sockets, those trials, are a part of the Christian walk and the Christian life. We are conformed into the image of Jesus Christ by learning to trust Him through them, not by avoiding them. It takes those brass sockets to make us stand securely. Look at how James described this truth in James 1:2-4:

> **Consider it all joy, my brethren, when you encounter various trials, knowing that the testing of your faith produces endurance. And let endurance have its perfect result, so that you may be perfect and complete, lacking in nothing.**

Paul echoes that in Romans 5:3-5, where he says:

> **And not only this, but we also exult in our tribulations, knowing that tribulation brings about perseverance; and perseverance, proven character; and proven character, hope; and hope does not disappoint, because the love of God has been poured out within our hearts through the Holy Spirit who was given to us.**

Paul was not a masochist. He was not going around hitting himself, insisting that it actually felt good. That is not what is meant here. God is working gloriously through the difficult things that happen to us. Growth cannot happen any other way, so we exult in our tribulations. We exult because we know that God is going to produce incredible fruit in our lives through these trials. Glory hallelujah! Therefore, not only can we tolerate it, we can actually consider tribulations to be joy because of the spiritual growth they will inevitably produce in us.

Nobody really *wants* difficulties. No one endures difficult times by saying, "Oh, this is fun! This pain is actually pure joy!" But what you *can* do is, through the eyes of faith, look to the future and say, "God is faithful. God is true to His Word. God loves me. Christ lives in my heart. I am part of His family. I am a piece of that wall. Therefore, I know God is doing something so glorious and so awesomely wonderful in the realm of the Spirit in my life that I can have joy." It is placed into the basket entitled "future joy" because that is what those brass sockets produce.

The Philippians 3 Wall

Paul makes a statement about his own walk that beautifully outlines the tabernacle wall. He says in Philippians 3:10-11:

> **… that I may know Him and the power of His resurrection and the fellowship of His sufferings, being conformed to His death; in order that I may attain to the resurrection from the dead.**

We all like the part of that verse about knowing Jesus. We can really get excited about that! Oh, yes, and we like the part about the power of His resurrection. But how many of us cling to the promise of fellowship in His sufferings? And, oh, that part about being conformed to His death—that is even *worse*.

But do you know what you have portrayed in that verse? You have the wall of the tabernacle. We can start at the top and work down.

"**… that I may know Him,**" is the silver, those bands and hooks. I know Him through His redemption of my life.

"**… and the power of His resurrection,**" is the white linen. That is the manifestation of Christ.

"**…and the fellowship of His sufferings, being conformed to His death,**" is the bronze sitting right there on the ground.

What is the result of that? "**… that I may attain to the resurrection from the dead.**" That is full-on salvation. It is all represented right there in that tabernacle wall.

Along that line, I like this little word of encouragement:

> **After you have suffered for a little while, the God of all grace, who called you to His eternal glory in Christ, will Himself perfect, confirm, strengthen and establish you.** (1 Peter 5:10)

You see, the Lord has bands around us. He knows what He is doing in our lives. These things will not go unchecked. He will accomplish what He sets out to do. He will perfect, confirm, strengthen, and establish us. That is our sure hope. This is our testimony to the world, by the Holy Spirit.

A Convicting Witness

Do you remember when Jesus was talking to His disciples about when the Holy Spirit would come upon them? He said in John 16:8-11:

> **"And He, when He comes, will convict the world concerning sin and righteousness and judgment; concerning sin, because they do not believe in Me; and concerning righteousness, because I go to the Father and you no longer see Me; and concerning judgment, because the ruler of this world has been judged."**

It is right there, brethren; that is the convicting work of the Holy Spirit through a believer. What does the wall do? It is a testimony of the tabernacle to the camp. People are convicted concerning sin **"because they do not believe in Me."** There is the silver. Christ is our redemption.

"... and concerning righteousness," there is the fine, white linen curtain wall. Ours is the righteousness of Christ because He has gone to the Father.

"... and concerning judgment," there are the bronze sockets; the prince of this world has been judged at the cross.

The Wall Leads to the Gate

What does the wall do? It does not just keep people from coming into the tabernacle area; it actually leads them to the way in. If you walk up to that wall, wondering how to get into the place, you will follow it until you eventually get to the gate. The wall will lead you to the gate.

There are a whole bunch of poles all lined up, leading in the same direction. I love it. As God uses the body of Christ to lead natural man to Christ, He uses us together. Very rarely is any one person, all by himself, responsible for the conversion of another believer to Christ. It is typically a team effort under the guidance and direction of the Holy Spirit. So, there we are, leading people to the gate.

I once heard a wonderful story about how God uses us, even at times when we are not aware of it. There was a fellow who lived in London. Like many Londoners, he would take the subway to and from work, morning and evening. Going to work in London in the morning and getting on the subway is probably a lot like our traveling the freeways to get to work. During rush hour traffic you can see so many people waiting in traffic who just look like death warmed over. They look like zombies.

Anyhow, every day as this man would purchase his subway ticket, he looked forward to seeing the lady cashier who sold him his ticket. She was the bright spot in his whole day. Whenever he came up to the ticket booth, she always had a smile and a friendly word. She was a bright spot, a flower in a gray place. After a while, he began to wonder why she was so different. He didn't know anyone else like her. As he went to buy his ticket one day, sitting right beside her was her Bible. He decided that must be it. She must be one of those Christians. It touched his heart, and he decided to find out more about it. He bought a Bible and visited a church where they shared the truth of the gospel, and he got saved. He became a born-again believer and it changed his life.

As soon as that happened, he could not wait to get back to the ticket place to tell her the news. When he got there to purchase his ticket, she was gone. Had God planted her there just for him, he wondered? Certainly God used her in his life.

There is more to this story. Some months later this born-again gentleman was walking down a busy London street when he recognized the ticket lady walking the opposite direction. He turned around, chased her down, tapped her on the shoulder and apologized for startling her. He then shared his testimony of how she had affected his life. It must have made her day! But if they had not accidentally crossed paths on that busy London street, she would never have known about how she had witnessed of Jesus just by showing up to work with a smile.

This is similar to the story in Acts about how Philip approached an

Ethiopian eunuch on the Gaza Strip, told him about Jesus, and as soon as the eunuch believed on His name, Philip baptized him—and then he was gone. The Ethiopian came out of the water and wondered where Philip had gone. Philip was used by the Lord, and then disappeared out of his life.

How often does God use us when we do not even know it? We will only know when we get to glory! It is exciting to be a Christian. We are just one of those poles, all lined up. The ticket lady in London was one pole, Philip was one, and you are another—all pointing to Jesus Christ, who is the door.

> **So Jesus said to them again, "Truly, truly, I say to you, I am the door of the sheep."** (John 10:7)

Brethren, I just want to encourage you. The Great Wall of China notwithstanding, you are a part of the greatest wall in the history of this world. You are one of those poles, lined up, holding up the reality of Jesus Christ to the world. Though you may not be a missionary or Billy Graham, you are just as much a part of His great witness in this world as any other believer in history.

In the next chapter, we will be looking at where that wall leads a person. We will look at the gate into the tabernacle.

Chapter Four

The Gate

*"I am the door;
if anyone enters through Me,
he will be saved ... "*

Jesus in John 10:9

The Only Way Inside

The tabernacle wall which we have seen, representing a believer's witness to an unbelieving world, led those on the outside to the only way inside, to the only way to communion with God. The wall led people to the gate of the tabernacle, the one and only entrance. There were no back doors and no windows; there was no other way to sneak inside. The only way in was through the door that faced the east. This fits perfectly with the gospel of Jesus Christ.

In John 14:6, Jesus said:

> "I am the way, and the truth, and the life; no one comes to the Father but through Me."

Jesus could not have put it any more clearly when He said **"but through Me."** I love the gate of this tabernacle because it represents Jesus. As people would walk into the tabernacle, which was the dwelling place of God, they went through the gate. Jesus said, **"I am the way."** You cannot *get* to the Father except through Jesus.

> **For the gate of the court there shall be a screen of twenty cubits, of blue and purple and scarlet material**

> and fine twisted linen, the work of a weaver, with their four pillars and their four sockets. (Exodus 27:16)

There was a multi-colored screen in front of the gate that was held up by four pillars. Like the wall, the screen was made of white twisted linen, but there was more to it than that. The white linen of the gate was adorned with blue, purple, and scarlet which are scripturally significant colors.

The Colors of Jesus

Blue

Just as the sky is blue, blue speaks of that which is heavenly. Jesus is the only man who came directly from heaven to dwell on earth.

> **In the beginning was the Word, and the Word was with God, and the Word was God. ... And the Word became flesh, and dwelt among us, and we saw His glory, glory as of the only begotten from the Father, full of grace and truth.** (John 1:1 & 14)

> **"For I have come down from heaven, not to do My own will, but the will of Him who sent Me."** (John 6:38)

Purple

Purple speaks of royalty. Descended from the line of David, Jesus is the nation of Israel's promised Messiah and King, and He is King of kings and Lord of lords.

Scarlet

The scarlet threads interwoven throughout the screen, of course, speak of the blood of Jesus who came to die and to shed His blood for our redemption. So, the Son of God, who *is* the King of kings, the Messiah, came to shed His blood for us.

White

The gate was also made of fine white linen. The white speaks of His righteousness. Jesus could die for us because He was perfectly righteous Himself. If I wanted to die for you to reconcile you to God, I could not do it because I am under the death sentence myself. I would have to die for me. Because Jesus is righteous and pure Himself, He has no judgment upon Himself. So He could take our place; He could die for us.

This scene, foretold in Revelation 5:9-10, takes place in heaven:

> **And they sang a new song, saying, "Worthy are You to take the book and to break its seals; for You were slain, and purchased for God with Your blood men from every tribe and tongue and people and nation. You have made them to be a kingdom and priests to our God; and they will reign upon the earth."**

Jesus came from heaven as God manifested in the flesh (blue). He came as king (purple). He was perfectly pure (white). His blood was shed for our redemption (scarlet). So what we have in that screen is a beautiful picture of our Lord and Savior, of Jesus Christ. You could not pick, scripturally, four other colors that picture the work of Christ and who He is any better than those four colors.

Jesus said:

> **"I am the door ... "** (John 10:9)

The Four Pillars of the Gospels

The screen was held up by how many pillars? Four. This is interesting because Christ is revealed to us in the four gospels. They tell us what He was like, who He was, and what He accomplished on the cross. These pillars represent the gospels, which reveal to us the person of Jesus Christ. So in the screen of that gate are four colors which picture Christ. That screen is held up by the four pillars representing the four gospels.

Did you ever wonder why there are four gospels in your Bible and not just one? Why did God want four separate accounts? Why didn't He just put them all together and give us one account?

By giving us the story of Jesus encased in four different gospels, we get a more complete view of who He is and why He came because each gospel looks at Jesus from a slightly different perspective. You know how it is. If four people were asked to describe any person at all, say their Aunt Sally, and then were asked to sit down and write about her, the result would be four different descriptions of Aunt Sally. One niece who burns water might be impressed by Sally's cooking skill; a nephew who can't remember a joke for more than thirty seconds might admire her humor;

another nephew who grew up in a comparative pigsty might take note of the cleanliness of Sally's home; and yet another niece, who also happens to be a couch potato, might marvel at the fact that Aunt Sally is also very athletic. Each description happens to be a true, but a very different slant on the same person. By considering them all, we learn a great deal about Aunt Sally, much more than we would by reading only one description of her. Likewise, the gospels offer four God-inspired perspectives on the Savior of the world, Jesus Christ, the Messiah of Israel.

Matthew presents Jesus as the King of Israel. There are more cross-references to the Old Testament in Matthew than the other three gospels put together. At the beginning of the book, Matthew is meticulous in pointing out that Jesus descended from the line of David. He is the King.

Mark, the shortest gospel, presents Jesus as the perfect servant, the one who laid down His life for us.

In Luke, Jesus is presented as the perfect man. Luke often referred to Jesus as the "Son of Man." Jesus was perfectly human. He was fully man.

In John, of course, Jesus is deity, God manifested in the flesh. There is no doubt about it: He is the Son of the Living God.

Jesus is presented as wholly man in Luke and wholly God in John. So when you read John, you come to realize that Jesus was and is the Living God. When you study Luke, you understand that He was also wholly human.

With all this in mind, look at the beginning of Revelation chapter 4 where John is translated into heaven. He sees the very throne room of God Himself in heaven. He sees the multitude of angels. He sees the twenty-four elders who represent the body of Christ, the church. Then he sees these characters, called the **"four living creatures,"** which are actually angelic beings who are situated in the closest proximity of all to God Himself at His throne. Look at how they are described.

> **… and before the throne there was something like a sea of glass, like crystal; and in the center and around the throne, four living creatures full of eyes in front and behind. The first creature was like a lion, and the second creature like a calf, and the third creature had a face like that of a man, and the fourth creature was like a flying eagle.** (Revelation 4:6-7)

Notice, the first creature was like a lion. Jesus is shown in the gospel of Matthew as the lion of the tribe of Judah, the King of Israel. (Matthew depicted Him as the perfect king.)

The second creature was like a calf. A calf is an animal of servitude that was slain in the tabernacle for sins. (Mark depicted Him as the perfect servant.)

The third creature had a face like a man. (Luke depicted Him as the perfect man.)

The fourth creature was the flying eagle, which is a picture of that which is heavenly, His deity. (John depicts Him as the Son of God.)

In what order are these creatures presented in Revelation? First Matthew, then Mark, Luke and John, in the same order as the gospels appear in your Bible and mine. I believe that the Lord designed it that way on purpose.

These beings described in John's vision are the nearest beings to the throne of God. They reflect the glory of the Living God. So, it's interesting to note who exactly they do reflect: Jesus Christ. He is the Lord. He is Yahweh, the God of Israel. Jesus is God manifested in the flesh.

Those four gospels are represented in the tabernacle as the four pillars that are holding up the covering to the gate.

Interestingly enough, the colors and what they represent in Scripture correspond to the four living creatures in Revelation 4.

Purple is the color of royalty (the lion). That is Matthew.

Scarlet is the color of servitude to the point of death (the calf). That is Mark.

White is the color of righteousness (the perfect man). That is Luke.

Blue is the color of deity (the eagle). That is John.

So the colors illustrate the perspective of each gospel, as do the four living creatures. Four colors, four pillars, four gospels, four views of Jesus.

With that in mind, there is another little interesting side note. We often tell people when they become new Christians to read the Gospel of John first. Maybe there is something to that because the order of the colors in Exodus is first John (blue), then Matthew, Mark, and Luke (purple, scarlet, and white).

Answering the Ultimate Altar Call

When you first come to the tabernacle, the wall leads you to the gate, the only way in. Every Christian is an instrument of God to lead other people to the gate, to Jesus. Whether you merely reflect the righteousness and love of Jesus to your neighbor by the way you live your life, or if you directly invite someone to church, or reach out with the love of Jesus to a drunkard in the gutter where he lies, in effect, by your witness, what you are doing is leading them to the gate. At that gate, however, they are confronted with the truth and reality of the person of Jesus, and they must choose to either accept or reject that invitation to know Him, to go through that one and only gate (which is Jesus Himself)—or not. Here's how Jesus put it in John:

> **"I am the way, and the truth, and the life; no one comes to the Father but through Me."** (John 14:6)
>
> **"I am the door; if anyone enters through Me, he will be saved, and will go in and out and find pasture."** (John 10:9)

Until that person responds to Jesus, he will forever be on the outside looking in. When he does decide to go through that gate, when he responds to Jesus' invitation to enter in, immediately as soon as he steps through that door, he is standing before a huge bronze altar, the place of sacrifice; he is standing, as it were, at the foot of the cross—the place of salvation.

Without the shedding of blood, there is no forgiveness.

Hebrews 9:22

Chapter Five

The Altar

Standing at the Foot of the Cross

If you were to diagram the six pieces of furniture in the tabernacle, a startling truth becomes evident. Just inside the entrance was the **bronze altar**. Also in the courtyard was the **laver** (the washing basin for the priests). The remaining four furnishings were kept inside the tent. In the first of two rooms, on the left side, was the **golden lampstand**. On the right side was the **golden table of the bread of the Presence**. In the center, in front of the veil, was the **golden altar of incense**. Finally, in the last partitioned room, behind the veil, was the Holy of Holies where the **ark of the covenant** was kept. Diagram these items and you'll see that these items in the tabernacle literally formed the shape of a cross.

Therefore, anyone who would walk through that gate would, in this beautiful tabernacle picture drawn as only God could, be standing at the foot of the cross. (See the diagram on page 31.)

The Sacrificial Purpose of the Tabernacle

It's important to realize that Israelites went through that one and only gate into the tabernacle for only one purpose. They came to make a sacrifice to God. No one walked through the tabernacle just to take a tour. There were no tabernacle tour guides. Israelites did not go to the tabernacle grounds just to "hang out." Every person who entered the tabernacle had to bring a sacrifice with him, and once the sacrifice was made, he left.

Did you know this tabernacle is more significant to *us* than it was to the Israelites who lived around it? Today, there is no temple or tabernacle, and there is absolutely, positively no reason for one. It is interesting that the temple in Jerusalem was destroyed within the generation that Jesus was crucified, having fulfilled its purpose. The Jewish people have not had a temple since then.

> **And every priest stands daily ministering and offering time after time the same sacrifices, which can never take away sins ...** (Hebrews 10:11)

In that passage, the writer of Hebrews is stating that the tabernacle and the temple did not work. They just did not do the job. Why? Because all those things were simply a shadow, a form, a picture of the good things that were to come, all of which were fulfilled in Christ Jesus. The point is: the Old Testament tabernacle and the temple were shadows of the reality of Jesus.

When you see a shadow, you know there is some object causing light to be blocked. For instance, it seems the road crews are always doing repair on the freeways in California. The other day, I was driving and, because of repair work being done on the freeway, we were down to one moving lane. We were going about twenty miles per hour on the freeway. I thought perhaps there must be a big truck going slowly and holding up traffic. I looked at the shadows along the road and saw by the shadow that it was a car in front of the line of traffic moving so slowly. I knew something was causing the shadow, and I knew from the shadow, it was a car.

The tabernacle was simply the shadow of our salvation. The reality is Jesus Christ and our personal relationship with Him through the Holy Spirit. Jesus is the real structure. The shadow is nothing. As Christians, we live in the reality.

Jesus, Our Sacrifice

Jesus Christ is our sacrifice. He is why Christians do not need a tabernacle or a temple. He is why we do not have to take a lamb, go to an altar somewhere and make a sacrifice like they did in the Old Testament. Jesus is the fulfillment of that need of a sacrifice to be reconciled to God.

The things that happened at the tabernacle prepared Israel to understand what had to happen for sin to be forgiven. Get the picture the Lord painted with that tabernacle: there was a separation between the Israelites and God, and something had to happen to take care of sin. It involved death. It involved the shedding of blood. It involved an innocent victim. It involved a vicarious sacrifice in our place. It all pictured Christ.

It is no coincidence that within the generation that crucified Christ, the temple in Jerusalem, which replaced the tent tabernacle, was burned to the ground and dismembered stone by stone. Ever since that time, the Jews have not had a temple in which to make their sacrifices to God. So an Orthodox Jew today might wring his hands and worry, saying, "I hope synagogue will suffice, because I haven't got a temple in which to present a sacrifice for my sins."

But Christ has fulfilled that for us. He *is* that sacrifice for us. So now we are, in a very real sense, surrounded and robed in that white linen, which is the righteousness of Jesus Christ.

The moment an Israelite stepped through that tabernacle gate, he was confronted with a huge bronze altar directly in front of him, and he was staring, as it were, at what pictured the very cross of Jesus Christ.

Our Tour Continues at the Bronze Altar

With this in mind, our tour of the tabernacle picks up at the bronze altar standing just inside the courtyard to the tabernacle tent. There is no need to look to the right or to the left; the bronze altar is "in your face" as soon as you walk through the gate.

That altar, the place of sacrifice, is an interesting piece of furniture. Look at what God said to Moses about the altar in Exodus 27:1-8:

> "And you shall make the altar of acacia wood, five cubits long and five cubits wide; the altar shall be square, and its height shall be three cubits. You shall make its horns

> on its four corners; its horns shall be of one piece with it, and you shall overlay it with bronze. You shall make its pails for removing its ashes, and its shovels and its basins and its forks and its firepans; you shall make all its utensils of bronze. You shall make for it a grating of network of bronze, and on the net you shall make four bronze rings at its four corners. You shall put it beneath, under the ledge of the altar, so that the net will reach halfway up the altar. You shall make poles for the altar, poles of acacia wood, and overlay them with bronze. Its poles shall be inserted into the rings, so that the poles shall be on the two sides of the altar when it is carried. You shall make it hollow with planks; as it was shown to you in the mountain, so they shall make it."

The essence of what God said there is: "Make it just like I showed you on Mt. Sinai."

We are not exactly sure what a cubit was. Most scholars believe it was approximately 18 inches. A cubit was basically the distance from one's elbow to the tip of his finger. The Israelites, of course, had a standard measurement for it. So, if a cubit were 18 inches, which is probably fairly close, the altar would have been about 7.5 feet square. It would be about 4.5 feet high.

The altar was completely overlaid with bronze. Notice that everything associated with the altar was also made of bronze.

The sinner went through the gate and made his sacrifice at the altar. Making this sacrifice was the sole purpose for his being there. For the common Israelite man, that is where his access to the tabernacle ended, right there at the sacrificial altar.

God commanded five offerings for that particular altar. One was called the burnt offering. It is interesting that when the Holy Spirit refers to this altar in Exodus 38:1, He uses the term **"the altar of the burnt offering."**

> **Then he made the altar of burnt offering of acacia wood, five cubits long, and five cubits wide, square, and three cubits high.** (Exodus 38:1)

The burnt offering might be considered the main sacrifice. We will study all five of those offerings in detail in the next two chapters.

Look at what the writer of Hebrews has to say to Jewish Christians about that altar:

> We have an altar from which those who serve the tabernacle have no right to eat. For the bodies of those animals whose blood is brought into the holy place by the high priest as an offering for sin, are burned outside the camp. Therefore Jesus also, that He might sanctify the people through His own blood, suffered outside the gate. So, let us go out to Him outside the camp, bearing His reproach. For here we do not have a lasting city, but we are seeking the city which is to come. (Hebrews 13: 10-14)

The people the writer of Hebrews is writing about were caught up in the Jewish sacrificial system; yet they had no part in the real altar, which according to Hebrews 13:10 is Jesus. The bronze altar was simply a shadow of the Lamb of God, whom they rejected, and whom the altar and the sacrifice represented. For that reason, they had no right or privilege to eat of that altar, the real one. But we believers do because we have believed in the Lord Jesus Christ.

In the tabernacle, once the sacrifice was made, the blood had been shed, and the offering had been burned, the portions that were edible were taken to be used. Then the charred carcass was taken outside the compound and burned, consumed wholly by fire outside the camp because it was considered unclean. That is the analogy that the writer of Hebrews, by the Holy Spirit, is making for us. Jesus Christ, our Lord, took our sin upon Himself and thus became unclean. He was led outside the gate of the city to be crucified, to be consumed, to be destroyed, outside the gate, for our sin.

The point that the writer of Hebrews is making, particularly to Jewish believers, is that they are to go outside the fellowship of this world. They are to separate. To a Jew, this would mean they should not be afraid to go outside their strict Judaism and the fellowship of that Judaism, and embrace Jesus Christ and Him crucified. They should be willing to embrace the very rejection itself that Jesus endured. Go outside the camp and be one with Him.

> "If anyone wishes to come after Me, he must deny himself, and take up his cross daily and follow Me."
> (Jesus in Luke 9:23)

A Shadow of the Cross

Remember, the furniture was laid out in the very form of a cross. To come through the gate meant to stand at the foot of the altar (for us, the cross), that place where you would receive, by faith, the full effectiveness of what was accomplished at that altar for you. They received, by faith, the effectiveness of the altar.

It was possible that an Israelite would make his sacrifice, walk out of there and not believe it really worked for him, not believe by faith that his cleansing was possible. Yet another person could go in, make his sacrifice and, by standing on the Word of God, walk out of there realizing his sins were covered. He was acceptable to the LORD, the God of Israel, because of what he just did *and* the fact that he believed. You see, even in the Old Testament, their standing with God and their coming to God was totally based on faith. They had some things they had to do, but it was ultimately based on faith.

Our standing with God, our salvation, is based on faith also. It is receiving by faith the meaning which that altar represents. It is there at the cross that the adventure of the Christian life begins. That is where a believer is born again, into the family and the kingdom of God. He is born again when he stands in spirit at that altar, at the foot of the cross, and receives the effectiveness of what was accomplished at the cross for him. He is born again, receiving that salvation by faith. That, brethren, is "receiving" Jesus Christ.

By looking at that big bronze altar, the Holy Spirit gives us insight into the meaning of Calvary. For instance, what materials were used in the construction of the altar? It was made of acacia wood, completely overlaid with bronze. What a statement right there about Jesus Christ who became a man to bear the judgment of God for us. What does wood represent? Humanity. What does bronze represent? Judgment. He became a man to bear the judgment of God for humanity, just as the wood bore the bronze.

It is interesting that all the furniture in the outer court, everything, was covered with bronze. But if you could go into the two-room tent beyond the courtyard, as did the priests, you would see that everything there was covered with gold. Gold represents the deity of God, the glory of God.

Now, as a sinner, coming through that gate, everything in that courtyard was made of bronze, which speaks of judgment. It would have been very clear to him that something needed to be done about his sin, and that something would involve judgment. And there was the altar, right in his face at that point.

> **For the wages of sin is death ...** (Romans 6:23a)

Equal Access and Equal Need

With this background about the altar, there are some interesting points about it.

> **"And you shall make the altar of acacia wood, five cubits long and five cubits wide; the altar shall be square, and its height shall be three cubits."** (Exodus 27:1)

The altar was square. It was perfectly square all around. This is significant because it describes equal access. Whichever direction a man came from, whichever side was approached, the altar offered equal access.

So what does that say to us? God is not a respecter of persons. Anyone can come equally to God for his forgiveness.

> **Then He said to me, "It is done. I am the Alpha and the Omega, the beginning and the end. I will give to the one who thirsts from the spring of the water of life without cost."** (Revelation 21:6)

Our Lord will give to anyone who is thirsty from His water of life without cost. The only requirement is to be thirsty. "Without cost" means it is equally accessible to anyone. Anytime there is a cost attached to something it automatically begins to eliminate people. Some things are inexpensive; however, when there are bills to pay, it does not matter how inexpensive something is—if there is not enough money to purchase it, it cannot be had. Access to the living water of life is without cost, and that is one of the meanings of the four-square altar. Anyone can come, and come equally to God.

> **... for all have sinned and fall short of the glory of God ...** (Romans 3:23)

Not only is there equal access to God, but it is an indication that everyone equally *needs* to approach His altar. No one can circumvent it. No one can say, "Well, that's fine for them, but I don't need that. I think I'll just bypass the altar because I'm worthy." *Everyone* needs it. All have sinned and fallen short of the glory of God.

> **… as it is written, "There is none righteous, not even one …"** (Romans 3:10)

That means the altar is a need in everyone's life from good Nicodemus (John 3), to the Samaritan woman at the well (John 5), who had five husbands and was living with a sixth man out of wedlock. There is no difference. We all need what is offered at that altar equally. If good Nicodemus would have said, "I don't need salvation as much as they do," he would have been wrong. He needed it every bit as much as the worst of sinners.

Some years ago I was asked to go to the Nevada State Security Prison with a team that was putting on an evangelistic service. I was asked to give my testimony to the inmates there. Now, I was raised in a suburban middle-class Christian home. I came to the Lord on my mother's knee when I was three years old. I grew up in a Christian home and pretty much stayed out of trouble growing up. I was considered a "good boy" all my life. Yet there I was, asked to visit this prison and give my testimony to guys who were car thieves, burglars, and attempted murderers. I was not sure what to share. I depended totally on the Lord to guide me because I was very uncertain as to how I was going to relate to these guys.

Just about any activity in prison is well-attended because it gives the inmates an excuse to leave their cells for awhile. This service was no exception. I wish I could show you a video of the men who came, because they looked like they could have been cast in a sitcom about prison life. Every kind of prisoner you can imagine walked into the room. There were the real cool, tough guys with tattoos all over their bodies. There was one short, fat man who came waddling in. There was this one inmate who was 6'5", who must have worked out every day because he looked like 250 pounds of solid muscle; if looks could kill, every man in that place was dead. He looked at me and, for a moment, I thought I was a goner. Right in front of him was a little skinny 5'6" black man with a huge afro. One prisoner who looked like death warmed over (his eyes were sunken in and his face was absolutely white), just slumped into a chair.

When it was time for me to speak, I was introduced simply as "a pastor from Truckee who is here to share with you how God changed his life." As soon as I started speaking, I sensed an anointing was taking place. I am not even sure exactly what I said, other than sharing my childhood and what it was like when I was growing up. Somehow, though, what was coming across was that I was, in reality, no different from them. I was simply a sinner saved by God's grace. After I finished my testimony, I sat down and it was quiet for a moment. Nobody seemed to know what to do. Finally we prayed and finished the service. Then, one by one, the prisoners spoke to me as they walked out. It was obvious from what they said that the Lord had worked in their hearts. I knew the point had totally gotten across when a car thief walked up to me and said, "Hey man, you're *just* like me. Thanks for that."

After everyone else had left, the guy who looked like death warmed over was still sitting there, motionless in his chair. Finally he got up, walked over to me and said, I came here today with one purpose, to disrupt this meeting, and I couldn't move. All I could do was sit there. Why is that?" All I could do was witness to him of the power of Jesus Christ.

That bronze altar was square because we all need to come to the altar and stand at the foot of the cross on an equal basis. We cannot come to God in a spirit of "I'm better than you. Your side needs to be 7.5 feet long because you're a *real* sinner. But my side can be smaller because I'm already pretty good." No matter how well behaved you may think you are, that is simply wrong. Your need for God's forgiveness is just as great as someone like Charles Manson's; no difference. We are all equally in need of His saving grace.

Ground-Level Forgiveness

Another interesting point about this altar is that, unlike altars of pagan cultures, this altar rested right on the ground. That was very unusual for ancient altars. Altars were almost uniformly raised up with access via stairs or a ramp. I saw one artist's conception of the tabernacle in the wilderness that was wrong because the altar was raised up with ramps all around it. This thing was flat on ground level. It is important to understand the significance of this.

There is no working your way up to the place where you can be forgiven and receive the grace of God. There are no steps to climb, no works you can perform, to reach the level of sacrifice and forgiveness. As soon as you walk through that gate, you are standing at the level of that altar.

For someone who believes in Jesus, it is not a matter of getting good enough to be baptized. His grace has brought His forgiveness right down to where we are. We can go to a street gutter, reach out to someone who has hit absolute rock bottom, and we can share Jesus Christ to that person, right there, at ground level. That altar is perfectly within reach of that hurting, miserable person. That wretch can receive his forgiveness right there where he lies, just like you did.

Sometimes people say, "I've got to get my life back together again. I'll do that, and then I'll come to Jesus." That is a mistake. They are missing the whole point. Who waits until he is clean to take a bath?

Like the gate to the tabernacle in the wilderness, the gate for us is perpetually open, twenty-four hours a day. The altar is always open and ready and at ground level, right on the level where you are standing.

The Ties That Bind

> **You shall make its horns on its four corners; its horns shall be of one piece with it, and you shall overlay it with bronze.** (Exodus 27:2)

This altar had horns on each corner. Those horns actually served two purposes. The primary purpose of the horns was to bind the innocent substitute while its blood was being shed.

Secondly, it was a place of refuge in time of trouble. We read about this once in a while in the Old Testament. A person could come to the tabernacle and grab hold of a horn of the altar and cry for mercy. The altar was recognized as a place of refuge, a place of mercy.

In Matthew 26, when Jesus and His disciples celebrated the Passover together, Jesus was, in effect, telling them, "You may think this celebration just signifies the Passover from Egypt, but I've got news for you. It signifies something much more significant. It signifies My broken body and My shed blood for your eternal life." It was less than twenty-four hours later that the meaning of the Passover was fulfilled at Calvary. In Matthew, it says after they celebrated the Passover, they sang a hymn just before leaving. We even know what that hymn was. It was Psalm 118, because that is the closing hymn of the Passover. It includes these words:

> **The LORD is God, and He has given us light;**
> **Bind the festival sacrifice with cords to the horns of the altar.**
> (Psalm 118:27)

They went out from there and walked to Gethsemane where Jesus had the most intense prayer meeting of His earthly life. What were the "cords" that bound Jesus to the "altar" of the cross? Certainly not the Roman nails. It was His love. It was the love of God that bound Jesus to the cross.

Where did that binding take place for Jesus? I submit to you that the binding transpired in the Garden of Gethsemane as Jesus prayed through what He was about to do with such intensity that he literally sweat blood. It was there that He settled what He was going to do on the cross for us. He bound Himself to that altar with the cords of love. He lived out the Old Testament binding of the sacrifice right there at Gethsemane.

A Place of Merciful Refuge

The horns of the altar were also a place of refuge. Two guys who took advantage of that were Adonijah, David's son who tried to take the crown as the aging king laid on his death bed, and his aide in that play for power, Joab, David's commanding general (1 Kings 1:50-53, 1 Kings 2: 28). The altar was a place where the guilty could find mercy by grabbing those horns.

Years ago there was a Christian women's breakfast here in Truckee at which a particular lady was invited to share her testimony. She was a fiery red-head, probably in her mid-thirties. She had quite a testimony. This lady shared that she had lived on the wild side. She married at a very young age and had proceeded to have a couple of kids. It was a miserable marriage. Her husband worked nights, and she was a dancer in a bar. Their home life was miserable, and she was in a bad environment where she worked.

One night at the bar, some guy from Texas took a shine to her. He was a wealthy man who was in California on business. They struck up a conversation and she began to pour her heart out to him. At the end of their evening together, this man told her to go home and pack her bags because first thing in the morning he was going to pick her up and take her back to Texas with him. That sounded wonderful to her.

So, she did as he said. She went home late and started packing. She had two children, a four-year-old boy and an infant. As she hurried about packing, the baby would not stop crying. Determined to leave, she ignored the baby's cries and continued to pack. Eventually the baby did stop crying and she was able to get a little sleep herself. In the morning, she awakened the four-year-old, got him dressed and told him to go wake up the baby. The four-year-old came back to the room and told her the baby would not wake up. She discovered that her baby had died that night from sudden infant death syndrome, or crib death. She had ignored her baby while it was crying, and the child had died. Obviously, she didn't go to Texas.

The result of this tragedy was a new low in her life, and in that of her husband. In their misery, however, she and her husband drew closer together. She found out much later that they both felt responsible for the child's death. She was amazed that her husband bore the guilt himself because he believed he should have been home at night.

This hurting family lived across the street from a woman who often invited this bar-dancing wife and mother over to visit, and frequently asked her to go to church with her. She had never done either. One day, after the death of her child, the grieving mother asked her neighbor if the invitation to church was still open. In her shame, she found a seat in the very back row. After a time of worship, the pastor got up and some of the first words he uttered were, "Whatever you've done, Jesus Christ will forgive you." Those few words pierced her heart. She immediately stood up and walked down that aisle to the pulpit. The pastor hadn't even gotten into the meat of his message, and here was this lady walking down the aisle toward him with tears flowing down her face—all because she had heard that Jesus would forgive her.

The Holy Spirit was orchestrating this whole thing. The pastor, realizing that something heavy was going on here, stepped down from the pulpit and prayed with her right in front of the congregation. He led her to the Lord.

By her own description, she felt the lifting of a heavy, heavy weight. She felt so light as she went back to her seat that she felt like she was walking a foot off the ground. She wasn't sure what the pastor said during his sermon after that because she was just enjoying an overwhelming peace that she had never experienced in her life, especially since the death of her little baby. She walked out of the church and her world had changed. Suddenly, the birds were singing more beautifully. The trees appeared more beautiful and she noticed that the sky had never been so gorgeous. Everything around her reflected the glory of God.

That transformed woman went home and told her husband that she had become a Christian. At first he did not believe her, but soon he could not deny that he was married to a totally different woman. He had to go to her church to find out for himself what had happened to her. The result was that he, too, became a Christian. The Lord, in His great mercy, became their place of refuge and transformed both of their lives.

That is what the horns on the altar represent. They are something you can grab to receive the mercy of God, regardless of the condition of your life or your heart. It is right there through the gate, at that great big bronze altar.

An Equal Measure of Mercy

> "You shall make for it a grating of network of bronze, and on the net you shall make four bronze rings at its four corners. You shall put it beneath, under the ledge of the altar, so that the net will reach halfway up the altar." (Exodus 27:4-5)

In the center of the altar was a bronze grating. That is where the sacrifice would be laid. That is where the burnt offering would be made, right on that grating. That was the place of judgment.

If you could have a cubit measure and you were to measure half way up that altar, then run inside the Holy of Holies of the tabernacle where the Shekinah glory of God rested, and measure the level of the "mercy seat" (the lid of the ark of the covenant), it would be exactly the same height as the level of the grating. What does that say to us? It says that His mercy is equal to His judgments. Or, as Psalm 85:10 says:

> **Lovingkindness and truth have met together;
> Righteousness and peace have kissed each other.**

The justice, righteousness, and truth of God and His perfect mercy, peace, and lovingkindness have met together at the cross. We find refuge at the place of judgment. People ask why we Christians celebrate a death. It is because it is the place of judgment where we receive His mercy and are set free.

An Israelite would bring his sacrificial lamb, bind that lamb, and lay his hands on it to identify with it. This symbolized the transfer of his sin onto that innocent substitute. Then the lamb would be slain and its blood would be poured out. There was death by the shedding of blood. But there were certain criteria which had to be met for the sacrifice to be an acceptable sacrifice to God.

The Criteria for an Acceptable Sacrifice

The sacrifice had to be an innocent life to take the place of the one whose sins were in need of atonement. As such, it had to be a ram, calf, lamb, or turtle dove. It could not be a lion, a tiger, an eagle or any kind of carnivorous beast; the sacrificed animal had to be innocent, pure, and clean in the eyes of God.

Also, that sacrifice had to die. You could not make a partial sacrifice. You could not amputate one leg and just sacrifice a portion of the animal. It had to die, and it had to die with the shedding of blood. According to the writer of Hebrews in chapter 9, verse 22:

> ... without the shedding of blood, there is no forgiveness.

So, it had to be innocent, it had to die, and its blood had to be shed. Why? That sacrifice was a picture of Jesus Christ, bearing the sins of the world. It represented His innocent life freely sacrificed, and His blood shed for us, which is the basis of the new covenant.

Right there at Calvary, everything, every sin that could possibly separate me from God was dealt with and completely removed. The sentence of death was taken off of me and placed on Him. On the cross when Jesus cried out, **"It is finished,"** my sins were completely removed (not just covered, as they were at the tabernacle) by His blood. The condemnation that I totally deserve was forever lifted and taken away from me.

The fire of the altar burned in the center of the altar, in the very heart of it. It is well put to say that Jesus died of a broken heart. It was not the spikes in His hands, nor the Roman spear thrust into His side that killed Him. His love for you and me kept Him on that cross. Those were the cords that bound the sacrifice of the perfect Lamb of God to that altar.

Always Open

> "The fire on the altar shall be kept burning on it. It shall not go out, but the priest shall burn wood on it every morning; and he shall lay out the burnt offering on it, and offer up in smoke the fat portions of the peace offerings on it. Fire shall be kept burning continually on the altar; it is not to go out." (Leviticus 6:12-13)

That altar fire burned continually. What does that say to us? The effect of the altar was, and is, continually available to us. The smoke emanating from that altar and the glow of the fire would have been an indication to Israelites in the camp that they could come there and get right with God, any time at all. That sinner would not have to wait for the gate to be opened. He could come to the altar at the moment he recognized the need, just as we can come immediately to the foot of the cross. That fact certainly applied to the thief on the cross next to Jesus.

> And he was saying, "Jesus, remember me when You come in Your kingdom!" And He said to him, "Truly I say to you, today you shall be with Me in Paradise." (Luke 23:42-43)

In a sense, the thief entered, grabbed a horn and received mercy. He did not even know what was going on when he made that cry to Jesus.

Some time ago, I was talking to a lady whose father had passed away. He would have nothing to do with the Lord for a long time, but he prayed the sinner's prayer before he died. She was concerned because she was not 100 percent sure he was saved. I just wanted to encourage her in the Lord. God's Word tells us that whoever calls on the name of the Lord will be saved, regardless of when or where that call is placed.

That is what that bronze altar symbolizes. It is so easy, anytime, anywhere, under any circumstances to come to the Lord and be forgiven, to be cleansed before God.

It's All Ours Now

On the Day of Atonement, the high priest would take the blood of the sacrifice, sprinkle the other pieces of furniture in the tabernacle, go into the Holy of Holies and sprinkle the blood on the mercy seat. In doing so, everything having to do with the tabernacle was cleansed by that sacrifice at that altar. What this says to us, brethren, is once we have received that sacrifice on that altar for ourselves, everything else in the tabernacle is opened up to us. It all becomes available. We have total open access to God because of the sacrifice.

> **"You shall make poles for the altar, poles of acacia wood, and overlay them with bronze. Its poles shall be inserted into the rings, so that the poles shall be on the two sides of the altar when it is carried."** (Exodus 27:6-7)

When the Israelites moved from camp to camp, the priests would carry the altar. It would also be covered when it was moved so it would not be seen until it was set up and ready for the sacrifice (Leviticus 4: 13-14). How true that is for us: we really cannot see Christ and Him crucified unless we go through the gate. We cannot see Jesus from the world outside.

> **For the word of the cross is foolishness to those who are perishing, but to us who are being saved it is the power of God.** (1 Corinthians 1:18)

We walk through the gate and stand before that altar, and suddenly we realize the power of God.

This reminds me of a man here in Truckee who, the first time he walked into my office, looked much like that death-warmed-over inmate in the Nevada prison. As a drug-addicted, recently divorced husband and father with a failing business, his life was in shambles. A born-again friend convinced him to meet with me so that he could ask me the questions he couldn't seem to find answers for anywhere else. I did my best, but after we talked, he walked out, seemingly no different than he walked in. However, just two weeks later, he returned to my office, only this time he was radiant, wearing a huge "Jesus grin" from ear to ear. Obviously, he was a transformed man! I asked what had happened and he said, "I'm born again! I know Jesus now and He is in my heart!"

This man, who would eventually become an elder in our church, said that he had been plagued by many unanswered questions that were preventing him from coming to the Lord. After that first meeting with me, he sat down, wrote out those questions in the form of a business letter to God which he put in his top dresser drawer (where would he mail it?), and told God He had thirty days to answer each of those questions if He really wanted him to believe in Him. He went on with life but it wasn't long before this man had his own Damascus road experience, completely apart from that letter, gave his heart to Christ and immediately became a new man. Out of curiosity, he went back to his top drawer and opened up the letter to God. He realized that some of the questions had been answered right away, as soon as he was saved. He was confident that the ones that had not been answered yet would be in God's perfect timing; he just did not feel the need to know anymore. All that really mattered to him now was that he had Jesus in his heart.

As St. Augustine put it, "Don't endeavor to see so you can believe, but believe so you can see."

That is exactly like the tabernacle. The Israelites could not see anything until they had gone through the gate. Once they went through the gate, the altar was right there.

So, coming into a meaningful relationship with God begins by coming to the crucified Jesus Christ, the Savior and Lord of your life. You cannot circumvent that big bronze altar.

> "The Father loves the Son and has given all things into His hand. He who believes in the Son has eternal life; but he who does not obey the Son will not see life, but the wrath of God abides on him." (John 3:35-36)

How completely and perfectly Jesus' sacrifice was for us takes five sacrifices in the Old Testament to explain. We will look at those in the next two chapters.

Chapter Six

The Offerings of Non-Sweet Aroma

... for all have sinned and fall short of the glory of God ...

Romans 3:23

In the Old Testament law there are five different sacrifices that God required at the bronze altar. It took these five sacrifices to show us how completely the sacrifice of Jesus Christ has covered our needs spiritually, how fully our sins have been removed from us by the cross. These are described in the first seven chapters of Leviticus.

At this point, you might want to take the time and read Leviticus chapters 1 through 7. As you read, you will discover that three sacrifices are called "sacrifices of sweet aroma" (or "fragrant" or "soothing aroma," depending on your translation). They are the burnt offering, the grain offering, and the peace offering.

There are also two sacrifices of "non-soothing aroma" (or "non-fragrant" or "non-sweet"). They are the sin offering and the trespass offering.

There is no apparent reason why some of them would be considered fragrant offerings and some would be considered non-fragrant offerings, until you see what they symbolize in Christ. The fragrant or soothing offerings picture for us the beauty and the perfection of Jesus Christ Himself, who is our sacrifice. The non-fragrant or non-soothing offerings picture Christ as our sin bearer, with the emphasis being on Him literally becoming sin for us.

When God gave instructions to Moses regarding these offerings, He gave him the instructions for the soothing sacrifices first. These are the offerings which picture the perfection and beauty of His Son, Jesus

Christ. Then God gave Moses instructions regarding the non-soothing sacrifices which show the sin-bearing that His Son endured. When the Israelites brought these offerings (or sacrifices) to the tabernacle, they were brought in reverse order. The offerings and sacrifices of non-fragrant aroma were presented first, and then when that was complete, the sacrifices of soothing or fragrant aroma were brought before the Lord.

Now, to Israel, this was a ritual to be followed in obedience to the Lord. There was no understanding of the real significance of all this, other than God said to do it. That is the way they would express their faith in God.

But to us, these sacrifices speak volumes. What a phenomenal picture God has painted for us to show us what Christ means to us and means to the Father.

> **And there is salvation in no one else; for there is no other name under heaven that has been given among men by which we must be saved.** (Acts 4:12)

It also helps us understand the importance of His sacrifice more fully when we consider the words of Paul in 1 Timothy 2:5:

> **For there is one God, and one mediator also between God and men, the man Christ Jesus ...**

From these sacrifices we see a picture of Jesus, who is very precious to God, as He offered Himself to God as a sacrifice for our sin. He became the mediator between sinful, fallen man and a holy, righteous, and perfect God. It is pictured for us in the sacrifices of the bronze altar of the tabernacle. In reality, it was accomplished once and for all and forever at the cross.

In this chapter, we will look at the first two sacrifices, the offerings of non-sweet aroma. Remember, we are looking at this tabernacle from the perspective of the common man, and he would have presented the offerings of non-sweet aroma first.

The Sin Offering

The first offering the common man would have brought would have been the sin offering, which is described in Leviticus 4:1-6:

> Then the LORD spoke to Moses, saying, "Speak to the sons of Israel, saying, 'If a person sins unintentionally in any of the things which the LORD has commanded not to be done, and commits any of them, if the anointed priest sins so as to bring guilt on the people, then let him offer to the LORD a bull without defect as a sin offering for the sin he has committed. He shall bring the bull to the doorway of the tent of meeting before the LORD, and he shall lay his hand on the head of the bull and slay the bull before the LORD. Then the anointed priest is to take some of the blood of the bull and bring it to the tent of meeting, and the priest shall dip his finger in the blood and sprinkle some of the blood seven times before the LORD, in front of the veil of the sanctuary.'"

In the diagram on page 31, we see the outer court contained the gate, the bronze altar, and the laver. In the holy place of the tent tabernacle we find the golden lampstand, the table of the bread of the Presence, and the golden altar of incense. In the Holy of Holies, which was filled with the Shekinah glory of God, we see the ark of the covenant.

The Scriptures above tell us that the sacrifice was made in the outer court, but the priest was to bring some of the blood of the sacrifice and sprinkle it before the veil, before the very presence of God, but he could not go through the veil. He could not go into the Holy of Holies, but he was to go up to the veil and sprinkle the blood seven times before that veil.

> "The priest shall also put some of the blood on the horns of the altar of fragrant incense which is before the LORD in the tent of meeting ..." (Leviticus 4:7a)

So, once the priest sprinkled the sacrificial blood seven times before the veil, he was to smudge some of the blood on the horns on the altar of incense which was before the veil in the tent.

> "... and all the blood of the bull he shall pour out at the base of the altar of burnt offering which is at the doorway of the tent of meeting." (Leviticus 4:7b)

This Scripture tells us that the priest then returned, and all the rest of the blood was poured out at the foot of the big bronze altar.

> "He shall remove from it all the fat of the bull of the sin offering: the fat that covers the entrails, and all the fat which is on the entrails, and the two kidneys with the fat that is on them, which is on the loins, and the lobe of the liver, which he shall remove with the kidneys (just as it is removed from the ox of the sacrifice of peace offerings), and the priest is to offer them up in smoke on the altar of burnt offering. But the hide of the bull and all its flesh with its head and its legs and its entrails and its refuse, that is, all the rest of the bull, he is to bring out to a clean place outside the camp where the ashes are poured out, and burn it on wood with fire; where the ashes are poured out it shall be burned." (Leviticus 4:8-12)

So the priest then took from the inner portions, the fatty portions, and he laid them on the altar and he burned it as a non-sweet aroma to the Lord. The carcass and everything that was left was taken outside the camp and was burned to ashes outside the camp.

> "Now if the whole congregation of Israel commits error and the matter escapes the notice of the assembly, and they commit any of the things which the Lord has commanded not to be done, and they become guilty..." (Leviticus 4:13)

> "When a leader sins and unintentionally does any one of all the things which the Lord his God has commanded not to be done, and he becomes guilty..." (Leviticus 4: 22)

> "Now if anyone of the common people sins unintentionally in doing any of the things which the Lord has commanded not to be done, and becomes guilty ..." (Leviticus 4:27)

The point of these Scriptures is: it does not make any difference, in the final analysis, who commits the sin, whether it is an individual and the sin has been committed on an individual basis, or whether it involves the whole nation. It does not matter if it is a rich man or a poor man, a master or a slave, a priest or a common man, a law-abiding citizen or a flagrant moral pervert. Everybody needs the sin offering.

But the Scripture says if you sin "unintentionally" you must make this sacrifice. However, unintentional sins are often unrecognized sins.

The fact is, we may sincerely desire to be good Christian examples. We may want, with all our hearts, to be very kind, thoughtful, and caring. Even so, we may still find ourselves unintentionally hurting other people, or being thoughtless or uncaring without realizing it.

I remember a fellow in our church some years ago. I really liked this guy. He would come by the office and we would just sit and talk. He came in one time when something was obviously bothering him. My heart went out to him, so I said, "Hey, what's the matter with the big guy?" We talked a little bit and he left. I never saw him again after that. I found out through the grapevine that he was very offended, and he thought I was being condescending when I asked, "What's the matter with the big guy?" Apparently he thought I was putting him down or making a joke about a big strong guy having a problem. That was not in my heart at all. I just cared about him, but I was unintentionally belittling him. I was being insensitive toward his feelings. Consequently, he was offended and he never came back. When I learned what the problem was, I apologized to him, but it didn't make any difference. I had hurt someone unintentionally.

There have been times when a person approached me right before a service and asked if we could pray for someone in particular during the service, and I have agreed to do it. Then, during the service I have completely forgotten to do it. I had every intention of doing it, but I simply forgot. Sin has been defined as "missing the mark," and I "missed the mark." Sometimes we do things that inadvertently offend someone. We do not mean to do it and it is not in our heart to do it. But those acts are usually just that old sin nature coming out in us. We have just "missed the mark." The sin offering addresses that old sin nature. It was meant to cover unintentional sin and dealt directly with the inherent sin nature of man, inherited from Adam.

> ... as it is written, "THERE IS NONE RIGHTEOUS, NOT EVEN ONE; THERE IS NONE WHO UNDERSTANDS, THERE IS NONE WHO SEEKS FOR GOD; ALL HAVE TURNED ASIDE, TOGETHER THEY HAVE BECOME USELESS; THERE IS NONE WHO DOES GOOD, THERE IS NOT EVEN ONE." (Romans 3:10-12)

> ... **for all have sinned and fall short of the glory of God** ... (Romans 3:23)

There are times when, individually, you just need to get things right with God. For an Israelite to do that, a "sin offering" would be sacrificed. The emphasis of this sacrifice was to cover unintentional sins. For us, the "sin offering" pictures how perfectly and effectively the sacrifice of Jesus Christ has atoned for our old sin nature.

What a beautiful picture God has drawn for us. The common Israelite would bring his own sacrifice on an individual basis, thus identifying it with his own guilt before God. By bringing that sacrifice to the doorway of the tent of meeting that pictured Christ, he would be confessing the fact that he is a sinner in need. He would place his hands on the head of that sacrifice, identifying with that innocent substitute, as that animal died in his place. The priest would take some of the blood of that sacrifice and sprinkle it seven times before the veil. After that, the priest would take a little bit of that blood and smudge it on the horns of the golden altar of incense inside the tabernacle. The priest would then come out and pour out the remaining blood right there at the foot of that big bronze altar. Then the fat portions would be laid on the altar as a sacrifice to God. Finally, the rest of that carcass would be taken outside the camp and burned as unclean.

This is a picture of what Jesus has done for us. First of all, Jesus' blood was poured out at the foot of the cross, just like the blood of the sacrifice was poured out at the base of that big bronze altar. It is interesting that God told Moses to make sure the priests poured out all the blood at the base of the altar which is symbolic of the foot of the cross.

The fatty portions of that sacrifice were burned on the altar as an offering to God. From the Old Testament viewpoint, when "fat" is referred to, it refers symbolically to "the best." For instance, in Genesis 45:18 we see it used there as "the fat of the land." What did that phrase mean? It meant the Lord was giving the people the very best of the produce of the land.

What does that say to believers? It says that the Father has freely given the best *to* us through Christ, and Jesus Christ has given His best *for* us.

As the body was taken outside the camp and burned outside the camp, so Jesus bore the fiery judgment for our sin outside the gate of Jerusalem.

> For the bodies of those animals whose blood is brought into the holy place by the high priest as an offering for sin, are burned outside the camp. Therefore Jesus also, that He might sanctify the people through His own blood, suffered outside the gate. (Hebrews 13:11-12)

The carcass was burned to ash in a place outside the camp, in a place where the wind would come and just blow the ashes away. In the same way, because of Jesus, our sins are blown away and God remembers them no more.

The priest would take some of that blood inside the tabernacle and he would sprinkle it before the Lord.

> But when Christ appeared as a high priest of the good things to come, He entered through the greater and more perfect tabernacle, not made with hands, that is to say, not of this creation; and not through the blood of goats and calves, but through His own blood, He entered the holy place once for all, having obtained eternal redemption. (Hebrews 9:11-12)

So the priest would go in and sprinkle the blood at the veil before the Lord because he could not go behind the veil. Why sprinkle that blood there? It was for reconciliation with God, for the redemption and the forgiveness of those people before God.

> ... and without shedding of blood there is no forgiveness. (Hebrews 9:22b)

At this point, we come to an interesting thought. When a priest would devote himself to this service, he had to ceremonially cleanse himself. After the cleansing, he could not touch anything unclean until his service was completely finished, until he had done the work he was called to do. He had to remain aloof from common man to perform this service. With that in mind, it is interesting what Jesus said to Mary immediately after His resurrection in John 20:17, especially as it is put in the King James Version:

> Jesus saith unto her, "Touch me not; for I am not yet ascended to my Father: but go to my brethren, and say unto them, 'I ascend unto my Father and your Father; and to my God, and your God.'" (John 20:17, KJV)

The priest would take the blood of the sacrifice and go into the tabernacle and sprinkle the blood before the veil, while he himself remained clean and untouched by anything unclean that would taint that act of reconciliation before God for that person, or for the nation if it happened to be for the nation. It is interesting that in the same way, Jesus Christ, right after His resurrection, told Mary not to touch Him for He had to go to His Father.

It is hard to say because the Bible does not tell us, but it is possible that Jesus said that to her because He had not yet gone into the heavenly Holy of Holies as our High Priest to present His blood as the sacrifice for our sins there.

The one other thing the priest did with that sacrifice was to smudge the blood from the sacrifice on the horn of the golden altar of incense. When you read the chapter on the golden altar of incense, this will come alive to you. But, in a nutshell, that golden altar of incense is a picture of the prayers of the believers before the throne of God. That altar pictures the power of intercessory prayer before God. That golden altar of incense is kept burning because God wants us to know that our prayers are ever before Him. So when that blood is smudged on the horns of that altar, it symbolizes that through the shed blood of the sacrifice of the Lamb of God we now have open access to His throne through prayer. We have been given a place of authority in prayer before God.

Do you remember what the blind man who was healed by Jesus said to the Sanhedrin in the ninth chapter of John? He essentially said that God would not answer the prayers of an unrighteous man, but He *will* answer the prayers of a righteous man (John 9:31). The blood is what makes us righteous before Him, and it gives us power and authority in our prayer life. That blood smudged on that altar says you have a hotline to heaven. The way has been opened. There is nothing to prevent your prayers from being powerful before the throne of God, not because you have been "holier than thou" today, but because the blood of Jesus Christ cleanses you from all sin. His sacrifice made that way open for you.

So Jesus could say to His disciples in John 14:13:

> **"Whatever you ask in My name, that will I do …"**

Jesus said in Matthew 16:19:

> "I will give you the keys of the kingdom of heaven; and whatever you bind on earth shall have been bound in heaven, and whatever you loose on earth shall have been loosed in heaven."

He has given us a place of open access to His throne in prayer.

There is another thing about this sin offering that I appreciate. Every time the word "sin" is used in the Old Testament, it is the same word that is used for "sin offering." They are interchangeable. That is exciting to me, because Jesus, our sin offering, became sin for us.

What that means is, you cannot separate my sin from Him who is my sin offering. The moment He became sin, the whole weight of my guilt, my condemnation, my judgment, landed on Him. That propensity to sin, which is in all of us, was dealt with once for all at the cross. That which I do not want to do, I do. That which I want to do, I do not do (Romans 7:13-25). We are forgiven for this at the cross. Our old nature is atoned for by the blood of Jesus.

We struggle sometimes with how God can forgive us again, and again, and again, and again for the same thing, over and over. As a Christian, I know better than to do some of the things I do, yet I still find myself doing wrong. How can God forgive me repeatedly? I don't have a problem with His willingness to forgive me once, maybe a couple of times, but repeatedly? Why does He do that? Our Lord makes it clear in His Word, as many times as you need forgiveness, you have forgiveness. God is not counting. The reason He forgives repeatedly is because of what that sin offering represents. That very sin nature we all have is forgiven. That is the sin offering. That is what Jesus did for us on the cross.

The Trespass Offering

Now let's look at the other offering of non-sweet aroma, the trespass offering.

In Leviticus chapters 5 through 7, the trespass offering, or the "guilt offering," is described. It was very similar to the sin offering in what was required for the offering. You will notice as you read through these chapters that the trespass offering was given for some specific sins committed: for instance, not testifying when you should have testified, touching something unclean, swearing thoughtlessly, lying, robbery, embezzlement, extortion, things like that.

> "... then it shall be, when he sins and becomes guilty, that he shall restore what he took by robbery or what he got by extortion, or the deposit which was entrusted to him or the lost thing which he found, or anything about which he swore falsely; he shall make restitution for it in full and add to it one-fifth more. He shall give it to the one to whom it belongs on the day he presents his guilt offering." (Leviticus 6:4-5)

In our society, when someone finds something, there is a tendency to say, "Finders keepers, losers weepers." People often want to keep things they find for themselves. But that is unrighteous.

For example, I heard on the news about a guy who received a check for $5,000 from Southern Pacific Railroad. This check should have gone to a company that had the same name as his. Even though the money clearly was not his, he deposited the check, and then closed his account. That was wrong. He was trying to get away with money that was not his rather than sending it back.

The Lord expects us to be honest. When we find something, it may be a hassle, it may be trouble, it may mean you have to do things you do not want to do and did not plan to do. But when you find something that does not belong to you, you are suddenly under obligation to restore it to its rightful owner.

> "... or anything about which he swore falsely; he shall make restitution for it in full and add to it one-fifth more. He shall give it to the one to whom it belongs on the day he presents his guilt offering. Then he shall bring to the priest his guilt offering to the Lord, a ram without defect from the flock, according to your valuation, for a guilt offering, and the priest shall make atonement for him before the Lord , and he will be forgiven for any one of the things which he may have done to incur guilt." (Leviticus 6:5-7)

This trespass offering was very similar to the sin offering. But the emphasis of this offering was on the outward acts of sin, whether they be unintentional or intentional. It was that outward act of sin that was being addressed. The word for trespass or guilt is literally "a fault," a commitment of a fault. It is an outward sin. So the difference between the sin offering and the trespass offering is this: the sin offering was offered for the *root* of sin (in our hearts); and the trespass, or guilt offering, was offered for the *fruit* of sin (the outward act).

> **For I know that nothing good dwells in me, that is, in my flesh; for the willing is present in me, but the doing of the good is not. For the good that I want, I do not do, but I practice the very evil that I do not want. But if I am doing the very thing I do not want, I am no longer the one doing it, but sin which dwells in me. ... Wretched man that I am! Who will set me free from the body of this death?** (Romans 7:18-20, 24)

Paul continues this topic in Romans chapter 8 where he describes the victory we have in the Spirit of God. Romans chapter 7 depicts our struggle with sin and Romans chapter 8 describes how we can walk in the victory and power of the Holy Spirit.

The sin offering took care of the **"I am no longer the one doing it, but sin which dwells in me"** problem of chapter 7. And the trespass offering deals directly with the **"good that I want, I do not do"** part. Those offerings together thus become the bridge to chapter 8.

So, the sin offering covers that nature of sin that is within me. The trespass offering covers those acts of sin that I commit because of the nature of sin that is within me. The sin and the trespass offerings represent the nature and the act, or the root and the fruit of sin **"which dwells in me."** Therefore:

> **If we confess our sins, He is faithful and righteous to forgive us our sins and to cleanse us from all unrighteousness.** (1 John 1:9)

We have in 1 John 1:9 what these offerings effect: the forgiveness of God. These offerings cleared the air before God in the Old Testament. They illustrate for us, as New Testament believers, that the cross cleanses us before God in every way.

I remember hearing a story some time ago about two young city children who went to visit their grandparents on their farm. The little guy, Joey, was out behind the farmhouse playing with a slingshot, near where Grandma's pet goose also happened to be. What a dangerous combination! In a playful way, never believing he would ever be successful in hitting his target, Joey took aim at Grandma's pet goose. When he shot the slingshot, the stone hit the goose right in the head. The goose keeled over, stone dead. Joey was petrified! He had to hide the evidence, so he took the carcass of that old goose and hid it in the woodpile. Thinking all evidence was gone, he turned around to see Sara, his little sister, staring intently at him. Joey *begged* Sara not to tell their grandparents what she had seen. Sara said nothing, just smiled and walked into the house.

Joey found it difficult to enjoy dinner that evening. Finally Grandpa said to Grandma, "Why don't you and little Sara clean up the kitchen and let me take little Joey fishing?" Sara grinned and said, "Grandpa, Joey told me just this afternoon how he really *wants* to do the dishes tonight for Grandma and me. You *want* to do the dishes, *don't you* Joey?"

"Yes, yes, I want to do the dishes, Grandpa. I'm sorry, but you better go fishing without me tonight."

That was just the beginning. Every chore that little Sara had to do for the next few days, Joey did instead. She had her brother wrapped around her little finger. Finally, not able to take the pressure a minute longer, Joey walked up to Grandma in the kitchen and confessed everything with heartfelt tears. Grandma looked at Joey, put her arm around his shoulder, and said, "I saw you do it, Joey. I saw everything from this window. I want you to know that I forgave you the moment you did it. I was just wondering how long it was going to take for you to come tell me and make things right again." Joey was happy again. His relationship with his grandparents was restored, no more secrets, and his little sister had no more power over him for the rest of their vacation.

Just like Joey's grandma, our God, our loving Father, sees all that His children do, forgives instantly, and just waits for us to come to Him to set things right.

Because of what the sin and the trespass offerings mean to us in Jesus, we have come to a place where we can now walk in the new life. We can walk in His power and His victory. We can walk in Romans 8 because of what Christ accomplished on the cross.

Notice that in this trespass offering the Israelite bringing the offering had a specific procedure he had to go through. Look at that again in the light of what Jesus has done for us.

> "… then it shall be, when he sins and becomes guilty, that he shall restore what he took by robbery or what he

> got by extortion, or the deposit which was entrusted to him or the lost thing which he found, or anything about which he swore falsely; he shall make restitution for it in full and add to it one-fifth more. He shall give it to the one to whom it belongs on the day he presents his guilt offering. Then he shall bring to the priest his guilt offering to the LORD, a ram without defect from the flock, according to your valuation, for a guilt offering ..." (Leviticus 6:4-6)

There are actually three parts to this offering:

1. **Confession of Sin.** The first part was the confession of the sin. The very fact of bringing a trespass offering, in this case, was an open confession of sin. "Yes, I have done this and I am bringing this offering as a way of getting right before God for what I have done."

2. **Restitution for Sin.** Secondly, there was restitution for the sin. Whatever was taken or stolen, it was to be restored, plus one-fifth more in restoration.

3. **Presentation of the Offering.** Thirdly, there was the presenting of the offering itself before the Lord as a trespass offering.

That was the way to become completely free of that particular sin and walk away knowing you were free and that sin was not hanging over you. This is the spirit of the teaching of Jesus in the Sermon on the Mount:

> "Therefore if you are presenting your offering at the altar, and there remember that your brother has something against you, leave your offering there before the altar and go; first be reconciled to your brother, and then come and present your offering." (Matthew 5:23-24)

Notice that the presentation of the offering was the last thing to be done. There was confession, restitution, and then the presentation of the offering. Jesus is essentially saying, "There are times when I don't need your offering. Instead, I need you to get right with your brother. Then it can be settled with Me."

So how does this apply to a Christian?

1. **Confession of Sin.** First we are called to confess our sin. 1 John 1:9 tells us to confess our sin and He will cleanse us from all unrighteousness.

2. **Restitution of Sin.** There is a place for restitution, if restitution

is what is needed in a particular circumstance.

3. **Forgiveness of Sin.** Based on the cross, we can thank Jesus for His forgiveness of our sin. We are free of it.

In the area of confessing your sin, and getting right with a brother, ask God to lead you and direct you according to His will. That action is to be applied if your brother has something against you because of an evil you have done. If that happens, then swallow your pride and restore in abundance. However, if you just have private thoughts against someone and they do not know how you feel, don't go up after church and say, "I need to ask your forgiveness because I've been hating your guts!" That just makes things incredibly worse. If it is your private problem, and the other party doesn't know how you feel, then you take that to the Lord and ask for His forgiveness and for His cleansing. From that point on, just go be that person's brother and friend. Do not go confessing your inner feelings to every Tom, Dick, or Harry in the church. I have seen people do that and it causes all sorts of problems. If, however, they are fully aware that you have a problem with them, then do go to them and get it right.

I was in Santa Rosa some years ago to perform a wedding. The bride and groom were both Christians, but the rest of the family was not. The family threw them a very worldly wedding reception (kegs of beer were flowing at the reception, so it was a little startling when my four-year-old son walked up and said, "That punch really tastes awful." Oops!). There was a young hippy friend of the couple who had the joy of the Lord written all over his face. I asked him about himself and he told me an interesting story.

This young hippy said he had been working in construction, taking odd jobs here and there, when he got a job working for a contractor who was a really bad boss. The way he got even with this incredibly bad supervisor was to steal tools from him. This mean boss believed this hippy guy was faithful to him, so he would always blame someone else for the missing tools and fire them. Workmen were being fired left and right.

When this hippy became a Christian, he had all those stolen tools in his garage that belonged to his boss. The Lord would not let him rest because of those tools. One day, after work, he went to his garage, gathered up all the tools and took them to his boss and confessed.

He told the man that Jesus Christ now lived in his heart, so he had to confess about stealing and return all the tools. The boss cussed him up one side and down the other, and then fired him. Even though he was now unemployed, that hippy drove away a free man and, by his own testimony, filled with the joy of the Lord.

That is the spirit of freedom we have in Jesus Christ. Get it right before the Lord, and if anything has to be done, do it regardless of the response. Let the Lord free you. Allow the Lord to clear the air and make everything new for you. That is the heart of the sin and the trespass offering.

It is because of what Jesus accomplished on the cross that a guy like Tex Watson, the man who massacred those people under the direction of Charles Manson, today is a redeemed believer in Jesus Christ and an ordained minister in the California prison system. Jesus Christ set him free.

Brethren, the point is that Jesus Himself has become both our sin and our trespass offering before God, once and for all and forever. He made that sacrifice at Calvary and then He went in to the Holy of Holies, the heavenly Holy of Holies, and sat down at the right hand of God the Father.

> **Therefore He is able also to save forever those who draw near to God through Him, since He always lives to make intercession for them.** (Hebrews 7:25)

Hallelujah! We are set free in Jesus.

These are the offerings of non-sweet or non-fragrant aroma because they deal directly with our sin. Based on the work done for us at the cross, which these offerings foretold, the sin issue in our lives is removed completely, settled forever before God in heaven through Jesus Christ. With that settled, we come to the offerings of fragrant aroma to the Lord. That is what we will look at in the next chapter.

Chapter Seven

The Offerings of Sweet Aroma

... and walk in love, just as Christ also loved you and gave Himself up for us, an offering and a sacrifice to God as a fragrant aroma.

Ephesians 5:2

The book of Hebrews holds a major clue to unlocking the truths given to us through the tabernacle picture. It tells us that when we are talking about the tabernacle, we are talking about something which goes much deeper than the simple outward acts of sacrifice, service, and ritual performed in the Old Testament. Using the tabernacle sacrifices as examples, Hebrews says of Christ:

> ... **but now once at the consummation of the ages He has been manifested to put away sin by the sacrifice of Himself.** (Hebrews 9:26b)

The passage in Hebrews refers to the sacrifices of the tabernacle itself as simply a picture, a shadow of the sacrifice of Jesus Christ.

> **By this will we have been sanctified through the offering of the body of Jesus Christ once for all.** (Hebrews 10:10)

> ... but He, having offered one sacrifice for sins for all time, SAT DOWN AT THE RIGHT HAND OF GOD ... (Hebrews 10:12)
>
> For by one offering He has perfected for all time those who are sanctified. (Hebrews 10:14)

In the Old Testament tabernacle, the Israelites had five different sacrifices which were offered on an ongoing, continual basis, over and over and over again, through the years, through the generations. Christ, in one sacrifice for all time, removed all of our sins from us with His ultimate act of love.

> ... and walk in love, just as Christ also loved you and gave Himself up for us, an offering and a sacrifice to God as a fragrant aroma. (Ephesians 5:2)

Paul was addressing Gentiles, the Ephesians, in that verse. To a Gentile eye, that just seems like a flowery way of saying that Jesus is our sacrifice. But it would have riveted a Jew's attention because it was saying something about the entire sacrificial system and how Jesus Christ fulfilled it. To the Jew, this meant that Jesus not only was our sin-bearer and that He took care of our sins at the cross, but He also was the fulfillment of the three offerings of "fragrant aroma," or "sweet aroma." He did not just fulfill the requirements for the two non-sweet offerings that we looked at in the last chapter, but He also fulfilled the requirements for the three offerings of sweet aroma.

The offerings of fragrant aroma, in order, are: the burnt offering first, then the grain offering, and, finally, the peace offering.

The Purpose of the Burnt Offering

The Lord starts describing the burnt offering in the first chapter of Leviticus. Let's look at verses 3-9:

> "If his offering is a burnt offering from the herd, he shall offer it, a male without defect; he shall offer it at the doorway of the tent of meeting, that he may be accepted before the LORD. He shall lay his hand on the head of the burnt offering, that it may be accepted for him to make atonement on his behalf. He shall slay the young bull before the LORD; and Aaron's sons the priests

shall offer up the blood and sprinkle the blood around on the altar that is at the doorway of the tent of meeting. He shall then skin the burnt offering and cut it into its pieces. The sons of Aaron the priest shall put fire on the altar and arrange wood on the fire. Then Aaron's sons the priests shall arrange the pieces, the head and the suet over the wood which is on the fire that is on the altar. Its entrails, however, and its legs he shall wash with water. And the priest shall offer up in smoke all of it on the altar for a burnt offering, an offering by fire of a soothing aroma to the LORD."

Notice that the special purpose of this offering was that the individual would be accepted before the Lord. What we have in the burnt offering is a picture of Jesus Christ's perfect and total surrender of Himself to His Father. Jesus came to do His Father's will and God accepted and delighted in His sacrifice. It is a two-fold picture that goes together.

Notice in this sacrifice, the entire sacrifice was burned on the altar. Remember that only portions of the sin and the trespass offerings would be burned on the altar, and then the carcass would be taken and burned outside the camp. In this sacrifice, the whole carcass was burned on the altar.

Because this sacrifice represents the perfect and total surrender of Jesus Christ to His Father, and God's acceptance and delight in that sacrifice, the smoke goes up and it is an offering of fragrant aroma to God. It is called an offering of fragrant aroma because of God's delight and acceptance of the sacrifice. This sacrifice is wholly accepted. The whole sacrifice is offered on the altar and it is fully accepted by God.

So, as the sin and the trespass offerings symbolize confession and cleansing from sin, the burnt offering symbolizes our identification with Jesus Christ Himself, who is our offering.

The sin and trespass offerings focus on our sin. The burnt offering focuses on Jesus Christ. The emphasis is on Him who is the offering, our Lord, Jesus Christ. It is interesting that we as believers talk about accepting and receiving Jesus Christ as our Lord and Savior. Well, there are actually two parts to that process. The first deals with the confession of sin and thanking Him for forgiveness and the cleansing that He has accomplished for us. That is pictured in the Old Testament by the sin and the trespass offerings, i.e., the offerings of non-sweet aroma. The second part is opening the door to your heart, letting Jesus come in as Lord and Savior of your life, receiving Him and identifying yourself with Him. In the Old Testament, that is pictured in the burnt offering.

This idea is summed up in Paul's description of his own life's ministry in the book of Acts.

> … solemnly testifying to both Jews and Greeks of repentance toward God and faith in our Lord Jesus Christ. (Acts 20:21)

That Scripture contains the two parts of accepting Jesus into your life: repentance toward God and faith in our Lord Jesus Christ.

Repentance toward God is pictured in the sin and trespass offerings. I repent and I am forgiven of my sin. Faith in our Lord Jesus Christ, identifying with Him, believing and trusting in Him, being in union with Him, are found in the burnt offering.

An Acceptable and Delightful Sacrifice

On the basis of what Jesus has sacrificed for us, in Christ we are fully accepted and literally delighted over. The result is that the delight and the acceptance that the Father has for the Son, through the burnt offering (Jesus' sacrifice on the cross), is now extended to the believer.

> "Behold, My Servant, whom I uphold;
> My chosen one in whom My soul delights.
> I have put My Spirit upon Him;
> He will bring forth justice to the nations." (Isaiah 42:1)

> "And as the bridegroom rejoices over the bride, so your God will rejoice over you." (Isaiah 62:5b)

As the bridegroom rejoices over His bride, God says He rejoices over you.

> … and in Him you have been made complete, and He is the head over all rule and authority … (Colossians 2:10)

> I have been crucified with Christ; and it is no longer I who live, but Christ lives in me; and the life which I now live in the flesh I live by faith in the Son of God, who loved me and gave Himself up for me. (Galatians 2:20)

So the burnt offering represents Jesus Christ wholly giving Himself to God for us, and our identification with Him.

This means that the issue of being acceptable to God has been settled forever because Jesus is our burnt offering of fragrant aroma to God. As God fully accepts and is blessed by that sacrifice, He fully accepts us through the sacrifice of Jesus Christ. A believer in Jesus is never unacceptable to God. We were completely and permanently cleansed at the cross by the blood of Jesus. As the writer of Hebrews says in chapter 11, verse 16, because of our faith in Jesus:

God is not ashamed to be called their God.

The Five Sacrificial Animals for the Burnt Offering

Why was this offering such a soothing aroma to God? It may be better understood by looking at the five different animals which could be sacrificed as a burnt offering to the Lord because of what they symbolize. (Notice how these offerings contrast significantly with our own nature.)

1. Bull or ox. It is the bull, or ox, which pictures Christ as the patient and enduring servant, obedient even unto death. This characteristic stands in direct contrast to our tendency toward rebellion and disobedience.

2. Sheep or lamb. This animal pictured the quiet unresisting self-surrender of Jesus, even to death on the cross. What a contrast this is to our nature of self-will and self-centeredness.

3. Goat. The goat makes an interesting sacrifice. Remember in the parable of the sheep and the goats, the goats were the bad guys, the sheep were the good guys. The goat typifies the sinner. How does that picture Christ? In His sacrifice, Jesus was numbered with the transgressors.

> **... Because He poured out Himself to death,**
> **And was numbered with the transgressors ...** (Isaiah 53:12b)

> **He made Him who knew no sin to be sin on our behalf, so that we might become the righteousness of God in Him.** (2 Corinthians 5:21)

> **Christ redeemed us from the curse of the Law, having become a curse for us—for it is written, "CURSED IS EVERYONE WHO HANGS ON A TREE—**(Galatians 3:13)

Paul is quoting the Old Testament law (Deuteronomy 21:23) when he says in that verse, "Cursed is everyone who hangs on a tree." Jesus became that curse for us. So He willingly and freely took our place in death. This is such a contrast to our nature which leads us to save our own skin at all costs. What a difference.

4. and 5.   Dove and pigeon. These were the sacrifices for the poor folks who did not have a lamb, bull, ox, or goat. These sacrifices picture sorrowing innocence. What a contrast to our nature of belligerent guilt. (We may be guilty, but boy can we be belligerent about it!)

The dove and the pigeon were the poor man's sacrifice. I like that because He emptied Himself and became poor that we might be made rich. I like the way I heard one person put it, "The sacrifice of the poor man becomes the poor man's sacrifice." We are *all* poor men, and He is our sacrifice. He became poor for us.

Those were the animals that could be sacrificed in the burnt offering. Now let us get into some other details regarding this offering.

> **He shall then skin the burnt offering and cut it into its pieces.** (Leviticus 1:6)

The burnt offering was cut into pieces and the whole thing was burned on the altar. Nothing was taken outside the camp, as they were with the other offerings. The entire sacrifice was consumed on the altar. This was probably the reason the fire needed to be stoked, because the whole thing was going to be burned right there on the altar.

"Burnt," in Hebrew, literally means "ascending." It is a reference to the smoke which would ascend from the fire. It could be called the ascending offering. This is wonderful because it emphasizes the point that this was all for God, it was all given to God, and it ascended to Him. None was burned anywhere else and none of it was partitioned off for the priests or the people. It was given to God in its entirety. Indeed, Jesus Christ gave Himself up completely to the Father for His purpose and His glory. This pictures the total offering that was Christ.

Set Apart for God's Use

We, as believers, receive the benefit of that offering. That puts us in a very unique place with God because we now, literally, belong to God. We are His. We identify with Jesus and we are His. The Bible says that we are called "saints." That is a powerful word. It means "holy ones." Just as the parts of the tabernacle were dedicated and given over, completely sanctified for God's use in the tabernacle, and only for that purpose, we are also dedicated and given over, completely sanctified for God's use.

The average Israelite man could not run into the tabernacle and say, "Gee, I can't find my shovel and I've got to clean a mess up in our tent. Can I borrow the shovel that you use for the sacrifices? It's an old, beat up dirty thing anyway. Can't I just borrow it?"

The priest's answer to that question would have been: "No, you cannot borrow the utensils set aside as holy to God. You cannot use this shovel. I'm sorry that you don't have a shovel, that you can't clean up your mess. I understand that this is the only shovel around right now, that it is just sitting in the corner, not being used. Even so, you cannot use this shovel, because it belongs to God. It is for *His* use, in *His* tabernacle, *period.*"

That is what it means to be sanctified for the Father's use. That word "sanctified," referring to the believer, is the same word that is translated "holy." It is also the same word that is translated "saint." You are sanctified. You are set apart for God's use, and God's use alone.

Suddenly, you have a greater and deeper understanding of what God's acceptance of that burnt offering means in your life. It means you are now an instrument fit for the Master's use. You are an instrument for His use because God has accepted the burnt offering sacrifice represented in Jesus Christ, once and for all and forever, for you and me.

> **Or do you not know that your body is a temple of the Holy Spirit who is in you, whom you have from God, and that you are not your own? For you have been bought with a price: therefore glorify God in your body.** (1 Corinthians 6:19-20)

> **... and do not go on presenting the members of your body to sin as instruments of unrighteousness; but present yourselves to God as those alive from the dead, and your members as instruments of righteousness to God.** (Romans 6:13)

You belong to God now, so you present yourself to God and remind yourself that you are entirely His, to be used for His good purpose. You can do that. You *can* see your body as a temple of God's. You *can* present the members of your body as instruments to God for righteous use because of everything that the burnt offering signifies, because Jesus Christ is your burnt offering. It is an offering of soothing aroma which is fully acceptable to God.

Washed By the Word and the Spirit

Now, notice the first part of Leviticus 1:9. The priests were to wash the inner parts and the legs with water.

> **Its entrails, however, and its legs he shall wash with water.** (Leviticus 1:9a)

Interesting. Water symbolizes two things in the Bible:
1. The Holy Spirit.
2. The Word of God.

Indeed, the Holy Spirit and the Word of God go right together.

> **And take … the sword of the Spirit, which is the word of God.** (Ephesians 6:17)

In the armor of the believer, the sword of the Spirit is the Word of God. Jesus Christ, of course, was perfectly anointed by the Holy Spirit.

The inner parts and the legs of the burnt offering sacrifice were washed. As believers, when the heart (our inner man) has been touched and anointed by the Holy Spirit (washed in the water of the Spirit), when the Word of God has done its work in the heart, the result is Holy Spirit-anointed action (the legs). An anointed heart results in anointed service.

As we identify with Jesus, He gives direction, guidance, and power through His Spirit directly upon our hearts. As the Holy Spirit does that work *in* our hearts, and as the Word does that work *on* our hearts, it has the same result. It puts an anointing of the Spirit on our very actions.

That is why Jesus said, " ... apart from Me, you can do nothing." (John 15:5b)

You can do a lot of running around and a lot of work, but until that running around and that work is a direct result of the work of the Spirit in your heart, it is worthless, useless, and fruitless. But when those efforts are inspired by the Spirit in your heart, they result in actions, guided, led, and empowered by the Holy Spirit.

Paul says in Romans 12:1:

> Therefore I urge you, brethren, by the mercies of God, to present your bodies a living and holy sacrifice, acceptable to God, which is your spiritual service of worship.

So, I take this little life of mine and, in faith, I obey God. I lay my life down as a sacrifice, holy and acceptable. Why? Because of Jesus, not because of me. The perfections of Christ were offered on my behalf. Now this body of mine becomes a fragrant aroma unto the Lord in this world.

> **He shall then skin the burnt offering and cut it into its pieces.** (Leviticus 1:6)

> **Also the priest who presents any man's burnt offering, that priest shall have for himself the skin of the burnt offering which he has presented.** (Leviticus 7:8)

The sacrifice is skinned before being offered and the priest gets to keep the skin, obviously to make things like clothing, shoes, and coats. It is his part of the offering. This is a reminder that we are now clothed in the righteousness of Jesus Christ. We are covered in the righteousness of Christ.

Donald Barnhouse tells a story of going to a coal mining town in Pennsylvania years ago. With all the coal mining going on, there was a layer of gray soot on everything. It was even in the air. He saw this grayness on the cars, houses, trees, grass, and bushes. *Everything* was covered with this gray soot from the coal mine. He was walking down a street in that town one day when he noticed a bright white flower. It was the only thing that was not covered with gray soot, so it really stood out. Barnhouse turned to the man who was walking with him and said, "Wow, look at that white flower! It is untouched and it is brilliant."

His companion walked over to the flower, took a bunch of soot from the ground and poured it on the flower.

Barnhouse asked him what he was doing. "You have one beautiful flower in the whole town and you just covered it with soot."

The man said, "Wait! Watch what happens."

They watched the little flower for a few minutes, long enough to witness the soot slide off the petals. There was a consistency on the petals that was slippery to the soot. The flower became as white as before.

That is what the sacrifice of Jesus has done for you. We live in a dirty gray world. We are so easily tarnished and can so easily get polluted with the "soot" of the world. But believers are now clothed with the righteousness of Jesus Christ and that dirty gray soot of the world can no longer adhere to us. In Him, we are new creations.

> **Therefore if anyone is in Christ, he is a new creature; the old things passed away; behold, new things have come.** (2 Corinthians 5:17)

Every single day, it is wonderful to be able to get up in the morning and say "Thank you, Jesus, that all the old stuff has passed away and new things have come." With your faith in Jesus Christ, and a heart that is yielded to His influence and His direction, you are God's beautiful little flower, wherever you have been planted in this dirty, messy world. That is where He wants you to be. He does not expect you to be anywhere other than where you are. Just be wherever you are, right now, for Him. You can be that bright spot in your corner of the world because of what was accomplished for you at the cross.

Jesus Christ is our burnt offering. That fact qualifies and equips us to be that light of His in the context of our daily lives. We are equipped. We are qualified, in Jesus.

The Grain Offering

That brings us to the grain offering, the second of the offerings of sweet aroma.

> "Now when anyone presents a grain offering as an offering to the Lord, his offering shall be of fine flour, and he shall pour oil on it and put frankincense on it. He shall then bring it to Aaron's sons the priests; and shall take from it his handful of its fine flour and of its oil with all of its frankincense. And the priest shall offer it up in smoke as its memorial portion on the altar, an offering by fire of a soothing aroma to the Lord. The remainder of the grain offering belongs to Aaron and his sons: a thing most holy, of the offerings to the Lord by fire." (Leviticus 2:1-3)

> "No grain offering, which you bring to the Lord, shall

> be made with leaven, for you shall not offer up in smoke any leaven or any honey as an offering by fire to the LORD." (Leviticus 2:11)

> "Every grain offering of yours, moreover, you shall season with salt, so that the salt of the covenant of your God shall not be lacking from your grain offering; with all your offerings you shall offer salt." (Leviticus 2:13)

In Scripture you find the grain offering linked very closely with the burnt offering. They go together. This is kind of interesting because the burnt offering looks at the person of Jesus Christ (His beauty, His perfection, and our identity with Him as a person). The grain offering came from the labor of the field; consequently, it pictures the work of Christ. The person and the work of Christ, which go right together, are pictured in the burnt offering and the grain offering.

With that in mind, note that the grain offering is the only offering that does not have blood associated with it. There is no blood involved in this sacrifice. The emphasis of this sacrifice is on the life of Jesus, and its unique beauty before God and man.

> **And the Word became flesh, and dwelt among us, and we saw His glory, glory as of the only begotten from the Father, full of grace and truth.** (John 1:14)

In Jesus, we see God's glory, grace, and truth. In Jesus' life and in His ministry, we see the only begotten of the Father.

In the grain offering, part of the grain went on the altar as an offering to God, and part of the grain was given to the priests. So there was a sense in which this was an offering to God, but it was also an offering to man. In the same sense, the life and ministry of Jesus was very pleasing to His Heavenly Father, but it was also very pleasing to those to whom He ministered. His life was a perfect example of selfless love for others.

> " ... just as the Son of Man did not come to be served, but to serve, and to give His life a ransom for many."
> (Jesus in Matthew 20:28)

As the Heavenly Father said:

> "This is My beloved Son, in whom I am well-pleased."
> (Matthew 3:17b)

Even though there is no blood associated with this sacrifice, death is still seen in this offering because the grain was burnt on the altar. What we see in that is a life dedicated to total obedience to His Heavenly Father. It was a life and ministry which had no reservations in obedience to His Father. He entrusted Himself to His Father to the point of death at the cross.

Referring to Jesus, Peter says in 1 Peter 2:22-23:

> **... WHO COMMITTED NO SIN, NOR WAS ANY DECEIT FOUND IN HIS MOUTH; and while being reviled, He did not revile in return; while suffering, He uttered no threats, but kept entrusting Himself to Him who judges righteously ...**

He entrusted Himself to His Father as an example to us as believers. Paul said this to believers in Philippians 2:5-9:

> **Have this attitude in yourselves which was also in Christ Jesus, who, although He existed in the form of God, did not regard equality with God a thing to be grasped, but emptied Himself, taking the form of a bond-servant, and being made in the likeness of men. Being found in appearance as a man, He humbled Himself by becoming obedient to the point of death, even death on a cross. For this reason also, God highly exalted Him, and bestowed on Him the name which is above every name ...**

James said in James 4:10:

> **Humble yourselves in the presence of the Lord, and He will exalt you.**

As we feed our souls on Him, we are nourished. We are sustained, just as the priests were who ate of this grain offering. The priests were feeding on the same ingredients which were that soothing aroma to the Lord. It consisted of fine flour, oil, and frankincense, seasoned with salt.

Fine flour represents the evenness, the consistency, the unblemished character of our Lord's life.

Oil was poured on that fine flour. Oil in the Bible always represents the Holy Spirit. Jesus was conceived by the Holy Spirit, filled with the Holy Spirit, and led by the Holy Spirit in every detail of His life. He was the One who said, "I only do those things that I see My Father doing." Consequently, He was our perfect example. His was a 100-percent, Holy Spirit-filled, led, and anointed life.

Frankincense is a fragrant gum, a sweet gum. But there is something particularly interesting about frankincense: it becomes most fragrant when it is crushed and burned. It was through the trials and sufferings of our Lord that His beauty, His love, and His compassion became most evident.

> **But God demonstrates His own love toward us, in that while we were yet sinners, Christ died for us.** (Romans 5:8)

It is interesting that all the offerings at the altar are burnt offerings. One way or the other, something gets burned on that altar. This is a picture of Jesus. His life was a great offering, a soothing aroma to God. Both His life and His ministry were evidence of the offering of His life.

Finally, the grain offering was seasoned with salt. Salt is a preservative. His words were seasoned. As John put it, He was **"full of grace and truth"** (John 1:14).

When salt is added, it adds flavor to what was bland. The ministry of Jesus was perfectly seasoned. He knew just what was needed, what needed to be said, what needed to be done. His ministry was perfectly balanced in every way. His enemies were driven up the wall because everything He said and everything He did was just right. They could never catch Him in a mistake. Every time they tried to catch Him in sin or error, He would turn it around and make it just right, seasoned with salt. His ministry was one which uplifted, helped, and encouraged, bringing support and hope. No wonder the downtrodden of the earth flocked to Him. His was a ministry seasoned with salt.

Salt was also used as a preservative. The ministry of Jesus is preserved forever. His words are still of eternal value with applications for life that work in the real world. His words are consistently useful and workable.

So, the fine flour creates a beautiful picture of our Lord and His perfection. Jesus was anointed with oil, anointed by the Holy Spirit, in every way. The frankincense represents that beautiful giving of Himself that was gloriously fragrant, and perfected in His suffering. His ministry was seasoned with salt. His work was just right.

It is interesting to note what ingredients were *not* to be used in a grain offering. There was to be no leaven added to this offering. Leaven symbolizes sin.

> **Your boasting is not good. Do you not know that a little leaven leavens the whole lump of dough? Clean out the old leaven so that you may be a new lump, just as you are in fact unleavened. For Christ our Passover also has been sacrificed. Therefore let us celebrate the feast, not with old leaven, nor with the leaven of malice and wickedness, but with the unleavened bread of sincerity and truth.** (1 Corinthians 5:6-8)

> **And Jesus said to them, "Watch out and beware of the leaven of the Pharisees and Sadducees."** (Matthew 16:6)

> **"How is it that you do not understand that I did not speak to you concerning bread? But beware of the leaven of the Pharisees and Sadducees."** (Matthew 16:11)

Leaven is a symbol of sin, and a little leaven leavens the whole lump. Since the grain offering speaks of the perfection of Jesus Christ, God did not want any leaven in it. Jesus was kin to us, very human, but with no sin.

> **For we do not have a high priest who cannot sympathize with our weaknesses, but One who has been tempted in all things as we are, yet without sin.** (Hebrews 4:15)

There was also to be no honey in the grain offering. It might seem that honey should be in an offering to God because it is so good and sweet. But honey pictures the sweetness of natural man. In this sense, honey appears attractive to a godless world, but it has nothing of the divine nature of God. Honey represents those things of the natural man which are so attractive to others, but are not of God's Spirit. Honey has another interesting feature, it ferments. If honey is put in the fire, it becomes sour. Fire sours honey. Fire brings the depth of fragrance out of frankincense, but it will sour honey.

I remember hearing of a counseling session Chuck Smith had with a couple who were having a tough time in their lives and ministry. His comment was, "You know, these things will do one of two things. They will either make you better, or they will make you bitter. So how are you going to let it affect you? These things that are so distressing to you will either be a source of bitterness to you, or they can be a source to make you better." One is honey, and the other is frankincense.

Jesus Christ has come into our lives. He replaces the honey of our lives with the frankincense of His life. He wants to replace your honey with His frankincense.

So Jesus is our grain offering before the Lord. Again, the priests partake of this offering. Part of this offering is given to God and part of this offering is given to the priests.

> **"What is left of it Aaron and his sons are to eat. It shall be eaten as unleavened cakes in a holy place; they are to eat it in the court of the tent of meeting."** (Leviticus 6:16)

Learn about Jesus. Meditate on Him, on that which is the fullness and richness of Jesus. Soak it up. This is communion with Christ. This is spiritual food for our souls.

> **"Take My yoke upon you and learn from Me, for I am gentle and humble in heart, and YOU WILL FIND REST FOR YOUR SOULS. For My yoke is easy and My burden is light."** (Matthew 11:29-30)

Notice that the grain offering is only for the priests. It is not to be taken out into the camp. The priests cannot take their part of the grain offering out of the tabernacle in a bag or satchel to eat later in camp. They have to eat it in the court of the tent of meeting. They cannot eat it outside of the tabernacle.

The world knows nothing about this food. This food is that intimate communion we have with Jesus Christ, that partaking of Him and drawing from Him, being sustained and nourished by Him and by His Spirit. It is knowing Jesus better. When the revelation of Jesus Christ hits your heart with a new sense of fullness and understanding, it is a delightful thing. It is an enriching thing. You know when you have been nourished in the Spirit. But the world knows nothing of this food. It cannot even relate to it. As this food was to be eaten only in the court, not in the camp, and it was only for the priests, so it is something that is enjoyed in your relationship with the Lord that the world has no part in.

The grain offering is an offering of fragrant aroma. The fragrant aroma that the life of Jesus Christ was to His Heavenly Father is the fragrant aroma that the life of Jesus Christ is to us, through His Spirit.

The Peace Offering

After the burnt offering and the grain offering have been made, finally comes the peace offering. We read about the peace offering in Leviticus chapters 3 and 7.

The order of these offerings is very significant. After all your sin has been dealt with in the sin offering and the trespass offering; after we have been accepted by God in Christ through the burnt offering; after we have come to the place where we can partake in the beauty and the glory of Jesus Christ Himself as is represented by the grain offering, then, and only then, do we come to the peace offering.

1. **The Sin and Trespass Offerings** picture for us how Jesus has removed our sin from us.
2. **The Burnt Offering** illustrates that we are accepted as the beloved of God in Jesus Christ.
3. **The Grain Offering** pictures for us our ability to partake in the beauty and the glory of Christ.
4. **The Peace Offering** pictures our consequent peace with God through Jesus Christ and fellowship with Him and with one another.

> **Therefore, having been justified by faith, we have peace with God through our Lord Jesus Christ …** (Romans 5:1)

In this offering, the sacrifice was brought to the door of the tent of meeting, hands were laid on the sacrifice, and identification was made with the sacrifice, signifying that Jesus, our sacrifice, is our peace with God. I am not my peace with God. *He* is my peace with God. That is important. This means I always have peace with God. There is no question as to whether you are at peace with God today or not. Peace is established in Him. Anything that could in any way come against peace in me, He took at the cross. So, if I do not have peace in my heart, whatever is robbing me of that peace in my heart, has already been taken care of at the cross for me.

Some wives may say, "It is my husband that is robbing me of peace in my heart." No, this is not true. It is not your husband that is robbing you of peace in your heart. It is your attitude about your husband. Your husband, or anyone else for that matter, does not have the power to rob your heart of peace. The peace in your heart is yours alone, to have or not to have.

Nothing out there can rob you of the peace of God in your heart. Whatever is threatening to steal your peace, He took care of at the cross. You have the privilege of having peace *with* God and the peace *of* God any time, under any circumstance. That is your inheritance. If you do not have the peace of God in you, it is because you are buying into a lie. You are believing something that is robbing you of that peace, instead of resting in that peace you have in Him. Your peace offering was made in Jesus. Peace has been established.

The bottom line of the cross, in the final analysis, when all is said and done, is that God has come to you and said, "Peace." There is no more condemnation. There is no more guilt. There is no more judgment. There is no more animosity. Now, there is peace, real peace, in Christ Jesus.

> **"Peace I leave with you; My peace I give to you; not as the world gives do I give to you. Do not let your heart be troubled, nor let it be fearful."** (John 14:27)

> **Therefore there is now no condemnation for those who are in Christ Jesus.** (Romans 8:1)

> **Be anxious for nothing, but in everything by prayer and supplication with thanksgiving let your requests be made known to God. And the peace of God, which surpasses all comprehension, will guard your hearts and your minds in Christ Jesus.** (Philippians 4:6-7)

"Be anxious for nothing," Paul said in Philippians 4:6. Do you know what was accomplished at the cross for you? Peace was given to you. If you know Jesus as your personal Lord and Savior, His peace is your inheritance. It's a peace that surpasses human understanding. His is the peace of God.

> **Finally, brethren, whatever is true, whatever is honorable, whatever is right, whatever is pure, whatever**

is lovely, whatever is of good repute, if there is any excellence and if anything worthy of praise, dwell on these things. The things you have learned and received and heard and seen in me, practice these things, and the God of peace will be with you. (Philippians 4:8-9)

Notice, at first, Paul says, "If you're anxious about something, pray about it. You can have the peace of God." Then he says, "Those things that are good, and right, and of the Lord, let your mind dwell on those things. Practice these things that you have learned from me through the Spirit, and the God of peace will be with you." I like that, you go from the peace of God to the God of peace abiding in your heart. That's a victorious life, an abundant life!

The inner portions of that sacrifice were put on the altar and sacrificed to God as a peace offering. The implication there is that God the Father is the only one who fully appreciated the inner sufferings that His Son endured on the cross for our peace. He is the only one who truly understood.

Furthermore, through this offering we now have fellowship with God. This is the offering that brought fellowship.

> "Now if his offering is a sacrifice of peace offerings, if he is going to offer out of the herd, whether male or female, he shall offer it without defect before the Lord. He shall lay his hand on the head of his offering and slay it at the doorway of the tent of meeting, and Aaron's sons the priests shall sprinkle the blood around on the altar. From the sacrifice of the peace offerings he shall present an offering by fire to the Lord, the fat that covers the entrails and all the fat that is on the entrails …" (Leviticus 3:1-3)

> "Now this is the law of the sacrifice of peace offerings which shall be presented to the Lord. If he offers it by way of thanksgiving, then along with the sacrifice of thanksgiving he shall offer unleavened cakes mixed with oil, and unleavened wafers spread with oil, and cakes of well stirred fine flour mixed with oil. With the sacrifice of his peace offerings for thanksgiving, he shall present his offering with cakes of leavened bread. Of this he shall present one of every offering as a contribution to the Lord; it shall belong to the priest who sprinkles the blood of the peace offerings. Now as for the flesh of the

sacrifice of his thanksgiving peace offerings, it shall be eaten on the day of his offering; he shall not leave any of it over until morning." (Leviticus 7:11-15)

Notice that this offering is the only offering in which God gets His portion, the priests get their portion, and the person making the offering also gets a portion for himself and his family to enjoy, to celebrate.

What a picture of fellowship with God, and in Jesus, fellowship with God's people. We have now been restored into fellowship with God through Jesus Christ who is our peace offering. Because of Jesus we have peace with God and fellowship with Him and with one another.

Fellowship was very significant to the Jews. According to the Jewish mindset, when you broke bread with someone, when you ate with them, or partook of the same dinner with them, you were, by the act of breaking bread and sharing it with someone else, becoming one with that person. The bread that I am eating is the bread that you are eating. The meat that I am eating is the meat that you are eating. The same thing is in both of us. We are one. That is why first century Jews would not eat with Gentiles. The Jews felt that they were separated unto God and they could not be one with the Gentile.

So there was a real sense in this offering of recognizing a oneness. Remember, part of that offering went to God, and part of that offering went to the people themselves, so there was a sense that they were one with their God. They were one with one another. They were one with the priests. There was a sense of oneness. That is fellowship.

There is a fellowship that comes from being in the Lord. I am in fellowship with my Lord. You are in fellowship with our Lord. Therefore, we have fellowship one with another. If I am not in fellowship with Him, that will hinder my fellowship with you. So when there is a problem on the horizontal level between believers, it is because there is a problem in the vertical level with God. When the vertical (our relationship with God), is in order, the horizontal (our relationships with our brothers), will be in place.

"Behold, I stand at the door and knock; if anyone hears My voice and opens the door, I will come in to him and will dine with him, and he with Me." (Jesus in Revelation 3:20)

If you open the door of your inner life to Him, the Lord will come in and dine with you. That is a rich way of saying that you will have intimate fellowship with Him. You will break bread together. You will be one with Him. This is the essence of the peace offering, taking the meal of the peace offering and enjoying it together.

The peace offering is a beautiful picture of Communion, because we partake together of the bread which symbolizes the body of Christ. What is the peace offering? It is Christ Himself, our peace offering. As we take that offering and we eat of it, that is our Communion.

The five offerings of the tabernacle are all represented in Jesus Christ and the work He did at the cross for us when He became a sacrifice for us. That five-in-one sacrifice of Jesus Christ removes anything that could be a hindrance to our fellowship with God and our fellowship with one another. Every sin is removed at the cross, totally, in every possible way and shape. The sacrificing ends with Communion. We celebrate a feast of the very sacrifice itself, which is Jesus Christ.

Now, as an aside, when the Israelites brought those offerings, there were certain requirements given in Exodus and Leviticus. They could not be brought by an unclean person. In many cases, the priests themselves had to be sure that they were cleansed before they performed these services. In addition, the people had to engage in ceremonial cleansing before partaking. Notice what Paul says to Christians regarding Communion:

> **Therefore when you meet together, it is not to eat the Lord's Supper, for in your eating each one takes his own supper first; and one is hungry and another is drunk. What! Do you not have houses in which to eat and drink? Or do you despise the church of God and shame those who have nothing? What shall I say to you? Shall I praise you? In this I will not praise you.** (1 Corinthians 11:20-22)

> **For as often as you eat this bread and drink the cup, you proclaim the Lord's death until He comes. Therefore whoever eats the bread or drinks the cup of the Lord in an unworthy manner, shall be guilty of the body and the blood of the Lord. But a man must examine himself, and in so doing he is to eat of the bread and drink of the cup. For he who eats and drinks, eats and drinks judgment to himself if he does not judge the body**

rightly. For this reason many among you are weak and sick, and a number sleep. But if we judged ourselves rightly, we would not be judged. But when we are judged, we are disciplined by the Lord so that we will not be condemned along with the world. (1 Corinthians 11:26-32)

Paul wrote 1 Corinthians 11 about the Lord's Supper because they were taking this supper in the wrong spirit. He even told those Corinthians not to call their feasting "the Lord's Supper." In the way of correction, he told them to examine themselves. There were some who were sick and some who had died because they were not taking the Lord's Supper in the right spirit. That is pretty heavy. Examine yourself and so partake of the Lord's Supper.

Paul does not say to partake only if you are "qualified." The Scripture does not say that. I have seen Christians come to a Communion service who will not partake in the celebration of the Lord's Supper because they do not feel they are "right with the Lord." That grieves me. The whole premise of Communion is that we *are* unworthy. We need the fullness of His sacrifice to be in fellowship with Him, to be forgiven of our sins, to be in a right relationship with Him. There is never a situation when it is best to say, "I am not worthy to take Communion today." To say that is to say the cross is not quite enough for me—and that is blasphemous!

When Paul says to "examine" yourself—what does that mean? Open your heart before your Lord, let the Holy Spirit search your heart, and see if there is anything there that needs to be confessed. Make sure everything is laid bare before Him and you have received His forgiveness. Remember, He died for *all* your sins.

As many times as you need forgiveness for anything in your life, as many times a day, for the rest of your life, it is forgiven by your Heavenly Father. As many times as you need to say, "Lord, I confess my sins," you are forgiven.

So Paul says to examine yourself. Come in that spirit to the Lord. Come in with an open heart before the Lord to partake. Communion cries out forgiveness, restoration, and fellowship. You can partake in that spirit and walk away from that feast renewed and refreshed.

As I was growing up, I loved Communion Sunday because it meant a short sermon and a snack before leaving. When I went to college, I attended a different church that treated Communion much differently than how I was accustomed. One Communion Sunday I was just broken before the Lord. Tears were running down my face for no reason at all, except that I finally grasped the reality of what I was doing by partaking of those Communion elements. I took that little bit of bread and that little bit of grape juice, and I was renewed in the Lord. I walked out of there brand new.

As a pastor, I have prayed that Communion in our church would be a special time of refreshing and celebration; of full, rich fellowship with God and each other, because we are all partaking together. There are many different ways to take Communion. It is not *how* you take it that matters. It is the fact that you are doing it and you are doing it in fellowship. In our church, I like to have everyone partake of the elements all at the same time because it exemplifies the fact that we are one together in Christ.

Paul was telling the Corinthians to come in the right attitude of heart. It helps when we understand that Old Testament picture of those sacrifices and how Jesus has fulfilled them all completely and perfectly. We do that in our hearts. We celebrate Communion simply in remembrance of His finished work for us on the cross. It is all five Old Testament offerings wrapped up in Jesus. It is taking for ourselves that which was sacrificed on our behalf.

Notice that the peace offering had to be eaten on the day of the offering. So they would invite all of their relatives, family and friends, to get together and have a feast. A peace offering was made and there was a lot of meat to be eaten. It was like a major barbecue. The sacrifice had to be eaten that day, because God wanted to make sure that the partaking was tied closely with the sacrifice that had been made. God did not want the connection to be lost.

Similarly, we are to be tied closely as a community in Christ. We are to be tied closely to the cross. The cross was the place of peace with God and fellowship with the redeemed. So when we take Communion, we are receiving all that Jesus is to us. True fellowship is now open and available. Fellowship with my Father, and fellowship with my brothers and sisters in Christ is now mine.

So those are the five sacrifices. Those sacrifices give us a fuller idea of what happened at the cross for us. But the bronze altar of sacrifice was as far as the common man went in the tabernacle. When we go on from this point, we are going to have to slip into the sandals of the priests, which is interesting because in the New Testament, what are we told by Peter?

> But you are A CHOSEN RACE, A royal PRIESTHOOD, A HOLY NATION, A PEOPLE FOR GOD'S OWN POSSESSION, so that you may proclaim the excellencies of Him who has called you out of darkness into His marvelous light; for you once were NOT A PEOPLE, but now you are THE PEOPLE OF GOD; you had NOT RECEIVED MERCY, but now you have RECEIVED MERCY. (1 Peter 2:9-10)

We are God's **"royal priesthood,"** born again into the family of the great High Priest. So in the next chapter, we will look at the high priest and his sons and we will see there an awesome picture of Jesus Christ and born-again believers.

Chapter Eight

The Priesthood of the Tabernacle

But you are a chosen race, a royal priesthood, a holy nation, a people for God's own possession, so that you may proclaim the excellencies of Him who has called you out of darkness into His marvelous light ...

1 Peter 2:9

As we continue our tabernacle tour, which is really a comparison of the Old Testament tabernacle to becoming and living as a New Testament believer in Jesus Christ, we have reached the point where we have accepted the invitation to enter through the one and only gate (which is Jesus), and have been confronted with the big bronze altar, and have stood, as it were, at the foot of the cross. There we saw the five sacrifices for sin to reconcile us to God—five because it took that many to fully explain and picture the significance of the one sacrifice of Jesus Christ at Calvary some 1,500 years later. The New Testament reality of this Old Testament shadow is that the person who walked in, separated from the Heavenly Father because of his sin, is now at peace with Him and is eternally saved by the sacrifice of Jesus Christ. The free gift of eternal life in Christ has been formally received "at the foot of the cross."

The result is that there now exists a new person who has been spiritually revived and transformed by the power of God, one who has now been born again into the family of God. According to the tabernacle picture, this is a very significant point, because that altar is as far as the common man could go. At this point, the common Israelite would have to leave the tabernacle courtyard; he was never, ever, allowed into the Holy Place and the Holy of Holies located inside the tent. Only the priests themselves could go beyond the altar. Only the priests were allowed into the tabernacle tent, and only the high priest was allowed into the Holy of Holies, and that only once a year on the Day of Atonement, Yom Kippur.

Only sons born into the family of Aaron could be priests. There was no school to attend to qualify for priesthood. One was either born into the family of Aaron, or not.

So, when a person comes to the Living God through Jesus Christ, a dynamic change takes place in his life and he is literally born again into a new family, the family of Jesus Christ.

> **Jesus answered and said to him, "Truly, truly, I say to you, unless one is born again, he cannot see the kingdom of God."** (John 3:3)
>
> **For you are all sons of God through faith in Christ Jesus.** (Galatians 3:26)
>
> **See how great a love the Father has bestowed on us, that we would be called children of God; and such we are.** (1 John 3:1)
>
> **So then you are no longer strangers and aliens, but you are fellow citizens with the saints, and are of God's household…** (Ephesians 2:19)

When you accept Jesus Christ as your Lord and Savior, you are born again into His family, the family of Him who is our "great High Priest" (Hebrews 4:14). You are thus born into the priesthood of Christ, as

Aaron's sons were born into that Old Testament priesthood.

> But you are A CHOSEN RACE, A royal PRIESTHOOD, A HOLY NATION, A PEOPLE FOR God's OWN POSSESSION, so that you may proclaim the excellencies of Him who has called you out of darkness into His marvelous light ... (1 Peter 2:9)

So now the Levitical priesthood takes on a whole new significance. Now we will look at our priesthood as it relates to that tabernacle priesthood, because the Levitical priesthood pictures for us a born-again believer in his relationship with God.

In this chapter, we will look at two aspects of that:

1. Aaron and his sons as priests; and
2. Aaron's special garments, the beautiful and costly garments of the high priest.

Aaron and His Sons

> "Then bring near to yourself Aaron your brother, and his sons with him, from among the sons of Israel, to minister as priest to Me—Aaron, Nadab and Abihu, Eleazar and Ithamar, Aaron's sons. You shall make holy garments for Aaron your brother, for glory and for beauty." (Exodus 28:1-2)

The Lord emphasizes two things in this verse: the priest and the priest's garments. Exodus chapters 28 and 29 give us details on the garments and the priesthood; more detail is found in Leviticus chapters 8 and 9.

Aaron, the brother of Moses, was Israel's first high priest, chosen by God. As high priest, he was the head of and in charge of the other priests, all of whom were his sons. Aaron, as the high priest, was the only person allowed to enter the Holy of Holies, and then only once a year. He could not just trip in to the Holy of Holies any time he felt like it, sit down on the mercy seat, and have a chat with God. He could only go in once a year on Yom Kippur, the Day of Atonement, and that was simply to sprinkle the blood of atonement on the mercy seat for the sins of the nation of Israel, and then get out.

Along with the general oversight of all the priests, Aaron had three primary functions as high priest:

1. He was to make the sacrifice for the nation on the Day of Atonement.

2. He was to pray for all the people at the golden altar of incense inside the tabernacle. He was primary intercessor for the people of Israel at the altar of incense.

3. He was to have a special compassion for the ignorant and misguided. He would speak for them. He would give guidance to them. He was their special friend (Hebrews 5:1-2).

What a wonderful picture of Jesus Christ!

Therefore, since we have a great high priest who has passed through the heavens, Jesus the Son of God, let us hold fast our confession. (Hebrews 4:14)

Unlike the high priest in the tabernacle who would pass through the veil into the Holy of Holies once a year, our great High Priest, Jesus Christ, passed through the heavens, into the very presence of God, into the real Holy of Holies. The Holy of Holies in the tabernacle on earth was simply a shadow or a picture of the heavenly throne room of God. The writer of Hebrews says, in essence, "Since Jesus is our true High Priest before the throne of God, hold fast your confession of Him as Lord. Keep your faith, your commitment to Him. Hold fast because we have a *great* High Priest."

Israel would look at their high priest as their man before God. He was one of them, but he would go into the presence of God for them. He was to have special compassion for the weak. He interceded for them. He was "their man" before God. The writer of Hebrews essentially says, "That was an earthly man, going through a veil into an earthly tabernacle. Our High Priest, Jesus—with more compassion and more love than that high priest ever had—became a man, *the Man,* for us. Jesus, who is God incarnate, became a servant of men and humbled Himself to death, even death on a cross. On the third day He rose again, and has passed into the very throne room of God in heaven. So, hold fast to your confession because *our Man* is at the throne of heaven for you. You cannot lose."

The book of Hebrews draws out the point that the Levitical high priest, of which Aaron was the first, is a type, a picture, a symbol, of the real one who is Jesus Christ. When you begin to look to Jesus as your great High Priest, the Old Testament functions of the priesthood come to life.

1. The high priest made a sacrifice for the sin of the nation on the Day of Atonement.

Jesus Christ *is* the sacrifice for our sin. He completely fulfilled that function. No one is required to take a bull, a lamb, an ox, a goat, or anything else to the tabernacle and slay it anymore because Jesus fulfilled, once and for all, that function. His one sacrifice put away our sin forever.

2. The high priest was to pray for all the people at the altar of incense inside the tabernacle. He was primary intercessor for the people of Israel at the altar of incense in the tabernacle. In Hebrews 7 we read regarding Jesus:

> **Therefore He is able also to save forever those who draw near to God through Him, since He always lives to make intercession for them.** (Hebrews 7:25)

Jesus always lives to make intercession for us. What the high priest would go in and do, often in a cursory way on occasion for his people, Jesus does continually in the presence of our Heavenly Father on our behalf.

3. The high priest was to have a special compassion for the ignorant and misguided. He would speak for them. He would give guidance to them. He was their special friend.

> **For every high priest taken from among men is appointed on behalf of men in things pertaining to God, in order to offer both gifts and sacrifices for sins; he can deal gently with the ignorant and misguided, since he himself also is beset with weakness ...** (Hebrews 5:1-2)

Talk about compassion for the weak, the ignorant, and the misguided! Jesus knows the stuff we are made of, as it says of God in Psalm 103:14:

> **For He Himself knows our frame; He is mindful that we are but dust.**

There is an understanding and a compassion that Jesus has for our frail frame. He made us. He understands. He has been here. He knows what it is like to be human.

> **Therefore, He had to be made like His brethren in all things, so that He might become a merciful and faithful high priest in things pertaining to God, to make propitiation for the sins of the people. For since He Himself was tempted in that which He has suffered, He is able to come to the aid of those who are tempted.** (Hebrews 2:17-18)

Jesus understands temptation. He has been there and He wants to help us. He is not standing over us just waiting for an opportunity to condemn us. He is not going to stand off at a distance and tell us to get our act together. Quite the opposite. He understands and wants to help us. He wants to help *you*. That is so awesome!

Jesus prayed for Peter in Luke 22:31-32. He told Peter that Satan wanted to sift him like wheat. He did not tell Peter to "tough it out" if he was going to qualify to be on the Jesus Team. Jesus did not tell Peter to "show himself worthy." No, He told Peter in verse 32:

> **"... but I have prayed for you, that your faith may not fail; and you, when once you have turned again, strengthen your brothers."**

That's compassion, understanding and helpfulness. That is the kind of High Priest I like. That is the kind of High Priest I need. He is "my Man" before the throne of God.

> **Therefore, since we have a great high priest who has passed through the heavens, Jesus the Son of God, let us hold fast our confession. For we do not have a high priest who cannot sympathize with our weaknesses, but One who has been tempted in all things as we are, yet without sin. Therefore let us draw near with confidence to the throne of grace, so that we may receive mercy and find grace to help in time of need.** (Hebrews 4:14-16)

Some people look at that statement and their impression is that He cannot understand what we are going through because He did not sin. Jesus faced temptation in every area that we have ever faced temptation and He experienced it to its complete limit. He knows temptation more than we know temptation, because we have a tendency of giving in to it. He never did give in to temptation, not one time. He knows temptation. He knows how it affects you, what it does to you. He understands.

He says we are to draw near with confidence to the throne of grace (notice, it is *not* the throne of judgment). It is at the throne of grace that we may obtain mercy and find grace to help in time of need.

That phrase "in time of need" in the Greek is a colloquialism, and the best English translation is **"in the nick of time."** Mercy and grace are supplied as they are needed, right then, right there. There will be grace to help you in the moment you need it, in the nick of time.

So these are what you find when you come to Him, when you turn to Him in your time of weakness. First of all, you come to a throne of grace. He is not there to condemn, accuse, or judge. He is there to help. It is a throne of grace. What are you going to find when you come to the throne of grace? You will obtain mercy first, and then you will find grace to help in the time of need.

The difference between mercy and grace, put very simply is: mercy is not getting what you deserve, and grace is getting what you do not deserve. So, I may deserve to be tied to a post and whipped. Instead I get mercy. I do not get what I deserve. Conversely, I do not deserve His compassion, His understanding, His help, His forgiveness. Yet that is what I get, I find grace at His throne. So, He is telling us not to be afraid to come to His throne.

Remember what the high priest represented to Israel, in the tabernacle. He was their man. He made sacrifice for them. He prayed for them. He was a special friend to the weak. That is what Jesus, as our High Priest, is to us. He is our Man. He made the sacrifice for us, once and for all. He intercedes for us continually. He is our special friend. He is on our side before God. We do not deserve His intervention for us. But He is in the presence of God intervening on our behalf (1 John 2: 1-2). He is our perfect High Priest.

Believer-Priests

If Aaron was a picture of Jesus Christ for us in his functions and duties as a high priest, then the priesthood, that is his sons, his family who were called of God to help in the ministry of the tabernacle, become a beautiful picture of born-again Christians who are now in the family of

Christ, serving, ministering, and living in the name of Jesus Christ.

> **But you are A CHOSEN RACE, A royal PRIESTHOOD, A HOLY NATION, A PEOPLE FOR God's OWN POSSESSION, so that you may proclaim the excellencies of Him who has called you out of darkness into His marvelous light ...** (1 Peter 2:9)

You, as a believer, are in the priesthood. You are special, chosen, a royal priesthood, that you might declare the excellencies of Christ to our generation.

A priest's job in its lowest common denominator is two-fold:
1. He represents the people before God.
2. He represents God before the people.

Indeed, that is what God has called us to do. Notice, He has declared that we are a royal priesthood. Because the King Himself is the High Priest, that makes His priesthood royal.

Aaron and his sons were ordained by God as priests in the tabernacle. The sons were ordained as priests in the tabernacle under the headship of Aaron. All of that is simply a shadow. God put all of that in the Old Testament simply to draw a picture for us on whom the end of the age has come. The reality is Jesus Christ Himself and us as believer-priests. We are the priests of God to this generation. That is why, in the body of Christ, there is not a priesthood. Each and every believer is a priest of God to this generation.

As an overview, let us look at Aaron and his sons as this theme of the family and the priesthood is developed. Obviously, they are of the same family. This priesthood is comprised of Aaron and his boys. This is family, not employer and employees. This is not master and slaves. This is *family*: Aaron and the boys, his sons. There is a close family association. Hallelujah, we are family with our High Priest!

> **So then you are no longer strangers and aliens, but you are fellow citizens with the saints, and are of God's household ...** (Ephesians 2:19)

It is important to realize that when it comes to the body of Christ, the family of God, and your relationship with God through Jesus Christ, you are not a stranger. You are not an alien. You are not an outsider. You are not just one in a crowd. You are no longer a stranger-alien, but you are a fellow citizen with the saints and you are of God's household (Ephesians 2:19). Every citizen of heaven is a member of the household of God. He is family. We even carry the family name, "Christians."

There are four things which are particularly interesting about Aaron's sons and their position in the priesthood:

1. They were commissioned. God commissioned them to His work.

> **So Jesus said to them again, "Peace be with you; as the Father has sent Me, I also send you."** (John 20:21)

It is the same commission because the sons were under the direction of the high priest; they went about doing his work. They were simply the arms and legs of the high priest, doing his work in his name. So is the body of Christ, serving in the name of Jesus Christ, each one of us divinely commissioned.

2. They were specially clothed.

> **"For Aaron's sons you shall make tunics; you shall also make sashes for them, and you shall make caps for them, for glory and for beauty. You shall put them on Aaron your brother and on his sons with him; and you shall anoint them and ordain them and consecrate them, that they may serve Me as priests."** (Exodus 28:40-41)

Aaron and his sons wore the same white tunics with sashes. What Aaron wore, the boys wore. White represents righteousness and purity.

Similarly, we have been clothed in the righteousness of Christ. We have been clothed for His use. Notice that the purpose of the clothing was for glory and for beauty. I love that. We are clothed for His use, set apart to Him. We are in a place where we can be an instrument of and reflect the glory of God. This clothing is to bring glory to our God. The clothing is also for beauty. We show forth His beauty. We see that same beauty in the white linen wall that went around the camp. That linen wall was probably made of the very same material as the priest's tunics.

We show forth the beauty, the glory, and the excellencies of Jesus Christ, not because it is in us to be able to do that on our own, but because we have been clothed in His righteousness. You may not *feel* as though you are clothed in the righteousness of Jesus. But it does not matter how you feel. Believers in Jesus are washed clean and clothed in

His righteousness.

Because we have been born again into His family and are clothed in His righteousness, we can go about our daily business and say, "I wonder what God is going to do here?" Everywhere you go the demons tremble because you now represent Him.

3. They were anointed. God said that the sons of Aaron were to be anointed in two ways, with blood and with oil (Leviticus 8:30). Aaron's sons were anointed with the same blood as Aaron when they were consecrated to their priestly office. It was the blood of the sacrifice which was used to anoint them all. To us, that means the sacrificial blood of Jesus is upon us, it is over us. That is why John could say that **"the blood of Jesus His Son cleanses us from all sin"** (1 John 1:7). There is an anointing of His cleansing blood.

They were anointed with the same oil. The oil that was used to anoint Aaron was the same oil that was used to anoint his sons. Oil, of course, represents the Holy Spirit. The oil of the Holy Spirit which anointed Jesus is the same anointing of the Holy Spirit which is in our lives.

With that in mind, there is a little detail which is kind of interesting. When Aaron and his sons were anointed with the oil, Aaron was anointed before the sacrifice was actually made. Then came the sacrifice, after which the sons were anointed with the same oil.

Similarly, Jesus received the Holy Spirit (His anointing) for His ministry at the Jordan River at the beginning of His ministry. He later died on the cross as our sacrifice for sins. Then, after His resurrection, He told His disciples to wait in Jerusalem until they received the Holy Spirit (their anointing). Ten days after His ascension into heaven, on the day of Pentecost, the believers were anointed with that same "anointing oil." That scenario is perfectly pictured in what happened in the wilderness. Aaron was anointed, the sacrifice was made, and then the sons were anointed (Leviticus 8:12, 30).

So these priests, these sons of Aaron, were anointed by the blood and anointed with the oil. What does that mean to you? To be anointed by the blood of Jesus means you are cleansed and qualified. You are cleansed before God and you are qualified to be a priest of the Most High God, a servant of the Living God, useful to Him in an eternal way. Anointed by His Spirit means you are not only cleansed and qualified, but you are equipped and empowered.

Do you know what the anointing means for you as a believer? It means everything has been done for you so that you can be effective for the glory of God and reflective of the beauty of Jesus Christ, as the priests' garments were **"for glory and for beauty."** *Everything* has been accomplished for you to have an effective and meaningful life of service for the Lord. The mission is accomplished. Jesus said, **"It is finished"** on the cross, and He meant it (John 19:30).

There are a couple of little things that are interesting about this anointing with the oil. First, Aaron got the greater anointing. Similarly, it is interesting that in John 3:34 we are told that Jesus received the Spirit without measure.

Secondly, the Lord made it very clear that this anointing oil was never to be used on common people or foreigners. It was not for them. It may have had a nice fragrance, but it was not to be used as a perfume. It was not to be used as a medicinal ointment. No. It was only for the priests and their anointing for service. As New Testament believers:

> **Now we have received, not the spirit of the world, but the Spirit who is from God, so that we may know the things freely given to us by God, which things we also speak, not in words taught by human wisdom, but in those taught by the Spirit, combining spiritual thoughts with spiritual words. But a natural man does not accept the things of the Spirit of God, for they are foolishness to him; and he cannot understand them, because they are spiritually appraised.** (1 Corinthians 2:12-14)

The gift of the Holy Spirit is for the redeemed in Jesus Christ and is not given to the world in general. No unbeliever can say, "Oh, I have the Spirit of God." It cannot happen. He may have a spirit of some sort, but it is not the Spirit of God.

4. They were representative. The sons were representative of the high priest. They ate the same meals that the high priest ate. It is interesting that, in a spiritual sense, Jesus desires to "dine" with us.

> **Behold, I stand at the door and knock; if anyone hears My voice and opens the door, I will come in to him and will dine with him, and he with Me.** (Revelation 3:20)

Remember that in the Jewish mindset, to dine together was to be as one. The sons and the high priest ate the same meals and they were involved in the same work. The sons were simply the helpers, the arms and legs for the high priest to do his work.

As Jesus was in this world, so are we, as His ambassadors.

> **Therefore, we are ambassadors for Christ, as though God were making an appeal through us; we beg you on behalf of Christ, be reconciled to God.** (2 Corinthians 5: 20)

We are in this world in the name of Jesus. God calls you to draw close to Christ, to receive His forgiveness and His eternal life, and to grow in Him. This is not just Brian Larson telling you it would be a nice thing to do. This is God Himself, reaching out to you and calling you to be reconciled to Him and to serve Him, your God.

What a blessing, what a high calling, what a privilege has been given to us through Jesus Christ. We have a special place in God's work and God's economy, in what God is doing. No one in the body of Christ is an "also-ran"—you are an integral part of God's work and plan. You are a commissioned, clothed, and anointed representative of Him. You are a member of His royal priesthood.

> **... and from Jesus Christ, the faithful witness, the firstborn of the dead, and the ruler of the kings of the earth. To Him who loves us and released us from our sins by His blood—and He has made us to be a kingdom, priests to His God and Father—to Him be the glory and the dominion forever and ever. Amen.** (Revelation 1:5-6)

The Garments of the High Priest

According to Exodus 28:2, the special garments of the high priest were **"for glory and for beauty"** also. This was the special clothing that Aaron was to wear when he ministered in the tabernacle in the name of the Lord.

There were five pieces to his special garments. They were very beautiful and costly. (These are apart from the white linen tunic that would now become the undergarment for the high priest.)

1. The blue robe, which went over the white linen tunic.
2. The ephod.
3. The breastplate.
4. The sash or the belt of the ephod.
5. The turban with the gold crown.

In these garments, God has given a wonderful picture of Jesus Christ as our great High Priest.

1. The Blue Robe

Over the white linen tunic was laid a solid blue robe.

> "You shall make the robe of the ephod all of blue. There shall be an opening at its top in the middle of it; around its opening there shall be a binding of woven work, like the opening of a coat of mail, that it will not be torn." (Exodus 28:31-32)

This blue coat would signify that which is of, or from, heaven. Only the high priest would wear that blue coat. The color blue signifies that which is of heaven. The point is that only Jesus Christ came from heaven for us, to reach us, to minister to us.

> **No one has ascended into heaven, but He who descended from heaven: the Son of Man.** (John 3:13)

> **For I have come down from heaven, not to do My own will, but the will of Him who sent Me.** (John 6:38)

> **You shall make on its hem pomegranates of blue and purple and scarlet material, all around on its hem, and bells of gold between them all around: a golden bell and a pomegranate, a golden bell and a pomegranate, all around on the hem of the robe. It shall be on Aaron when he ministers; and its tinkling shall be heard when he enters and leaves the holy place before the LORD, so that he will not die.** (Exodus 28:33-35)

Hanging around the hem of this blue robe were, alternately, little golden bells and cloth pomegranates. These gold bells speak of the deity of God. The bell itself would signify proclamation or declaration, a sounding forth.

What a picture we have there of God's Word being proclaimed or declared.

The common Hebrew man could not go inside the tabernacle. But he could hear the high priest as he ministered in the tabernacle on his behalf, representing him before God.

Similarly, we can not physically see Jesus Christ before the throne of God, but we hear His Word. It is in the hearing of His Word that we know Him, and we know of His service and intercession for us. We know that He is interceding before the throne of God on our behalf right now.

> **Therefore He is able also to save forever those who draw near to God through Him, since He always lives to make intercession for them.** (Hebrews 7:25)

The pomegranate is a picture of the fruit of His ministry for us. These pomegranates which were hanging from the hem of the blue robe were of blue, purple, and scarlet material. The blue signifies His heavenly power. The purple signifies His royalty, His authority as King of kings. And the scarlet signifies His sacrifice for us. He came in the royalty, the power, and the authority of the Living God to be our sacrifice.

The bells and the pomegranates hung at the hem of the blue robe around the feet. This is a picture of His going around and doing good, with a perfect complement of the words spoken to the actions done. It was not just the words He spoke, but His words matched His actions perfectly. The actions of Jesus were deeds done on our behalf. His words were pure and true, every one of God. His deeds were fruitful, as were His words.

> **So will My word be which goes forth from My mouth;**
> **It will not return to Me empty,**
> **Without accomplishing what I desire,**
> **And without succeeding in the matter for which I sent it.**
> (Isaiah 55:11)

That little bell dings and then there is fruit, faithfully, each time.

> **So faith comes from hearing, and hearing by the word of Christ.** (Romans 10:17)

> And do not be conformed to this world, but be transformed by the renewing of your mind, so that you may prove what the will of God is, that which is good and acceptable and perfect. (Romans 12:2)

The fruitfulness of His Word in the life of a believer transforms the mind, bearing fruit for the kingdom of God. So there is the divine Word given, the proclamation (golden bells), followed by fruit in the lives of His children (pomegranates).

Now, as Israel delighted in their high priest, knowing that He was ministering for them, and that He was meant to be a blessing to them, so is our relationship with Jesus Christ. Jesus is our great High Priest, ministering for us and His ministry is always effective, bearing fruit. That is why we love and follow Him, because of who He is.

2. The Ephod

> They shall also make the ephod of gold, of blue and purple and scarlet material and fine twisted linen, the work of the skillful workman. It shall have two shoulder pieces joined to its two ends, that it may be joined. (Exodus 28:6-7)

> You shall take two onyx stones and engrave on them the names of the sons of Israel, six of their names on the one stone and the names of the remaining six on the other stone, according to their birth. As a jeweler engraves a signet, you shall engrave the two stones according to the names of the sons of Israel; you shall set them in filigree settings of gold. You shall put the two stones on the shoulder pieces of the ephod, as stones of memorial for the sons of Israel, and Aaron shall bear their names before the LORD on his two shoulders for a memorial. (Exodus 28:9-12)

The ephod was a sleeveless outer garment which hung to about knee level. It had a front part and back part, and it was fastened at each shoulder with an onyx stone set in gold. Each stone had engraved on it six of the tribes of Israel.

The ephod had strands of gold and white linen that were woven together and it was embroidered with blue, purple, and scarlet material. The gold speaks of the deity of God. The linen speaks of the sinless humanity of Christ. They are distinct, God and man, but they are woven together. To try to separate the gold from the linen would destroy the garment. Jesus Christ is wholly God and wholly man. If you try to separate them, you destroy who He is, and you destroy the very essence of the gospel. You cannot diminish His humanity by saying, "Well, He *was God*, after all, just with a man's uniform on." And you cannot say, "Oh, He was a man just like us, and because of the things He did He gained godhood." To do that would be to destroy Jesus Christ and who He is. He is a man just like us, but He is also God. His deity and His humanity are so woven together that they cannot be separated.

The ephod contained the blue, the purple, and the scarlet which signified the message and purpose of Jesus. The blue color means He came from heaven, from God. The purple means He came as King. The scarlet means He came to be the sacrifice for our sin.

> **… namely, that God was in Christ reconciling the world to Himself, not counting their trespasses against them …** (2 Corinthians 5:19)

The ephod was held together at the shoulder with the onyx stones in settings of gold, and the twelve tribes were engraved on those stones. The shoulder is the place of strength. It is the place of bearing the burden, giving support. Jesus Christ carries all His people and their burdens on His shoulders. Every tribe was written on those shoulders, each tribe was dear to God. And so it is that God cares for each of us.

> **… casting all your anxiety on Him, because He cares for you.** (1 Peter 5:7)

The Lord wants to take your burdens, your cares, your anxieties upon Himself and bear them for you. When you are not sure Jesus would want your burdens, just remember those onyx stones on that ephod with the names of the tribes of Israel engraved right on the shoulder. He wants to carry your burdens for you.

The onyx stones were set in gold. Gold represents, as well as deity, that which is precious, valuable, and costly. So we are very precious, very valuable, very costly to Him. We are His prized possession of all creation. He carries us, and nurtures us, and loves us.

You've probably read the prose entitled "Footprints," which has been sold for years now on plaques and greeting cards in most Christian bookstores. It tells of a man walking in the sand by the sea who looks back at his walk to discover two sets of prints following him in the sand (representing Jesus and himself). Then, when things got tough, there was only one set of prints in the sand. When the man asked the Lord where He went when things got tough, the Lord tells the man that those footprints are His, because Jesus was actually carrying the man during those times. It is a nice thought, but, according to what God is telling us in the tabernacle and what the Word says, that is not fully accurate. There would never be two sets of prints in the sand because Jesus is *always* carrying us. He never puts us down.

> 'Do not fear, for I am with you;
> Do not anxiously look about you, for I am your God.
> I will strengthen you, surely I will help you,
> Surely I will uphold you with My righteous right hand.'
> (Isaiah 41:10)

The names of Israel were engraved on those onyx stones. They were permanently etched there. The names were not penciled in so they could be erased later. Once those names were engraved on those stones, they were there forever. Jesus says:

> "I WILL NEVER DESERT YOU, NOR WILL I EVER FORSAKE YOU." (Hebrews 13:5b)

3. The Breastplate

The breastplate was attached to the ephod, and it hung over the chest of the high priest.

> You shall make a breastpiece of judgment, the work of a skillful workman; like the work of the ephod you shall make it: of gold, of blue and purple and scarlet material and fine twisted linen you shall make it. It shall be square and folded double, a span in length and a span in width. You shall mount on it four rows of stones; the first row shall be a row of ruby, topaz and emerald; and the second row a turquoise, a sapphire and a diamond; and the third row a jacinth, an agate and an amethyst; and the fourth row a beryl and an onyx and a jasper; they shall be set in gold filigree. The stones shall be according to the names of the sons of Israel:

> twelve, according to their names; they shall be like the engravings of a seal, each according to his name for the twelve tribes. (Exodus 28:15-21)

So the beautiful breastplate was made of the same material as the ephod, but the breastplate was worn over the ephod. It was doubled over and had four rows of three precious stones in each row, each representing a tribe of Israel.

These stones create a beautiful picture for us. There were twelve distinct stones, one per tribe, right over the heart of the high priest. That tells me we are God's jewels. God sees us as His jewels, His precious stones. As one might delight in the beauty of a precious stone, so God delights over us.

Notice that each stone on the breastplate is different, just as we are each uniquely precious to Him. I cannot take your place and you cannot take mine. We are uniquely precious to our Lord. We are loved with an everlasting love.

These stones, interestingly enough, are the very same stones which, in the book of Revelation, represent the glory of God Himself. These are the same stones John describes when he sees the glory of God in heaven (Revelation 21:18-20).

Picture the high priest walking around in his beautiful high priestly garments out there in the court of the tabernacle before the people of Israel with the light of the sun reflecting off those stones. He must have sparkled with the colors of the rainbow. As the light would catch those stones, it must have been brilliant.

As we are in Jesus and His light shines in us, we sparkle with the glory of God. Sometimes something will happen in a particular situation and I will realize that the Lord was magnified there. Sometimes events just happen to the glory of God in our lives. Those special times are just a little sparkle of the glory of God.

The two onyx stones which were worn at the shoulders each contained six names of the twelve tribes of Israel. But on the breastplate, each stone is different from one another, in appearance and in glory. There is diversity. The onyx stones tell us we are all equal in Christ, equally valued and equally loved. But each breastplate stone shows that each one of us is used by the Holy Spirit in a unique way to bring glory to God. We are uniquely loved by Him and uniquely used by Him to shine forth His glory.

So when you think of the onyx stone, you are reminded that the strength of our Lord and His support for us is limitless. When you think of the breastplate stones, you are reminded that His love is manifested uniquely in us and through us individually. It has a rainbow effect to the glory of God. Each stone of the breastplate was quite beautiful. But when all the stones were put together, it was an awesome sight, and all to the glory of God. That is the way God intends to use us. Each of us is different, each is precious, and equally loved, each on His heart. If you are a ruby, do not try to be an amethyst. He made you a ruby and He wants you to be a ruby. He needs you to be a ruby right where He has placed you.

The Urim and the Thummim

The breastplate was folded over, and there was a little pouch within the breastplate.

> **You shall put in the breastpiece of judgment the Urim and the Thummim, and they shall be over Aaron's heart when he goes in before the LORD; and Aaron shall carry the judgment of the sons of Israel over his heart before the LORD continually.** (Exodus 28:30)

The Urim and the Thummim were kept in that little pouch. Although we do not know exactly what the Urim and Thummim were or how they were used, we do know what the words themselves mean: "lights and perfections."

There are a few other things we do know about the Urim and the Thummim. We know they were used to discern the will of God. The high priest used them to discern God's will in certain matters. How he did that we do not know. Most Bible scholars (and I think Hebrew tradition is behind this, which carries a lot of weight) think they were stones of some sort. Although we do not know exactly how they worked, a very simplified possibility is this: on each stone there would be something that signified a "yes" on one side and a "no" on the other side. Perhaps they would be cast before the Lord, and if a "yes" and a "no" came up there would be no specific answer from the Lord. If they both came up "yes," then this would be considered an affirmative answer from the Lord. If they both came up "no," this would be considered a negative answer from the Lord. The way we see them used in the Bible lends to that kind of thinking because the questions were generally yes- and no-type questions that were brought before the Lord when the Urim and the Thummim were used. But the bottom line is we just do not know for sure.

But I do not have to know how they were used. I just know they were used to determine the will of God and they were kept in a pouch in the breastplate, next to the heart. This pictures for me the ability and promise of Jesus Christ to guide my life according to His love for me. He is ever faithful to lovingly guide my life.

> **And do not be conformed to this world, but be transformed by the renewing of your mind, so that you may prove what the will of God is, that which is good and acceptable and perfect.** (Romans 12:2)

"**Good**" means that something is beneficial to you. It is for your benefit.

"**Acceptable**" means that not only is something good for you, it is also pleasant. It is well pleasing. It is not just castor-oil good, but it is pleasing to you.

Some people act as if God were dishing out castor oil for all their needs. I have actually had people come to me and say, "I think God is telling me to marry this person." When I ask them why, they say, "Because I can't stand him." These type of people think that if there is something they really want in their life, it must not be from God, it must be their flesh. But if they hate something, that must be what God wants for them. This is wrong thinking. The will of God is good and it is acceptable. It is well pleasing.

We have a brother in our church who loves to say that the reason he took so long to finally come to Christ and give his heart to the Lord is because he was afraid God was going to ask him to go to Africa as a missionary. He kept saying he did not want to go to Africa. We kept explaining that God's will is good and it is acceptable and it is perfect for each individual. And finally it sunk in and he gave his heart to the Lord. Not long after he was born again, Ken's heart totally changed toward Africa. We could not talk Ken out of going to Africa. He got it in his heart that he was going to Africa, and it was not castor oil to him. He *wanted* to go and serve. He *could not wait* to go. The Lord opened the door for Ken to go to Africa, and the Lord put the desire in Ken's heart to go. Since then, he and his family have spent years in Uganda as missionaries. It has been **"good and acceptable and perfect"** for Ken to be there.

"Perfect" is that word which means complete, just right, made for you. It is not a "one-size-fits-all" situation. It is tailor made for you. It is just right.

The Urim and Thummim, which signifies your Lord's clear direction and guidance in your life, rests right over the heart that says, "This is because I love you so much. This is because, when all is said and done, I want to bless the socks off of you." So, thank You, Lord, for Your good and acceptable and perfect direction in our lives. So, ...

> **Trust in the LORD with all your heart**
> **And do not lean on your own understanding.**
> **In all your ways acknowledge Him,**
> **And He will make your paths straight.** (Proverbs 3:5-6)
>
> **Your ears will hear a word behind you, "This is the way, walk in it,"** **whenever you turn to the right or to the left.** (Isaiah 30: 21)

God will guide you.

People frequently ask me, "How come I don't hear God telling me exactly what I want to know?" The answer is that He guides us one step at a time. We must constantly look to Him and rely on Him for the next step. That is abiding in Him.

I like the way one believer described the Urim and Thummim. Some liberal churches have gotten away from the Word of God and the ministers are more impressed with their own intellect than they are with the authority of the Word of God. So there was this one godly Christian fellow who loved the Lord and loved the Word of God. He was a real student of the Bible. Although his church was one of those liberal churches which had departed from the Word of God, he felt like God just wanted him to keep going there.

Well, his church hired a new pastor who was a young preacher right out of seminary. This new pastor loved to debate this godly Christian because he was impressed with this guy's knowledge of the Word and with his wisdom. But to the preacher it was just a game. Every time the young pastor would come up with some theological question, this guy seemed to know Biblically how to address it. He really had a grasp of the Word, much more so than did this kid preacher with the seminary degree.

So the pastor was studying one day and he realized that no one knows exactly what the Urim and the Thummim were and how they were used. He was sure he could stumble his learned parishioner on this one. So he dropped by the guy's work place on a pastoral courtesy visit and said, "I was reading in the Bible about the Urim and the Thummim. What are they?" It was asked in the same spirit that the Pharisees used when they tried to trip up Jesus.

The guy did not realize that this was a setup. He was just transparent before the Lord, and his comment was classic. "You know, I really don't know what the Urim and the Thummim actually were back then, but I'll tell you this. It was used to discern the will of God. And God has given to us His Book, and by Usin' and Thumbin' through this book you are going to find God's will for your life."

4. The Sash

That sash was the belt around the ephod and the sash speaks simply of service. Jesus girded Himself with a towel and washed the feet of the disciples. The sash reminds us of the commitment of Jesus to serve His own.

> " ... just as the Son of Man did not come to be served, but to serve, and to give His life a ransom for many."
> (Matthew 20:28)

The colors of the sash are the same that we have studied: blue, purple, and scarlet. He serves as God in the authority and power of God Himself (blue). He serves as King, King of kings and Lord of lords with all commensurate authority given to Him by the Father (purple). He serves sacrificially (scarlet). The service of Jesus is sacrificial. He has and He does give Himself completely in service and in ministry for our benefit.

That is why we are told in Hebrews to:

> **Pray without ceasing.** (1 Thessalonians 5:17)

That is why we are also told in Hebrews:

> Therefore let us draw near with confidence to the throne of grace, so that we may receive mercy and find grace to help in time of need. (Hebrews 4:16)

He welcomes us to the throne of grace. He is there to serve, with our best interest always in His mind.

5. The Turban

> "You shall also make a plate of pure gold and shall engrave on it, like the engravings of a seal, 'Holy to the LORD.' You shall fasten it on a blue cord, and it shall be on the turban; it shall be at the front of the turban." (Exodus 28:36-37)

The turban itself was white. The gold crown was fastened to the white turban with a blue cord. This represents to us that Jesus is God Himself, who came from heaven, is forever tied to heaven, and that He became the perfect man. The words on the gold crown "Holy to the Lord," represent Jesus Christ, the head of the church, Son of the Living God.

> **Christ also is the head of the church, He Himself being the Savior of the body.** (Ephesians 5:23b)

The turban was worn on the head of Aaron, who was set apart to the Lord as high priest. Similarly, Christ is the head of the church, and He is Holy to the Lord.

So, from the garments of the high priest, we understand a little better what it means for Jesus Christ to be our great High Priest. This should add a little depth to our understanding of Hebrews 4:14-16. What an awesome, *great* High Priest we have!

> Therefore, since we have a great high priest who has passed through the heavens, Jesus the Son of God, let us hold fast our confession. For we do not have a high priest who cannot sympathize with our weaknesses, but One who has been tempted in all things as we are, yet without sin. Therefore let us draw near with confidence to the throne of grace, so that we may receive mercy and

find grace to help in time of need. (Hebrews 4:14-16)

There they are, the high priest and his sons, clothed for the Master's use—clothed, but not quite ready, not at this point. Before they venture into that tent and all it means, before they begin their service unto the Lord, they have to be consecrated to that work. So, in the next chapter, we will take a look at the consecration of the priests. It will reveal to us a beautiful picture of Jesus' consecration for His earthly ministry, and our consecration to the service of our Lord, and into the blessings and inheritance He has for us.

Chapter Nine

Consecration Into Service

For both He who sanctifies and those who are sanctified are all from one Father; for which reason He is not ashamed to call them brethren ...

Hebrews 2:11

When a Christian is born again of the Spirit into God's spiritual family, in many ways it is like it was to be born into the Old Testament Levitical family of priests in the tabernacle. The picture God painted for us in the tabernacle comes alive because we realize that we have been born into the family of Jesus Christ Himself, our High Priest.

> ... and from Jesus Christ, the faithful witness, the firstborn of the dead, and the ruler of the kings of the earth. To Him who loves us and released us from our sins by His blood—and He has made us to be a kingdom, priests to His God and Father—to Him be the glory and the dominion forever and ever. Amen.
> (Revelation 1:5-6)

We ARE the Real Thing

Aaron and his sons were a mere shadow of the reality which is

Jesus and His church of believer-priests. Aaron and his sons were the shadow; we, as believers, are the real thing. With those tabernacle priests, God painted a physical picture of what we have as the spiritual reality. I am fascinated by the idea that the physical can be a mere picture of a spiritual reality. So many people, Christians included, think something has to be manifested physically to be "real." Anything that is not physical is categorized as fantasy and unsubstantial—*not* the "real thing." It is interesting that in God's economy, He uses the physical, which is not the real thing, to describe and picture the reality, which is spiritual.

> **… while we look not at the things which are seen, but at the things which are not seen; for the things which are seen are temporal, but the things which are not seen are eternal.** (2 Corinthians 4:18)

Eternal things are the things we cannot see and touch. They are the real things, the lasting things. What an example the tabernacle is of that truth.

> **Therefore, since we have a great high priest who has passed through the heavens, Jesus the Son of God, let us hold fast our confession. For we do not have a high priest who cannot sympathize with our weaknesses, but One who has been tempted in all things as we are, yet without sin. Therefore let us draw near with confidence to the throne of grace, so that we may receive mercy and find grace to help in time of need.** (Hebrews 4:14-16)

In other words, using the analogy given in Hebrews, in the reality of the spirit, go boldly into the tabernacle, into the very presence of God, whenever the need is there. Because it is there where you will receive mercy. It is there where you will obtain grace to help in time of need.

Mercy is the passive. Grace is the active. Mercy is the withholding. Grace is the giving. And so we obtain mercy, the withholding of that which we deserve as punishment. And grace is the active, helping, powerful, energized-by-the-Spirit hand of God, working in our lives, to work His miracles, His way. That is grace.

Before a priest could go traipsing off into the tabernacle, however, or begin performing any of the priestly duties, he had to be ceremonially consecrated to that position of priesthood. Even though he was born into that family, there had to be the consecration of the priest to the priesthood. According to Merriam-Webster, the term "consecration" means being "devoted irrevocably to the worship of God by a solemn ceremony." At the tabernacle, it was God Himself who did the consecrating of those tabernacle priests to their ministry and service unto Him. Likewise, it is still Him who consecrates believer-priests to serve Him today.

> But you are A CHOSEN RACE, A royal PRIESTHOOD, A HOLY NATION, A PEOPLE FOR GOD'S OWN POSSESSION, so that you may proclaim the excellencies of Him who has called you out of darkness into His marvelous light ... (1 Peter 2:9)

Believers have been called by God and are consecrated, or dedicated, to Him by His Holy Spirit into this priesthood. Because of that, the consecration of the priests in Leviticus is very enlightening to us. God commanded some very specific things to be done in their consecration, which gives a picture of our consecration into service for His glory, only ours is in the spiritual realm.

There are four major parts to the Levitical consecration into the priesthood: the washing with water, the sacrifices, the anointing with oil, and a seven-day feast.

Consecrated By the Water of His Word

The priests were washed with water.

> Then the LORD spoke to Moses, saying, "Take Aaron and his sons with him, and the garments and the anointing oil and the bull of the sin offering, and the two rams and the basket of unleavened bread, and assemble all the congregation at the doorway of the tent of meeting." So Moses did just as the LORD commanded him. When the congregation was assembled at the doorway of the tent of meeting, Moses said to the congregation, "This is the thing which the LORD has commanded to do." Then Moses had Aaron and his sons come near and washed them with water. (Leviticus 8:1-6)

> ... Christ also loved the church and gave Himself up for her, so that He might sanctify her, having cleansed her by the washing of water with the word, that He might

> **present to Himself the church in all her glory, having no spot or wrinkle or any such thing; but that she would be holy and blameless.** (Ephesians 5:25b-27)

The water in this context is a reference to the Word of God. The washing with water is the cleansing effect of the Word on our lives.

This is interesting because God is telling us something here which is very important. His Word is an integral part of our consecration to Him. There can be no consecration apart from the effective working of His Word in our lives. They go together.

> **So faith comes from hearing, and hearing by the word of Christ.** (Romans 10:17)

This reminds me of the story of the Roman centurion Cornelius that is told in Acts chapter 10. Peter went to Cornelius' home in Caesarea, only after the Lord convinced him in a vision that he could even enter the home of a Gentile, let alone preach the gospel to one. Once there, he shared the good news of Jesus Christ. Peter had not even given an "invitation" to receive the Lord, hadn't even finished his sermon, before the Holy Spirit fell upon Cornelius and the others who had gathered with him. They started speaking in tongues as they were filled with the Holy Spirit on the spot. Their new-birth experience was so unmistakable that Peter immediately baptized with water his very first Gentile converts. It was the Word of God that pierced Cornelius and his friends and brought them to the Lord. As it says:

> **… the Holy Spirit fell upon all those who were listening to the message.** (Acts 10:44b)

They were simply "listening to the message."

As an Augustinian monk, Martin Luther was desperate to find a way to make peace with God. He did everything he could think of, including beating himself, to be more acceptable to God. One day, as he was reading the Word, he came across Hebrews 10:38 (KJV) where it says, **"The just shall live by faith."** Suddenly the meaning of those words became clear to him in a dramatic way for the very first time. He finally realized that he could only be redeemed to God by faith alone, and not by his many works. Penance could not save him. Pilgrimages to Rome would not save him. The light dawned in him that salvation does not come by fulfilling a bunch of regulations and traditions imposed by an organization, even a church. Salvation comes by faith in Jesus Christ alone.

Martin Luther never wanted to leave the Catholic Church. He was just excited about the great news he found in that passage of Hebrews. It was a wonderful, liberating truth that he just had to share. He was shocked by the response he got when he did; eventually he was forced out of the Catholic Church. If Luther was going to follow the Lord, he would have to do it completely apart from the Catholic Church. Thus began the Protestant Reformation that changed history. Don't miss the point that it was the Word that worked such a miracle in the heart of Martin Luther, and through him, in the world.

I remember another story of the miraculous effect the Word can have on a life. This one was told to me by a counselor for a Christian high school youth camp. One of the campers was quite an athlete and very popular with the girls, but he had no interest in the purpose for this camp. He just came to hang out and be cool. One of the camp requirements, however, was that all campers must attend all meetings for teaching and worship. The leaders assured the kids that there would be an abundance of fun and activities, but attendance at the meetings was required to remain at the camp.

Even so, this popular athlete skipped out of the Friday night meeting and goofed around instead. Then he opted not to participate in the Saturday morning meeting either. He came in for a short time, but then he slipped out the back to hang out with some guys who hadn't come to the meeting at all.

Aware of this, this counselor prayed about what to do with this particular young man. Should he send him home, as he could easily do? The expectations of the campers were clear to all, and the consequences for not abiding by them were equally clear. Or should he speak to the youth? Finally, the counselor went up to him, because it was obvious the young man had no interest in, or intention of, going to any of the meetings. In addition to being a good athlete, he knew the boy was also very smart. So the counselor made him an offer the young man couldn't refuse.

"If you will go into the woods and completely read this little booklet—it will take you an hour or two—you can miss all of the rest of the meetings, with my full consent and permission."

The counselor handed him a little newsprint booklet published at the time by Calvary Chapel that contained the full gospel of John, but presented in a comic book style with colorful drawings.

The young man agreed, and walked off into the woods with the gospel of John in hand. After a couple of hours, he returned absolutely transformed. The Word turned his heart and his life around on the spot. He did not miss a meeting after that. When the invitation was given on Saturday night, he publicly made a profession of faith in Jesus Christ. It was the Word of God that made such a phenomenal transformation in this young man's life.

Sometimes on Sunday morning when I am teaching the Word, I'll notice someone who is sleeping, while the person sitting right next to him is literally on the edge of his seat soaking in every word I say. One Sunday, many years ago, a visitor came to church at the encouragement of his friend. Immediately after the service, the guy who brought this visitor came to me and asked me to come talk to this friend. I went outside to find his friend leaning against the wall because he literally could not stand up. The Word had so pierced him that all strength had left his legs. I talked to him and shared more of the Word with him before he went home. His neighbor later prayed with him to receive Christ. There is nothing more exciting to me than seeing the Word of God do its powerful work in individual lives!

The point I want to make is that consecration to God does not happen apart from the Word of God working in your life. They go together.

> **All Scripture is inspired by God and profitable for teaching, for reproof, for correction, for training in righteousness; so that the man of God may be adequate, equipped for every good work.** (2 Timothy 3:16-17)
>
> **Your word I have treasured in my heart,**
> **That I may not sin against You.** (Psalm 119:11)
>
> **Your word is a lamp to my feet**
> **And a light to my path.** (Psalm 119:105)

It is the Word that gives guidance as we travel down the road of life; it also provides light for our steps, to keep us from stumbling.

> For the word of God is living and active and sharper than any two-edged sword, and piercing as far as the division of soul and spirit, of both joints and marrow, and able to judge the thoughts and intentions of the heart. (Hebrews 4:12)
>
> ... like newborn babies, long for the pure milk of the word, so that by it you may grow in respect to salvation ... (1 Peter 2:2)

The place the Word has in our consecration to the Lord cannot be minimized.

It is interesting that Moses washed Aaron and his sons together. I think this points out our oneness with Jesus Christ, our High Priest, in our consecration. It is clear that we are consecrated by the Word, but there is also a oneness in Christ. There is no consecration apart from intimate union with Jesus Christ Himself.

> "Sanctify them in the truth; Your word is truth. As You sent Me into the world, I also have sent them into the world. For their sakes I sanctify Myself, that they themselves also may be sanctified in truth." (Jesus in John 17:17-19)

In this Scripture, Jesus is praying for our sanctification through the Word of God (the truth). Notice what He said there, **"For their sakes, I sanctify Myself that they may be sanctified in truth."** Jesus is saying He is with us, even as He sends us out. We are in this together. This whole consecration is in oneness and unity with Jesus Himself.

> **For both He who sanctifies and those who are sanctified are all from one Father; for which reason He is not ashamed to call them brethren ...** (Hebrews 2:11)

This verse tells us that we are not alone. Jesus is with us in our sanctification, our cleansing, and our being set apart unto the Lord. The whole consecration ceremony emphasizes that we are set apart, yet there is a oneness in this union with Jesus Christ Himself.

You see, the Christian life should not be lived in an attempt to please God by our own strength and ability. Instead, it is a life lived in Jesus Christ, in oneness with Him. He is the one who abides in our hearts. We are one, and that is the issue: we can depend on Him, totally.

> "... All authority has been given to Me in heaven and on earth. Go therefore and make disciples of all the nations, baptizing them in the name of the Father and the Son and the Holy Spirit, teaching them to observe all that I commanded you; and lo, I am with you always, even to the end of the age." (Jesus in Matthew 28:18b-20)

Jesus is the One who is with us in this commission of our life, this great consecration. So, as we are told in Hebrews 4:16:

> **Therefore let us draw near with confidence to the throne of grace, so that we may receive mercy and find grace to help in time of need.**

He is saying that you can depend on Him to come through. After all, it is His ministry and His work.

When Moses consecrated these men for the priesthood, Aaron was right there as high priest. He was consecrated with them. He was washed with the same water.

Hudson Taylor, one of the first Christian missionaries to China in the nineteenth century put it so well: "If we are obeying the Lord, the responsibility for the work rests with Him, not us."

In other words, if we are seeking our direction from the Lord, if we are obediently laying our lives down to the Lord, He will work His work in His way. If we turn our lives and our hearts over to Him, the responsibility for that work rests with Him. That sets us free to simply be available to Him.

We are consecrated with Jesus Christ Himself to the great service of representing the Living God in this unbelieving world. And this is exactly how Jesus prayed for us:

> "As You sent Me into the world, I also have sent them into the world. For their sakes I sanctify Myself, that they themselves also may be sanctified in truth. I do not ask on behalf of these alone, but for those also who believe in Me through their word ..." (John 17:18-20)

The High Priest is Anointed With Oil

The first part of the consecration ceremony for those tabernacle priests involved being washed with water. Next, dressed in his high priestly garments, Aaron was anointed with oil. The sons, however, were not anointed with oil at that time. The sacrifice had to be made for them first.

Oil symbolizes the Holy Spirit, so it is interesting that Aaron alone received a generous anointing of that oil before the sacrifices were made. His anointing of oil occurred after the washing with water, but before the sacrifices.

> **Then he poured some of the anointing oil on Aaron's head and anointed him, to consecrate him.** (Leviticus 8: 12)

Consecrated By the Blood

Next in the ceremony, a sacrifice was made.

> **Then he brought the bull of the sin offering, and Aaron and his sons laid their hands on the head of the bull of the sin offering. Next Moses slaughtered it and took the blood and with his finger put some of it around on the horns of the altar, and purified the altar. Then he poured out the rest of the blood at the base of the altar and consecrated it, to make atonement for it.** (Leviticus 8:14-15)

> **Then he presented the ram of the burnt offering, and Aaron and his sons laid their hands on the head of the ram. Moses slaughtered it and sprinkled the blood around on the altar.** (Leviticus 8:18-19)

> **Then he presented the second ram, the ram of ordination, and Aaron and his sons laid their hands on the head of the ram. Moses slaughtered it and took some of its blood and put it on the lobe of Aaron's right ear, and on the thumb of his right hand and on the big toe of his right foot. He also had Aaron's sons come near; and Moses put some of the blood on the lobe of their right ear, and on the thumb of their right hand and on the big toe of their right foot. Moses then sprinkled the rest of the blood around on the altar.** (Leviticus 8: 22-24)

The shedding of blood is always central to what happened at the tabernacle. The blood is a reminder to us of the centrality of the cross in our relationship with God, our fellowship with Him, and our spiritual walk as believers in Jesus. We cannot separate these things from the centrality of the cross.

That is why Communion needs to occur on a regular basis in the spiritual life of a believer. Communion brings you back to the cross, mentally. The cross is the center of it all. All life, all service, all ministry, all fruit emanate from what Jesus accomplished at the cross. This means that it is through the blood, not our works, that we have been consecrated. We have been consecrated, by His blood, as servants and as priests of God. It has nothing whatsoever to do with our efforts or our works.

> **For if the blood of goats and bulls and the ashes of a heifer sprinkling those who have been defiled sanctify for the cleansing of the flesh, how much more will the blood of Christ, who through the eternal Spirit offered Himself without blemish to God, cleanse your conscience from dead works to serve the living God?** (Hebrews 9:13-14)

In the phrase **"cleanse your conscience from dead works,"** the reference to **"dead works"** is not a reference to sinful activity. This is a reference to nice "religious" things that you do in service to God to show your righteousness before men. Those works are useless and worthless. It is by His blood you are cleansed from that and set apart so you can serve the Living God effectively. By the blood you are consecrated so that God can now work in you according to His perfect will.

The blood of Jesus was shed for you, and you (if you are a believer in Jesus Christ), right now, are an instrument fit for the Master's use.

Notice the application of the blood. Blood was applied to the right ear lobe, the right thumb, and the right big toe. In other words, this consecration by the blood came upon the ear, the hand, and the foot. What a picture of Jesus' ministry on earth.

Jesus' ear was always, constantly, continually tuned to His Heavenly Father.

> **"I can do nothing on My own initiative. As I hear, I judge; and My judgment is just, because I do not seek**

My own will, but the will of Him who sent Me."** (John 5:30)

His hand was consistently directed by the Spirit in doing good.

> **Therefore Jesus answered and was saying to them, "Truly, truly, I say to you, the Son can do nothing of Himself, unless it is something He sees the Father doing; for whatever the Father does, these things the Son also does in like manner.** (John 5:19)

Jesus did nothing of His own initiative. He saw what the Father was doing, and that was what He did. What an example to us. Everything He did was under the guidance of the Heavenly Father through the Holy Spirit. That is His example to us as believers. His hand was so guided by the Spirit, that everything He touched and everything He did was directed by the Spirit in doing good, for the glory of God.

His feet were also guided by the Spirit.

Remember the story of Lazarus who was sick unto death (John 11)? Mary and Martha had sent an urgent message to Jesus to come quickly because Lazarus was dying. Jesus was down by the Jordan River and it was a couple of days' journey from there to Bethany. He purposely waited two days so that four days had elapsed by the time He returned. He delayed so that God would be glorified when He raised Lazarus from the dead.

The human tendency would be to expect Jesus to gather His disciples, drop everything, get on their camels, and ride. (I am asking for some poetic liberty here!) Just picture it: sweat drips from their brows, as the camel hoofs pound the dirt roads on the way to Bethany. Jesus and His boys make their entrance into town in a cloud of dust, and head straight for Lazarus' house. It's Jesus to the rescue! Lazarus will not die today!

It may be human nature to think that God should work that way, that He should do everything in His power to prevent His own from suffering pain and death. But the Spirit leads in a different way and Jesus' steps were always guided by the Spirit, to the greater glory of God. He purposely waited until Lazarus had died, to bring all the greater glory to His Heavenly Father.

Have you heard the phrase "the tyranny of the urgent?" God calls us to a walk, not a run. We do not have to succumb to a frantic pace in life, we can daily *walk* with Him.

As Aaron was consecrated by blood, his sons were consecrated with exactly the same blood. The consecration that Jesus had on Him is the consecration that was put upon us through His blood. I am not worthy of that. I do not deserve it, but it has been given to me by His blood.

The Blood Lets Us Hear

First, by the consecration of the ear we are now able to hear His Word. There is an ability to hear and understand His Word which was not in us before.

> **Now we have received, not the spirit of the world, but the Spirit who is from God, so that we may know the things freely given to us by God, which things we also speak, not in words taught by human wisdom, but in those taught by the Spirit, combining spiritual thoughts with spiritual words.** (1 Corinthians 2:12-13)

It is by the work of the Holy Spirit in you that you are now able, because of His blood shed for you, to hear His Word. It is a Word the world cannot understand. Jesus said, regarding those who would believe in Him:

> "My sheep hear My voice, and I know them, and they follow Me …" (Jesus in John 10:27)

I believe it is Donald Barnhouse who told the story of visiting the Middle East and seeing, first hand, several different flocks of sheep go up to the same watering hole. All of the sheep from every flock became completely intermingled. This is something that has happened since time immemorial. In fact, you may remember the Old Testament story of Jacob moving the rock so the sheep could be watered. Other shepherds were there, waiting for the rest of the shepherds to get there so they could move the rock and let everyone's flocks drink together.

As Barnhouse watched these flocks coming together, being watered at the same time, he wondered how they would ever be able to again separate the sheep by flock. After a time of watering, one of the shepherds walked a short distance from where the watering hole was and made a call. It was a unique call. It was *his* call. Immediately some sheep perked up and moved toward the sound of the shepherd's call. Then another shepherd moved out and gave his own unique call, and so on. Each sheep recognized the voice of his own shepherd and followed where he led.

That is exactly what Jesus meant in John 10:27. His sheep hear His voice. He knows them, and they follow Him. It is the consecration of His blood that gives you that ear to hear.

In Revelation chapters 2 and 3, Jesus repeatedly says:

> **"He who has an ear, let him hear what the Spirit says to the churches."**

By His blood, the ear of the believer has been consecrated to hear **"what the Spirit says to the churches."**

The Blood Qualifies Us To Serve

Secondly, your hand is now qualified to be able to truly serve the Lord. The blood Moses applied to the hand of each of Aaron's sons represents how the blood of Jesus qualifies you, as a believer-priest, to serve Him.

The Blood Prepares Us To Walk By the Spirit

Thirdly, you have also been prepared to be guided by the Holy Spirit in your walk, by the blood of Jesus. That is symbolized in the blood that was put on the big toe during the consecration in the Old Testament.

> **Trust in the LORD with all your heart**
> **And do not lean on your own understanding.**
> **In all your ways acknowledge Him,**
> **And He will make your paths straight.** (Proverbs 3:5-6)

In Acts, we see examples of the faithful leading of the Holy Spirit.

> **They passed through the Phrygian and Galatian region, having been forbidden by the Holy Spirit to speak the word in Asia; and after they came to Mysia, they were trying to go into Bithynia, and the Spirit of Jesus did not permit them; and passing by Mysia, they came down to Troas. A vision appeared to Paul in the night: a man of Macedonia was standing and appealing to him, and**

> saying, "Come over to Macedonia and help us." When he had seen the vision, immediately we sought to go into Macedonia, concluding that God had called us to preach the gospel to them. (Acts 16:6-10)

Notice the guiding of the Holy Spirit there. There are times when the Spirit tells us not to do anything in a certain situation, or not to go to a certain place. That happens when He is leading us in another direction. That guiding is by the Holy Spirit, because your feet have been consecrated by His blood to the service of the Lord and they are thus fit to be guided by the Spirit.

There is absolutely no reason for the Spirit not to be guiding your life, because you have been set apart to that. The Holy Spirit is the One who sets up those divine appointments in your life. We have been made fit for the Master's use. We are consecrated by the blood of Jesus Christ.

For our part, it is simply faith in His shed blood that is the key to our recognition of His consecration of us for service. The burden is off of you. His blood shed for you has consecrated you to service for Him.

The Sons are Anointed With Oil

After the application of the blood, there was the anointing of the oil.

Once the sacrifices were made and the blood was applied, now Aaron's sons were included in this anointing of oil. What a beautiful picture of Christ. Jesus was born of the Holy Spirit. At the Jordan River, at the beginning of His ministry, the Spirit came upon Him. After that came the sacrifice at Calvary. And then, after the sacrifice, at Pentecost the anointing of the Holy Spirit fell upon the believers. This is all pictured in the anointing of the priests for service at the tabernacle.

It is the Holy Spirit that brings that power and that spiritual reality to your service for God. It is the Holy Spirit that brings to life the ministry He has for you. The blood means you are now fit for the Master's use. The oil means you are now equipped by the Holy Spirit for the Master's use. The blood makes you fit, and the Holy Spirit (the oil) equips you.

Once again, Aaron is included in this second anointing. He is part of it. Look at what Jesus said to His disciples when He commissioned them. He ended the commission with these words:

> "... lo, I am with you always, even to the end of the age." (Matthew 28:20b)

Jesus told us He is in our Holy Spirit-guided,-directed,-anointed service. Apart from Him we can do nothing.

> "I am the vine, you are the branches; he who abides in Me and I in him, he bears much fruit, for apart from Me you can do nothing. (John 15:5)

It is that anointing of oil that brings home the realization that what we are being called to do goes beyond our natural abilities. It means God is doing His work through us. Anyone can give someone else a glass of cold water when he is thirsty. But it is only the Holy Spirit that can make that a divine transaction with eternal implications. We cannot do that.

Years ago, when I lived in southern California, I knew a man who was a Peruvian aristocrat. Every so often he would call me and ask me to do things with him. I was not at all close to him, we had little in common, but he continued to pursue our friendship. Juan seemed to like being my friend, which left me scratching my head in wonder because we were so different. Even after I got married, Juan kept in touch once in a while.

One day Juan called and invited my wife and I to a completely worldly party at his house. I did not think we should go to such a worldly party but, at that moment, I could not think of an excuse not to go. So I accepted his invitation, which concerned my wife Joyce when I told her we were going to Juan's party. We even prayed that God would get us out of going, that something would happen to make it impossible. We would have even been happy with a flat tire on the way there. For a week, we prayed with great faith for God to deliver us from that party. No good excuse presented itself, so we believed that God, for some reason, wanted us to be at that party.

We drove from Bellflower to the party in North Hollywood, believing that the Lord had us there for a reason. Even so, we planned to be there for just a short while and leave as quickly as we could. I felt like a fish out of water—totally out of place. It didn't help that one of Juan's favorite things to do was to try to get me to drink alcohol without my knowing it. I chose long ago not to imbibe, and he knew it. Thankfully, I could always smell the alcohol right away, so he never "got me."

I grabbed a Coke and sat down on the sofa to watch the other people who were crowding together in the kitchen and living room. A girl sitting on the other end of the sofa looked over at me and asked, "What do you do for a living?"

"I'm a minister."

"A minister?" she asked, amazed. "Do you mean a priest or something? Whoa, what in the world ever got you into that line of work? I have always wanted to talk to someone like you, just to find out what would possess someone to do that."

I thought, "Thank you, Lord, it is personal testimony time." So I sat there and started sharing my testimony with her. She was clearly interested, so I started to give her the longer version. I got so involved in what I was saying, and her interest in it, that it took me a while to realize that the place had gotten completely quiet. Everyone there was listening and gathering around to hear me share my testimony with this girl. I told her how I came to know Jesus and about His call on my life to teach the Word of God. They all seemed mesmerized. When I finished, it was totally quiet for a few seconds, then it was like someone flipped a switch and the party started up again. The music came back on, and people moved away to start new conversations. But as Joyce and I prepared to leave, I cannot tell you how many people came up and thanked me for sharing. One person commented, "You don't know what it meant to me to hear you say that tonight!" We walked out of the place just smiling about what the Lord had done. That event, which neither of us wanted to attend, was a divine appointment for us. God had a reason for it.

It is exciting to be led by the Spirit of the Lord. There are times when we are going through the day, seemingly as usual, totally unaware of how His Spirit is guiding and using us. Some day we will stand before Him in glory and He is going to unravel all the reasons why. We will fall on our faces, take the crowns off our heads, cast them before the throne, and give praise, honor, and glory to God in thanks to Him (Revelation 4:10-11). Lord, forgive us for ever doubting You for a moment in our lives.

This is the anointing of the Holy Spirit, the "oil" upon our lives. Thus, the blood has made us fit for the Master's use, and the oil, equipped for the Master's use. Do you think, after all that, He is not going to use you?

I like the way Charles Spurgeon put it. "Organizations without the

Holy Spirit are like mills without power. Even a church that is thoroughly orthodox and accepts Biblical standards is as useless as clouds without rain until endowed with power from on high." That is the anointing of the oil.

A fellow named A.C. Dickson said: "When we rely on an organization, we get what an organization can do. When we rely on education, we get what education can do. When we rely on eloquence, we get what eloquence can do. When we rely on the Holy Spirit, we get what God can do."

> "You shall anoint Aaron and his sons, and consecrate them, that they may minister as priests to Me. You shall speak to the sons of Israel, saying, 'This shall be a holy anointing oil to Me throughout your generations. It shall not be poured on anyone's body, nor shall you make any like it in the same proportions; it is holy, and it shall be holy to you." (Exodus 30:30-32)

Likewise, there is a spiritual reality here also:

> **For the flesh sets its desire against the Spirit, and the Spirit against the flesh; for these are in opposition to one another, so that you may not do the things that you please.** (Galatians 5:17)

Notice, the holy anointing oil could not be poured out on the flesh. And so it is, when someone lives according to the flesh, is in the flesh, guided by the flesh, and given over to the flesh, he cannot have that anointing, because that oil, God's Spirit, is not for worldly uses.

If you are thinking, "But, man, I am so fleshly. How can I ever get that anointing?"

I like what Dwight L. Moody said. He took a glass and put it on a table. He then asked his congregation how one might remove the air from out of the glass. Different people had different ideas. Some said to suck the air out. Others said that to suck the air out would implode the glass. Some said that you just could not get the air out of the glass. Mr. Moody said, "I'll show you how to get the air out of this glass," and he poured water into it. The air was out of the glass because it was filled with water. The air was replaced with the water.

It is the same with us. Your flesh will be in control of your life, unless the Spirit is given control of your life. It will be one or the other. You cannot just get rid of the flesh anymore than you can empty the air from the glass. But you can replace the flesh with the guiding and empowering of the Holy Spirit.

Wilbur Chapman, a Bible-teaching preacher of the early twentieth century, was already in the ministry when he was filled with the Holy Spirit for the first time in his life. He said it happened after someone asked him, "If you are not willing to lay down everything to the Lord, are you willing to be made willing?" He thought that seemed easy enough. Alone in prayer, he surrendered everything, willingly giving up his time, his pleasures, his ambitions, and his family. When he got to the point where he had, as best he knew, laid every part of his life on the altar, he said, "Lord, I give it up. It's all yours." Then, without any great emotion, he humbly asked the Holy Spirit to fill him and take charge of his life. That simple step was the major turning point of his life and ministry.

Sometimes people feel they must have an incredible experience, be "slain in the Spirit," or burst out in laughter, or speak in tongues if it truly is "a work of the Spirit." Being filled with the Holy Spirit does not require an emotional response, but it does require faith.

That is exactly what happened in my own life. I had a choice to make. It was in March 1970 when I prayed a prayer much like Wilbur Chapman's. I had to decide whether I was going to take God at His Word that He would fill me with His Spirit because I sincerely asked Him to, or depend on my own feelings to tell me whether God had done as He promised. I was so totally desperate that I was willing to take God at His Word. The evidence did not come immediately. I had no emotional experience at all after praying that prayer. However, later that day I led someone to the Lord for the first time in my life and my life has never been the same since that day.

Do you believe His blood, shed for you, has saved and separated you unto Him? In the same way, put your faith in His Spirit to equip you for service. You *are* equipped by the Holy Spirit even if you do not feel like you are. It just requires faith in His Spirit, just like the faith you have in His blood.

Furthermore, we read in Exodus regarding that holy anointing oil:

> "… it is holy, and it shall be holy to you. Whoever shall mix any like it or whoever puts any of it on a layman

shall be cut off from his people." (Exodus 30:32b-33)

Similarly, regarding the Holy Spirit:

> But a natural man does not accept the things of the Spirit of God, for they are foolishness to him; and he cannot understand them, because they are spiritually appraised. (1 Corinthians 2:14)

As the oil was only for the priests, what the Lord offers here, in the way of application and anointing of the Spirit, is a gift to those who are born again into the family of God by faith in Jesus Christ. It is a gift for believers. It is not for natural man. Natural man cannot comprehend it nor can he have it. It is a gift to the body of Christ.

The Lord also said that a likeness is not to be made of that oil. To you, I say, beware of concoctions. Beware of that which has the appearance of the "anointing oil," of being of the Holy Spirit, but is not the true anointing on God's people. There are concoctions. Beware.

> "For false Christs and false prophets will arise and will show great signs and wonders, so as to mislead, if possible, even the elect." (Matthew 24:24)

Probably the most important way to test a spirit is that the true "anointing oil," that which is truly of the Holy Spirit, will have the clear example and vindication of the Word of God behind it. You'll see the Spirit working in the same way in the Bible.

So, Aaron's sons were washed with the water, anointed with the blood and the oil, and thus they became consecrated priests unto God. There is one other aspect of that ordination which I find particularly interesting.

A Feast of Consecration

The consecration was concluded with a seven-day feast for the high priest and his sons. They were not allowed outside that tabernacle compound for seven days of feasting before the Lord.

> Then Moses said to Aaron and to his sons, "Boil the flesh at the doorway of the tent of meeting, and eat it there together with the bread which is in the basket of

> the ordination offering, just as I commanded, saying, 'Aaron and his sons shall eat it.' The remainder of the flesh and of the bread you shall burn in the fire. You shall not go outside the doorway of the tent of meeting for seven days, until the day that the period of your ordination is fulfilled; for he will ordain you through seven days." (Leviticus 8:31-33)

The Bible tells us that someday Jesus Christ is going to come into the air and call all believers to be with Him. He will then take us into heaven where we will celebrate the marriage feast of the Lamb. This feast will last seven years. Then, the great High Priest Himself, our King Jesus Christ, will return in glory and power, back to this earth, and we will come with Him.

> **Now it came about on the eighth day that Moses called Aaron and his sons and the elders of Israel ...** (Leviticus 9:1)

In the Old Testament, what follows happened on the eighth day. The seven days were completed. The number eight signifies a new beginning. Regarding that eighth day:

> "... for today the Lord will appear to you." (Leviticus 9: 4b)

> **Moses and Aaron went into the tent of meeting. When they came out and blessed the people, the glory of the Lord appeared to all the people. Then fire came out from before the Lord and consumed the burnt offering and the portions of fat on the altar; and when all the people saw** *it,* **they shouted and fell on their faces.** (Leviticus 9:23-24)

What a picture of that future, glorious day. Out of the most holy place, Jesus Christ, our great High Priest, will appear in glory to all the earth.

> "For just as the lightning comes from the east and flashes even to the west, so will the coming of the Son of Man be." (Matthew 24:27)

> "And then the sign of the Son of Man will appear in the

sky, and then all the tribes of the earth will mourn, and they will see the SON OF MAN COMING ON THE CLOUDS OF THE SKY with power and great glory." (Matthew 24:30)

On that great day of the return of the Lord, Jesus will make His awesome appearance on the "eighth day." All the earth will see the glory of the Lord when Christ returns. It is then that swords will be beaten into plow shares and spears into pruning hooks, and the earth will be full of the knowledge of the Lord. We will be with Him and inherit that new kingdom, under the authority and power of Jesus Christ Himself. That is when serving as believer-priests will take an even richer, fuller meaning than it does in this life, as we rule earth with Christ, as His servants.

We are consecrated unto Him, and that consecration is freeing. It frees us to realize we are usable to the Lord, not because of our own merit, but because of the righteousness of Jesus. The blood and the oil of the Old Testament represent that consecration to us through the cross and the Holy Spirit. We just make ourselves available to the Lord, and look to Him to be used for His purposes. That propensity toward sinfulness is washed in the blood of Jesus Christ and we are made fit for His use by its application. By the blood of Christ, our ears have been sanctified to hear the Father, our hands made qualified and usable, and our feet ready to be guided by His Spirit. And by the anointing oil of the Spirit of God, we are empowered for that service. That is what Jesus has done for us. We just stand there, and the Lord washes us, puts His garments on us, and anoints us with the blood and the oil. And thus we are consecrated believer-priests. Thank you, Lord.

So we are chosen, redeemed, ordained, and consecrated. Just as God told Israel that He had chosen them as His own, physically redeemed them from Egypt, spiritually redeemed them in the sacrifices, ordained the family of Aaron, and consecrated them to be fit and ready for service.

At that point, the priests are almost ready to go into the main tent of the tabernacle and serve. As we continue our "tour," we will venture into the tabernacle tent itself with them, but we must first make one final stop before entering into that Holy Place. Our final stop in the courtyard will be at the laver, which sits right in front of the tabernacle door.

Chapter Ten

The Laver

If we confess our sins, He is faithful and righteous to forgive us our sins and to cleanse us from all unrighteousness.

1 John 1:9

The two-roomed tabernacle itself, wherein was the Holy Place and the Holy of Holies, was called the **"tent of meeting"** because it was the place to meet with the Lord. It was the place that represented intimate fellowship with God. Even after making a sacrifice for his sin, before a priest could physically walk into that tent, one more thing had to happen. That brings us to Exodus 30:17-18:

> The LORD spoke to Moses, saying, "You shall also make a laver of bronze, with its base of bronze, for washing; and you shall put it between the tent of meeting and the altar, and you shall put water in it."

The laver was put **"between the tent of meeting and the altar."** In drawings of the tabernacle, artists occasionally put their lavers in the wrong place, on one side or the other of the courtyard. Clearly, though, the laver is between the tent of meeting and the altar, and it was put right there for a reason: it was to be used and used often.

> "Aaron and his sons shall wash their hands and their feet from it; when they enter the tent of meeting, they shall wash with water, so that they will not die; or when they approach the altar to minister, by offering up in smoke a fire sacrifice to the Lord. So they shall wash their hands and their feet, so that they will not die; and it shall be a perpetual statute for them, for Aaron and his descendants throughout their generations." (Exodus 30:19-21)

So the priests were required to wash from the laver before they could either serve at the altar or enter the tent. They could not commune with the Lord nor truly serve Him until they had washed, every single time.

A priest could not say, "Well, I washed this morning so I don't have to wash again." No. Are you going to go into the tent? Wash again. Are you going to minister at the altar? Wash again. Are you going to serve? Wash again. The laver was filled with water, sitting on the dust of the earth directly in front of the tent tabernacle.

I believe what we have in the bronze laver is an explanation of why so many Christians can experience a nagging sense of powerlessness, frustration, or unfruitfulness in their relationship with God and in their service for God. They don't wash regularly at the spiritual laver of God.

In this chapter we will look at the laver itself and at the two washings required of priests.

The Water of the Word

There was water in that laver and we know that water symbolizes the Word of God.

> Husbands, love your wives, just as Christ also loved the church and gave Himself up for her, so that He might sanctify her, having cleansed her by the washing of water with the word … (Ephesians 5:25-26)

> "You are already clean because of the word which I

have spoken to you." (John 15:3)

The Word has a cleansing effect in our lives. We need to regularly be in the Word of God, reading, listening, studying, and meditating upon it.

That laver was positioned right in front of the tent. The priests of God did not go into the tent, the presence of the Lord, until they stopped first at the laver to wash. Similarly, we need cleansing by the Word of God on a regular basis.

A young lady named Nancy, who was a senior in high school, attended the youth group I led when I first started ministering as a youth pastor in southern California. I came on staff in the spring of the year and that following fall she started college. Since she was going to college locally, she stayed with the youth group. In college, Nancy found the studies to be intense. She had a heavy study load which caused her to miss most of our Friday night Bible studies. Finally, after a couple of months, she came back to our study and commented afterward that she had not realized how much she had missed coming to Bible study. She could see that she desperately needed that time in the Word, but she did not realize just how much she needed it until she was nourished and cleansed by sitting under the teaching of the Word once again.

It is easy for us to relegate to a level of unimportance the time spent in God's Word on a regular basis. We feel like we can skip a Bible study, or a church service, or time alone in the Word here and there, and it is no big deal. But that couldn't be further from the truth. That laver, placed right in front of the tent of meeting, tells us the place of God's Word in cleansing is crucial to our communion, fellowship, and service for Him—absolutely crucial.

Manna, the food from heaven that God gave the Israelites in the wilderness, provides a good example of how we need to stay in the Word. Just as water does in the Bible, manna can symbolize the Word of God. Consider that manna was necessary on a daily basis; however, it would only remain fresh on the very day it was gathered. Yesterday's manna would not sustain them tomorrow, nor would it be edible the next day if stored. The Israelites needed that manna from God every single day.

Similarly, being regularly in the Word of God is vital to our Christian walk, our service to the Lord, and our fellowship with Him. For example, if I start putting my daily time in the Word on the shelf, for a while I might believe that I am okay. "So what is the big deal? There is no problem with me. I am still a Christian."

But ever so gradually, if that continues, my spiritual walk can start getting a little stale, and my fellowship with the Lord and with other believers will not be as sweet as it was before. "What is the problem here?" Frequently the problem goes right back to not staying in that place of being daily in His Word, of being constantly refreshed and cleansed by it. His Word has a cleansing effect on your life.

I will give you an example of one way that cleansing effect of the Word can work in your own life. Bear in mind, however, that I am not encouraging the first part of this scenario. Think for a moment of the movies on television that are such trash. The next time you stay up late to watch one of them, and then go to bed with a sick feeling in the pit of your stomach because of the garbage you allowed in your mind, stay up for an extra half hour and bathe yourself in the Word of God. See if there is not a cleansing effect that takes place. Of course, you can spare yourself from a lot of filth by not watching the worldly junk which is on television in the first place. The point is that God's Word does cleanse. How much better, instead of feasting on some garbage for two hours in the evening, to feast on His living Word, and go to bed renewed and refreshed in spirit … and a little earlier at that!

The Water of the Spirit

The second thing that water, which fills the laver, represents in the Word is the Holy Spirit. As John recounts in John 7:37-39:

> Now on the last day, the great day of the feast, Jesus stood and cried out, saying, "If anyone is thirsty, let him come to Me and drink. He who believes in Me, as the Scripture said, 'From his innermost being will flow rivers of living water.'" But this He spoke of the Spirit, whom those who believed in Him were to receive; for the Spirit was not yet given, because Jesus was not yet glorified.

That water symbolizes the Spirit of God and that Spirit is like a well of water springing up into eternal life. What a picture! In that hot barren desert, right in front of the tabernacle was this laver, a basin filled with cool, clear water which represents the Holy Spirit. The presence and the work of the Holy Spirit is absolutely essential if we are going to commune with God and effectively serve Him.

In that Old Testament picture, it is as if God told Moses to put that laver directly in front of that tent so that nobody could get into the tent without tripping over it. The laver is essential to communion with Him and service for Him. It has always been that way. No one can do the works of God. Only the Holy Spirit can do the work of God through individuals. It is as simple as that.

That is what Jesus meant when He said in John 15:5:

> "I am the vine, you are the branches; he who abides in Me and I in him, he bears much fruit, for apart from Me you can do nothing."

Your contribution to the work of God—in and of yourself—amounts to absolutely "nothing." It is the hole in the donut. It is a zero to which someone came along and erased the line. It is nothing. Service to God *must* be through the work of the Holy Spirit.

When Israel came back from the Babylonian captivity, intent on rebuilding their temple, what did God tell them through Zechariah the prophet?

> Then he said to me, "This is the word of the LORD to Zerubbabel saying, 'Not by might nor by power, but by My Spirit,' says the LORD of hosts. (Zechariah 4:6)

That temple was not going to be built by the power of men, no matter how fervent or determined they might be. It would do no good to have the right people in the right places, or to get a large number of people committed to the project. Basically God told them, "By My Spirit that temple will go up." Against incredible opposition there was erected a temple in Jerusalem after the Babylonian captivity, the construction of which was directed and empowered by the Spirit of God.

It is the same with the work of God today. For communion with Him, and for service for Him, that continual renewal and refreshing comes through the Word and by the Spirit of God. His Spirit is absolutely essential—your spiritual life will be dry bones apart from the

Spirit working upon your heart through His Word.

The Water of Cleansing

Notice that even though the laver sat there on the hot barren desert floor, the water basin itself, containing that cool, clear water, was raised above the earth. That reminds me that God has called us to be in the world, but not of the world.

I am sure you have noticed how dust has the tendency of accumulating. You can dust your house and before long that thin film of dust will return. Just imagine Aaron and his sons as they worked in the tabernacle courtyard and tent. They would be clean and ready to serve, yet within a short period of time they would become dusty and dirty again. So God put the laver right out there in the middle of that courtyard, in front of the tent, and told the priests to use it frequently in their service.

What does that say to us? We have the same problem, but our dust and dirtiness is the defilement of sin. We can walk out of church so refreshed and cleansed, but before we even get home, we can be dusty and dirty. It can happen so quickly. Thankfully, there is the spiritual laver right there. If we turn to the Lord and confess that we are dusty and dirty, i.e., go to the laver, He is always faithful to forgive and cleanse, and we are renewed by His Spirit in our relationship with Him (1 John 1:9).

It reminds me of John 13:3-10, which tells of Jesus washing the disciples' feet. He made His way around washing each of the disciple's feet. Even though most of the disciples did not understand why, they let Him do it anyway. But Peter, the one disciple who always seemed to be afflicted with "foot-in-mouth disease," spoke up and told Jesus not to wash *his* feet. As their teacher and leader, He shouldn't do that. Jesus told Peter he would have no part in Him if He did not wash his feet. Then Peter told Jesus to wash his hands and head as well. Jesus explained to Peter that if he had bathed, he was clean, all he needed was a foot washing. What a picture that is for us! The cross cleansed us and reconciled us to God, once and for all. However, because that defilement of sin so easily attaches itself to us, we need occasional, regular cleansing at the laver. The laver—His Word and the ministry of His Spirit—cleanses and renews us daily, enabling us to commune with and serve the Lord.

That is why there was a laver in the tabernacle, and I am so *glad* that God put it in there. The laver tells us that we can enter in and commune with God any time. We can serve Him, today, right now. Because God put a laver right there in the center of the courtyard, directly in front of the tent, the priests could wash any time and then enter into the **"tent of meeting"** or go out and serve at the altar.

Any time a believer comes before his Lord open-heartedly, confessing sin, and allowing the Word of God and the power of the Holy Spirit to minister to his heart, he is going to be renewed and refreshed in the Lord, automatically, every time. The laver is always there.

David is a prime example. When David committed adultery, he murdered a man and then lied to cover his sin. Then, with a broken heart (when he was exposed), he turned to his God. David cried out to God and Psalm 51 came out of that broken heart before the Lord.

> **Wash me thoroughly from my iniquity**
> **And cleanse me from my sin.** (Psalm 51:2)
>
> **Purify me with hyssop, and I shall be clean;**
> **Wash me, and I shall be whiter than snow.** (Psalm 51:7)
>
> **Create in me a clean heart, O God,**
> **And renew a steadfast spirit within me.**
> **Do not cast me away from Your presence**
> **And do not take Your Holy Spirit from me.**
> **Restore to me the joy of Your salvation**
> **And sustain me with a willing spirit.** (Psalm 51:10-12)

God can and will forgive under any circumstance when we come to Him in that spirit. It is the laver of the tabernacle that pictures for us the reality that God will forgive, every time.

There is a super-dispensational kind of doctrine which has attained popularity in some circles. According to this doctrine, because of the cross, we as believers do not have to confess our sins to God anymore and we do not have to seek His forgiveness. This belief further says that because all our sins were removed at the cross, we do not have to, in any way, be concerned about sin any more. In fact, according to them, to even bring your sins up through confession is saying that the cross was not effective. They are against seeking God's forgiveness. If that doctrine were true, they just took the laver out of the tabernacle.

They are saying we do not need a laver, that the big bronze altar is all we needed. However, God put a laver in the tabernacle as a picture to us to say, "Wait a minute! Hold everything! You know yourself that you need that frequent cleansing of the Word and the Spirit, as well as the cleansing that comes from open and honest confession of sin. So you need to come to that laver and wash on a regular basis. That's why it's there."

The Mirroring Effect of God's Word

Now, it is interesting to note where the bronze was obtained for the construction of this laver. Look at Exodus 38:8:

> **Moreover, he made the laver of bronze with its base of bronze, from the mirrors of the serving women who served at the doorway of the tent of meeting.** (Exodus 38:8)

I love it! The ladies gave up their mirrors for the construction of the laver. I know from years of living with my wife and three daughters what a major sacrifice that must have been! But there is more to it than just that obvious sacrifice of some women giving up their mirrors. Think of how the Word of God has a mirroring effect in our lives. James says in James 1:22-25:

> **But prove yourselves doers of the word, and not merely hearers who delude themselves. For if anyone is a hearer of the word and not a doer, he is like a man who looks at his natural face in a mirror; for once he has looked at himself and gone away, he has immediately forgotten what kind of person he was. But one who looks intently at the perfect law, the law of liberty, and abides by it, not having become a forgetful hearer but an effectual doer, this man will be blessed in what he does.** (James 1:22-25)

The Word of God causes us to see ourselves as we really are. Perhaps you could say that these ladies who sacrificed their mirrors for the laver gave up that which reflects natural beauty in order that they might be used to reflect the truth of God's Word in their lives. Indeed, there are two ways to look at yourself. You can look at your natural beauty, or you can look at yourself with an honest look from the Word of God. When you look at yourself in the light of the Word of God, it is never pretty, not for one single one of us.

Job said he abhorred himself, yet Job seemed to be a righteous man. In Romans 7:18, the Apostle Paul said:

> "For I know that nothing good dwells in me ..."

In Isaiah 6:5, the prophet said:

> "Woe is me, for I am ruined!
> Because I am a man of unclean lips ..."

But God does not just leave you staring at your own unfit reflection in His Word. That is where the enemy would want to leave you. Satan would like you to stay in the place of seeing yourself only as a miserable wretch, a worthless piece of dust. But God does not leave us in that place. That is the purpose of the Old Testament laver. The laver is not just a place of introspection. It is a place of cleansing and refreshing.

1 John 1:9 Applied

The laver is 1 John 1:9 applied:

> If we confess our sins, He is faithful and righteous to forgive us our sins and to cleanse us from all unrighteousness.

In other words, we are to confess those things we know make us dirty and dusty, those sins that are all over our hands and feet, and we cannot miss them. We just confess those things to Him, whatever they may be, and immediately He is faithful to forgive. That means He will do it every time. There will never be a time when God will say, "No, not today. No, you have sinned too many times today. You will have to come back to Me next week on that one. Your quota is filled today." He will never say that. He will *always* forgive.

Notice that John said it is also **"righteous"** for God to forgive us. Because that sin was paid for at Calvary, it would be unrighteous for God *not* to grant you forgiveness. There's more in that verse. God cleanses us from all unrighteousness, not just that sin that led you to the point of confession. Do you know what that means? You bring to God that sin you need to confess and the Lord cleans the whole slate. It is all clean. So you do not have to go digging for that hidden sin that is preventing you from really getting into the Holy of Holies and back to Jesus. That verse says you are completely cleansed.

The laver pictures that kind of cleansing. It is a 1 John 1:9 cleansing. It comes by the Spirit upon your heart. It comes by the Word. God wants us to use the laver in our lives, and use it regularly. It is not a place of condemnation. It is a place of refreshing, renewal, cleansing and preparation. We can walk away after washing at the laver, knowing we are ready to just enjoy the fullness of that tent of meeting, or go out and be a servant of God.

A preacher had scheduled a week of evangelistic meetings down in the South somewhere, but little happened in the first four days. The services were kind of flat. There were not many salvations at all so he was concerned. He felt there was something hindering what God wanted to do there. On the fourth night, he encouraged Christians to really get right with the Lord, whatever it took.

There was a prominent businessman attending that service, and it really pierced his heart. He stood up before the congregation and said he had something he really needed to confess. Forty years before, he had embezzled money from his employer, and no one else knew about it. He opened his own business and was very successful. As time went by, he wanted to right the thing he had done wrong, but it was so embarrassing because it had been so long, and he had been a Christian for so long. He realized he needed to make that right with the Lord. It was not that the Lord had not forgiven him, he just realized this situation had to be made right.

That confession broke things loose and, one by one, others in the body started confessing things that were not right in their lives which they wanted to make right before God and their fellow believers. The *believers* had a revival. In addition, during the last two nights of these meetings, many came to the Lord. All the stops were pulled out and things started to happen.

It is interesting how we avoid the practical application of that laver. How often does God want to do something in our lives, but we are too proud, for whatever reason, to let Him do the work which would transform us?

The laver was a very practical piece of furniture in that tabernacle and it sat right there at the front of the tent of meeting. God has given the picture of the laver because He wants us to use the spiritual laver in our lives, and use it regularly. It is there to be used. After washing at it, we can walk away knowing we are ready to enjoy the fullness of that tent of meeting, or go out and be a servant of God. It is a glorious thing.

God has provided every Christian with a spiritual laver, a provision from Him on a daily basis for cleansing when cleansing is needed, renewing when renewing is needed, and refreshing from the defilement of sin in the world. But that spiritual laver is completely useless unless it is used.

I am reminded of a little class of Sunday School boys. After talking about the importance of the confession of sin and of receiving God's forgiveness, the Sunday School teacher asked the boys if they had anything they wanted to confess. This group of a dozen or so little boys just sat there, looking around with a stony, cold silence for a while. Finally one little boy raised his hand, and said, "Teacher, I really don't have anything to confess myself, but I know some people who do."

We are so like that! The laver must be applied to oneself. That laver is for you, it is not for you to apply that water to anyone else in the body of Christ. It is for you.

So, the spiritual laver is a necessary fixture that is given for moment-by-moment renewal in your fellowship with your Heavenly Father. It offers a renewal for effective service, the power of the Holy Spirit, and a renewal of worship. It's like God is saying, "You may not want to admit it, but you need it more than you know. So I put it right there on front of the tent. Use it."

The Washings

There were two ceremonial washings for the priests: the one-time washing at the ceremony of consecration and numerous daily washings. Many times throughout each day of service the priests washed their hands and feet before they would enter the tabernacle or serve at the altar.

What a picture of the Christian life!

As Christians, we are washed, cleansed, and sanctified once and for all and forever at the moment we are born again of the Spirit of God.

We call that "positional sanctification." It means you are forevermore sanctified unto God through Jesus Christ. That is where you stand in your relationship with Him. God has given the church a symbol of that positional sanctification; that symbol is water baptism.

> **Such were some of you; but you were washed, but you were sanctified, but you were justified in the name of the Lord Jesus Christ and in the Spirit of our God.** (1 Corinthians 6:11)

Now that is a spiritual fact. That is our standing before our God through Jesus Christ. We have been washed and set apart to Him; that is settled once and for all, forever.

But, obviously, sin is still at work within me. And I must wash frequently for my service and walk with the Lord.

> **For the good that I want, I do not do, but I practice the very evil that I do not want. But if I am doing the very thing I do not want, I am no longer the one doing it, but sin which dwells in me.** (Romans 7:19-20)

Paul is saying, "I've got this problem with sin in my life which dwells in me, causing me to do what I do not want to do, and causing me *not* to do what I really want to do."

That sin hinders my fellowship, hinders the ministry, and hinders the power of the Holy Spirit in my life. Sin hinders my service. It is a big dumb hindrance. That is where the laver comes in. It provides for that daily washing of the hands and the feet. The washing of the hands pictures our spiritual service to the Lord. The washing of the feet pictures our spiritual walk with Him.

That laver was placed right in front of the tabernacle which speaks of the need to regularly examine our lives in the light of God's Word. With the help of the Holy Spirit we should examine our service and our walk before the Lord.

Paul tells us that we are to examine ourselves at the Communion table. Don't just flippantly take Communion, but examine yourself.

> **Therefore whoever eats the bread or drinks the cup of the Lord in an unworthy manner, shall be guilty of the body and the blood of the Lord. But a man must examine himself, and in so doing he is to eat of the**

bread and drink of the cup. (1 Corinthians 11:27-28)

Examine yourself in relation to your service and in relation to your walk.

I remember hearing of a fellow who very much desired to enroll in Bible College. He was married and had a family. In order to attend Bible College, he would have to quit his job and move quite a distance away. Despite the hardship this was going to be on his family, he did it. He quit his job, uprooted everyone, and moved so that he might attend Bible College. From that point on, there was just one trial after another for his family. They were not making it financially, they were really suffering. His wife and kids were having an awful time. Personally, he was also struggling. So he sought counseling from someone on staff at the Bible College.

After hearing the man's story, the counselor asked him if he was sure this was what God really wanted him to do, because it just did not look like it was coming together for them. The counselor told him to really seek the Lord on this. The man had just assumed it was God's will for him to attend Bible College. But after he went out and sought the Lord, he realized he may have jumped ahead of the Lord. As he examined himself, he realized his place was to provide and care for his family, then to wait and see what the Lord would provide and direct from there.

When we are facing trials or difficulties, it is not a matter of blaming them on poor choices we make, and just living with the consequences. "Oh no, I made a mistake. I got off on the wrong road. Oh no, what am I going to do now?" It is just a matter of going to the laver and letting the Lord have it. Sometimes adults live as though we were still little children, rushing ahead of the Lord just as kids sometimes will enthusiastically jump into something they should not really attempt. "I'll do it. I'll do it." Then, when everything comes crashing in, we turn to our Father, "Oh Dad, will you fix it?" Thankfully our Father is faithful to come along and deliver us from the messes we create, once we surrender to His will.

We might think that going to Africa as a missionary would be the right thing to do. It is the big sacrificial thing to do, right? Living here and having a job, what is that to the Lord? That just isn't true. If you are going to serve God, you can serve your Lord from your work place and the environment in which you live right now.

Examine yourself in your daily activities. Apply 1 John 1:9:

> **If we confess our sins, He is faithful and righteous to forgive us our sins and to cleanse us from all unrighteousness.**

God said it, I believe it, that settles it. Or, more accurately, God said it and that settles it.

God intends His forgiveness to be a source of peace and assurance in your life, in your relationship with Him. Through that simple examination, that fellowship with Him, you are restored in full and you have the daily adventure of watching Christ do His works through your life.

That is the purpose of the laver, to bring you back in that place where you have that peace, that assurance, that fellowship with Him. You really *can* enjoy the daily adventure of seeing what Jesus wants to do with your life each day. You *can* rest in the knowledge that the events of each day are directed and guided by Him. The laver is there for our cleansing, so we can renew our relationship with Him and walk according to His direction. So use the laver and use it regularly.

First John is a very practical book. Notice the three verses preceding and including 1 John 1:9.

> **If we say that we have fellowship with Him and yet walk in the darkness, we lie and do not practice the truth; but if we walk in the Light as He Himself is in the Light, we have fellowship with one another, and the blood of Jesus His Son cleanses us from all sin. If we say that we have no sin, we are deceiving ourselves and the truth is not in us. If we confess our sins, He is faithful and righteous to forgive us our sins and to cleanse us from all unrighteousness.** (1 John 1:6-9)

Now, how important was it to regularly use that laver?

> **"So they shall wash their hands and their feet, so that they will not die; and it shall be a perpetual statute for them, for Aaron and his descendants throughout their generations."** (Exodus 30:21)

You know what that says to me? It says that communion and fellowship with our God is very important. The Apostle John said it so well. If you say you have fellowship with Him and you walk in the darkness you are lying. Your life is a joke. Your fellowship with Him and your service to Him is a farce. It says to me that communion with Him and service to Him is dead works without clean hands and feet.

The point in 1 John 1:9 is: you cannot really enjoy fellowship with Him and be used by Him unless you are clean before Him. He knows our condition. That is why the laver is there.

Regardless of how cold your own heart may seem at times, or how spiritually "blah" you may feel at times, just go to the Lord in full confession, open-heartedly, and every time He will instantly forgive, cleanse all, and empower you for worship and service. Period. You never, ever need to be "unworthy" or "unusable." That is why the laver is there.

Does it mean that every time we are going to go to prayer or commune with God or do any service for the Lord, we need to confess every one of our sins? Please know that the idea here is not some sort of legalistic or rote process of: "If you are going to commune with God or serve God, be sure you confess every single one of your sins first." That is not the point of it. This should not become a legalistic rote practice. Simply know that the laver is there to be used. It is a part of our Christian life and walk, to avail ourselves of the Word of God, receive that cleansing, and let it do its work on our hearts.

Sometimes you listen to a good message and you receive comfort and are built up. Other times you are convicted and admonished in that message and that, too, is the work of the Word, doing its work in your life. Let the Spirit do His work by keeping that avenue with Him open and allowing the Holy Spirit to fill you afresh, to guide and direct you. That is adequate use of the laver. It is not a meaningless ritual or rote process of confession that must be engaged in before ministering to others in His name. It is simply a matter of living cleansed lives before the Lord.

Only a simple little wash job is required on your hands and feet to cleanse you for service. Just wash your hands and feet, and you are ready to go into the tabernacle, to go forth and serve Him in the power of His name. You are ready. Remember, He is with you always, even to the end of the age.

Chapter Eleven

The Tent of Meeting

Christ Jesus Himself being the cornerstone, in whom the whole building, being fitted together, is growing into a holy temple in the Lord, in whom you also are being built together into a dwelling of God in the Spirit.

Ephesians 2:20-22

We are now going to look at the two-room tent itself. As usual, there were specific instructions about the tent. They are listed in detail in Exodus chapters 26 and 36. Let's look at the highlights here.

The tent was large and rectangular: 45 feet long, 15 feet wide, and 15 feet high. It was divided into two rooms. The outer room was 30 feet long and 15 feet wide. That outer room was generally called the Holy Place. There was a veil separating the outer room from the inner room of the tent of meeting. The inner room, with the space that was left, was a perfect cube: 15 feet by 15 feet by 15 feet. That room was called the Holy of Holies. There was a curtained door at the front of the tabernacle, so that what happened inside was not visible from the courtyard.

The walls of the tent tabernacle were made of acacia wood boards covered with gold. Everything in the courtyard was covered with bronze. But inside the tent everything was covered with gold, with the exception that the boards were set upright in silver sockets which sat on the ground. The boards were made secure with each other with bars, which were also made with acacia wood covered with gold. The bars connected the whole structure of boards together.

Right over the top of those golden overlaid acacia wood walls was a four-layer covering. The inner most or bottom covering was made of fine linen. The colors embroidered into the linen were purple, blue, and scarlet. Cherubim (angelic figures) were embroidered in the linen.

The layer over that was a layer of goats' hair.

Over that was a layer of rams' skins dyed red.

We cannot be certain exactly how to translate the word for the outer most covering. Every translation has a different idea of what the Hebrew word actually meant. The King James says **"badgers' skins."** But the best guess would be something in relation to the sea, like **"porpoise skins"** (NASB), or perhaps seal skin. Whatever it was, that outer layer was tough and durable, making a waterproof, protective covering for the tent.

Not Your Average Tent

If we could have the privilege of going back in time and seeing the entire tabernacle with all that pure gold, all that silver, all that costly material, it would be a mind-blower. For instance, there were forty-six solid silver sockets holding up the board walls of the tent. It is estimated that the sockets each weighed 125 pounds. That means that there were 5.5 tons of pure silver just in those sockets. When you throw in all of the gold and the various other materials that were used (the brass, the wood, the cloth, etc.), this edifice would have been worth millions of dollars. Obviously, the tabernacle was not your average desert tent.

So the question comes up: how did those ex-slaves out in the wilderness get that kind of wealth? The answer is that they took it from Egypt.

> **"Speak now in the hearing of the people that each man ask from his neighbor and each woman from her neighbor for articles of silver and articles of gold." The Lord gave the people favor in the sight of the Egyptians. Furthermore, the man Moses himself was greatly esteemed in the land of Egypt, both in the sight of Pharaoh's servants and in the sight of the people.** (Exodus 11:2-3)

In other words, the Egyptian people just unloaded on them. The Egyptians gave the Israelite slaves their own silver and gold. The Israelites did not leave Egypt empty-handed; they took much of that nation's wealth with them. The riches that they took were not used just for personal gain—much of that wealth was used in constructing the tabernacle. However, what was used was all freely donated by the people (Exodus 35:29).

Do you remember what silver represents? In the Old Testament, silver speaks of redemption. Where exactly did the silver for the tabernacle come from? The answer to that is given in Exodus 30 where we are told that every son of Israel, every man twenty years of age and older, paid a half-shekel of silver for his redemption. God redeemed them from Egypt, so they each paid the Lord a "redemption tax" because they belonged to Him.

This whole tent was based on, built on, and resting on silver. The whole tent structure is literally being supported by the silver. This reminds us, as believers, that we also were redeemed at a price, the price of Jesus' precious blood. Our fellowship with God is totally based on, literally rests upon, His redemption of us.

The precious gold, the metals, and the other valuable materials used to construct the tabernacle convey to us how rich and precious is our own salvation to us, and to God. God sees it that way. What He has given to us is extremely valuable and He wants us to comprehend it, to get a feel for the richness of the salvation we have been given.

> ... that the God of our Lord Jesus Christ, the Father of glory, may give to you a spirit of wisdom and of revelation in the knowledge of Him. I pray that the eyes of your heart may be enlightened, so that you will know what is the hope of His calling, what are the riches of the glory of His inheritance in the saints, and what is the surpassing greatness of His power toward us who believe. These are in accordance with the working of the strength of His might ... (Ephesians 1:17-19)
>
> **And my God will supply all your needs according to His riches in glory in Christ Jesus.** (Philippians 4:19)

God wants us to comprehend, spiritually, what a rich salvation He has for us. The tent tabernacle was built to give us a small idea of how precious and rich our salvation truly is. The tent was worth millions; our salvation is worth far more—it is priceless.

This tent represents two things, Jesus Christ and believers.

We see an awesome picture of Jesus Christ in the tent itself. The tent was God's dwelling place to be with His people. Jesus Christ came to tabernacle among men as God's dwelling place in the Spirit. In other words, He was God in our midst, tabernacling among men.

> **And the Word became flesh, and dwelt among us, and we saw His glory, glory as of the only begotten from the Father, full of grace and truth. ... No one has seen God at any time; the only begotten God who is in the bosom of the Father, He has explained Him.** (John 1:14, 18)

> **Jesus said to him, "Have I been so long with you, and yet you have not come to know Me, Philip? He who has seen Me has seen the Father; how can you say, 'Show us the Father'?** (John 14:9)

The tent is also a beautiful picture of believers, of the church, the body of Christ.

> **... in whom you also are being built together into a dwelling of God in the Spirit.** (Ephesians 2:22)

We, too, are the dwelling place of God, in the Spirit, in this world.

Now we will look at two major components of the tabernacle itself: the sides and the tent's four-fold covering.

The Tent Walls

> "Then you shall make the boards for the tabernacle of acacia wood, standing upright. Ten cubits shall be the length of each board and one and a half cubits the width of each board. There shall be two tenons for each board, fitted to one another; thus you shall do for all the boards of the tabernacle." (Exodus 26:15-17)

> "You shall make forty sockets of silver under the twenty boards, two sockets under one board for its two tenons and two sockets under another board for its two tenons ..." (Exodus 26:19)

> "Then you shall make bars of acacia wood, five for the boards of one side of the tabernacle, and five bars for the boards of the other side of the tabernacle, and five bars for the boards of the side of the tabernacle for the rear side to the west. The middle bar in the center of the boards shall pass through from end to end. You shall overlay the boards with gold and make their rings of gold as holders for the bars; and you shall overlay the bars with gold." (Exodus 26:26-29)

The boards of this tent tabernacle, made with wood and gold, draw a beautiful picture of Christ. In the Old Testament wood always pictures humanity, and gold pictures deity. So what a picture of Christ: wholly man and wholly God.

Those boards also provide an interesting picture of a redeemed believer. We are, in every sense of the word, common human beings. God said He purposely picked out the weak, the base, the lowly things of the world (1 Corinthians 1:27-29). So, when you were called by God, that is the category into which you fit.

Yet, we have been born again of the Spirit of God, and we are, by virtue of that birth, children of God. When God looks upon us now, all He sees is gold. Do you realize that? All He sees is gold. The wood of our humanity has been totally covered by the Person of Jesus and His righteousness. To have looked at that tabernacle board, you would not have known it was made of wood unless someone told you, for the wood was completely encased in gold. To look at it, that board would have appeared to be a solid gold plank. That is how God sees us—as solid gold.

How in the world did we get to that place where we have become a beautiful part of His tabernacle, serving mankind for the glory of God? How did we get there? Brethren, we each started out as a weather-beaten, gnarled, desert acacia scrub tree. Then we were cut down and stripped. Our lives are spent being molded into the size and shape He wants each of us to be.

As our God molds us, we cannot say, "Oh, *why* are you doing that? Why are you removing that part of me? Why don't you just leave *part* of me in tact? I want a little more left here—but you can take *that* away if you want." No. You are being molded by the Master Architect, Designer, and Builder, into the size and shape that He wants. He covers you with the gold of His presence so you can reflect the glory of the Living God. You are a work of God's. You are just a scrub tree and He has done the rest. He now has us standing upright in sockets of silver, resting firmly upon our redemption in Jesus Christ.

For several reasons, I love the fact that the silver for the building of the tabernacle came from the redemption money of Israel. First, I am thankful that the same amount of money was required of everyone. The rich did not pay more; the poor did not pay less. Everyone paid exactly the same amount. You see, all people are equally in need of His redemption. There is no one on earth that needs that redemption more than anyone else on earth. In addition, that silver redemption money was a symbol that they had been redeemed by God, unto God, for His purposes. It is a recognition that we are His, and that our redemption is for Him. Once we are redeemed, we understand we are completely His—redeemed by God, for God.

The redemption money was required of all men twenty years old and older. These were the fighting men who could be drafted into the service. We too, as His redeemed, are "saved to serve." It was Paul who told Timothy to be ready to endure hardship as **"a good soldier"** of the Lord (2 Timothy 2:3).

Our One Foundation

These silver sockets were the only foundation for those boards. They had no other means of support whatsoever.

> **For no man can lay a foundation other than the one which is laid, which is Jesus Christ.** (1 Corinthians 3:11)

There is no other foundation. Despite the howling storms of the wilderness, the strong winds, and the blasting sandstorms, these planks never blew over. They remained secure in those silver sockets of redemption.

Tenons of Faith

Each board had two tenons on the bottom of them, also covered with gold. These two tenons on the bottom fit into the silver sockets. The word **"tenon"** in the Hebrew literally means "hand." I like to refer to those tenons as hands of faith. There were two of them extending from the end of each board—not one, but two. Two, in Scripture, is the number of true witness. In other words, by the fact that there were two of them, we *know* that our salvation is secure in the redemption of Jesus Christ.

The Lord put two silver sockets down there for each board. No board was held by only one socket; each board rested in two sockets. Point: He gives equal grace to us all, not more to some or less to others. There is an equality of grace. There were two tenons fitted into those two silver sockets for every single board, just as everyone is given a measure of faith sufficient for their salvation.

When we look at the physical construction of the tabernacle, spiritual truths become so obvious. What a message it holds for us! The boards were not *suspended from* the sockets. The boards were not *holding onto* the sockets. The boards were *resting upon* the sockets. We can rest in the redemption God has given us. As we rest in His redemption, we stand upright and secure in His very presence.

> **So then you are no longer strangers and aliens, but you are fellow citizens with the saints, and are of God's household, having been built on the foundation of the apostles and prophets, Christ Jesus Himself being the corner stone, in whom the whole building, being fitted together, is growing into a holy temple in the Lord, in whom you also are being built together into a dwelling of God in the Spirit.** (Ephesians 2:19-22)

It is when we rest in His redemption that this verse from Ephesians becomes a reality in our lives. We are being built together, just like those planks were built together into the tabernacle of God in the wilderness. We are being built together as a dwelling of God in the Spirit, each one of us. We are part of the dwelling place of God, as we rest in the redemption of Jesus Christ. We are not Lone Ranger "boards" in the wilderness. We as believers are part and parcel of one structure, being **"fitted together"** into the body of Christ.

That fitting together was accomplished by five acacia wood bars covered with gold. There was one bar that went the full length of one side, through the center, and then four half-bars that went halfway along each side, above and below that center bar.

The Centrality of Christ

What a picture of Jesus Christ! It is Him, as the center of our lives, who bonds us all together. We are bound together in Jesus Christ. I don't believe we fully appreciate or comprehend how one we are in Jesus Christ, what kinship and family we are in Him. When Christians begin to taste that one, they long for Christian fellowship because it offers a richness the world knows nothing about. It is not "hanging out with the dudes, man." There is something there that is so rich to the heart and spirit and, consequently, the enemy wants to prevent that kind of "koinonia" (Greek for "fellowship") from developing in the body of Christ. It is too powerful. It is too binding when it is in Jesus Christ. He is the One who is in the center of our lives, and when He is in the center, we are bound together in Him.

Each of the boards were fitted with gold rings which the bars went through. A gold ring is an emblem of love, like the gold wedding rings married couples wear as a symbol of their love and commitment to each other. These boards were fitted with gold rings, a symbol of God's love, and the bars rested in those rings. Christians are called to love one another in the body of Christ.

> **… with all humility and gentleness, with patience, showing tolerance for one another in love, being diligent to preserve the unity of the Spirit in the bond of peace.**
> (Ephesians 4:2-3)

How the body of Christ today needs that love for one another! How churches need that love for one another. We need that love, with all humility. Do you know why there is strife in the body of Christ? In almost every case, someone in the church has dropped his humility somewhere. We are to love with all humility, gentleness, and patience. Never, ever stop being patient with the brethren in the body of Christ. Show tolerance or, as the KJV says, **"forebearing one another in love."** When someone offends or hurts you, let it go. Just let it go. Do not hold it against them. Let it be like water off a duck's back to you. Do not get all frazzled about it. Just let it go. Show forbearance to one another in love.

"Being diligent to preserve the unity of the Spirit in the bond of peace." How can you be diligent in preserving the unity of the Spirit and the bond of peace? By applying humility, gentleness, patience, and forbearance. Every one of those words cries out to "just love them the way they are." Don't do it in a condescending manner, either – don't act high and mighty. Just love them as is, for what they are and just the way they are.

That **"unity of the Spirit in the bond of peace"** is represented by the rings the poles slid through. That is what makes us part and parcel with the body of Christ, the dwelling place of God in the Spirit. It's His love bonding us together in Christ.

That unity of the Spirit in the bond of peace is so important for fellowship within the church body. It begins with the application of that humility, gentleness, patience, and forbearance.

It has been said that our churches would be perfect if it were not for the people. But the church *is* the people, so there must be humility. There must be gentleness. There must be patience. There must be forbearance. Without these you will never enjoy the koinonia, the fellowship of the brethren, the unity of the Spirit in the bond of peace, our oneness in Christ. All this is represented in those golden rings of the tabernacle tent structure.

The Four Short Bars of "Body Life"

The tent tabernacle wall also had four shorter bars in its structure. In Acts chapter 2 we read of four things that were hallmarks of the early church.

> **They were continually devoting themselves to the apostles' teaching and to fellowship, to the breaking of bread and to prayer.** (Acts 2:42)

I believe the four shorter bars represent the four tokens of the spiritual bond which are **"teaching," "fellowship," "the breaking of bread"** (Communion), and **"prayer."** These four tokens are what comprise the essence of what Christian "body life" should be, with Christ as our center (as illustrated by that long central bar), as it obviously was in the earliest days of the church. Those are the activities that any church that gathers in Jesus' name should be devoted to, first and foremost. At our church here in Truckee, and at Calvary Chapels in general, you will not find a preponderance of pre-packaged programs aimed at ministering to the latest social need or special interest group. Any group that does gather, even if it intends to minister to a select group of, say, young adults, recovering alcoholics, or married couples, are all basically doing at least three of these things (not all will share Communion, although they certainly could).

The Apostles' Teaching: A Healthy Diet of the Word

Once again we see the importance of the Word in a Christian's life and walk. Pastor Chuck Smith, founding pastor of the Calvary Chapel movement, has been asked, more than once I imagine, to what he attributes the phenomenal growth of first his own church in the 1960s in Costa Mesa, Calif., then the rapid spawning of new Calvary Chapels throughout the West, across the country, and now around the world. Surely, it must be because of some new or improved method for church growth that he could share with the body of Christ as a whole? His answer to that line of questioning has consistently been these three words: "Healthy sheep reproduce."

How *do* sheep, or believers, become and then remain healthy? His experience and that of Calvary Chapels has been that only a steady, uncompromised diet of the entire Word of God can produce spiritual growth in an individual and in a corporate body of believers. Absolutely nothing is more important to a body of believers than sitting under the regular teaching of the Word of God, because absolutely nothing else creates spiritual growth.

> … like newborn babies, long for the pure milk of the word, so that by it you may grow in respect to salvation, … (1 Peter 2:2)

That is why the primary focus of Calvary Chapels is the verse-by-verse teaching of the Word of God. Of course our corporate worship includes healthy doses of worship and prayer, but the teaching of the Word of God is always central. Why?

God promised in Isaiah 55:10-11:

> "For as the rain and the snow come down from heaven,
> And do not return there without watering the earth
> And making it bear and sprout,
> And furnishing seed to the sower and bread to the eater;
> So will My word be which goes forth from My mouth;

> It will not return to Me empty,
> Without accomplishing what I desire,
> And without succeeding in the matter for which I sent it."

In California, we see the truth of the dramatic effect of rain and snow. I recently drove to southern California with my son Dave. The hills around Interstate 5 were green. That doesn't happen very often! They're usually yellow or brown. When it rains on that brown, parched earth, life, beauty, and fruit spring forth. What a transformation that rain can make on that old ground that can be so dry and so barren!

God is saying, "My Word works the same way." He makes a guarantee here, in essence, "It will produce, in the very same way that rain will bring life and fruit out of dry, parched ground. My Word will do that in the hearts and souls of people. It will not return to Me void. It will accomplish what I sent it out to do."

I see a lot of people walking around who are like that dry, barren soil. There is such potential there! How sad it is to see a human being created in the image of God and yet he is barren. God says, "Let Me and My truth and My Word in there and watch what can happen, because it will not return to Me void. Out of that barrenness, suddenly, will come life and beauty." There *will* be fruit from His Word.

This is why I love teaching and sharing the Word so much! It's the *Word* that will not return void and will accomplish what God sent it out to do—and it offers so much!

> **For the word of God is living and active and sharper than any two-edged sword, and piercing as far as the division of soul and spirit, of both joints and marrow, and able to judge the thoughts and intentions of the heart. And there is no creature hidden from His sight, but all things are open and laid bare to the eyes of Him with whom we have to do.** (Hebrews 4:12-13)

The power of His Word is the difference between the religions and the philosophies of men, and the truth—the Living Water that's offered from God. The power of God is behind His Word. You can argue with someone up one side and down the other or just lay some of God's Word on him and let God's Word do the work.

When I was a youth pastor, my wife Joyce and I hosted a Friday evening Bible study for high school kids in our apartment living room.

I'll never forget a kid named Henry, a junior who was brought by a friend one Friday night. He seemed very interested in our study of the Word. After that, I saw Henry every week. He was obviously on fire for the Lord. After each study, Joyce would have cookies or cupcakes and the kids would hang out for a while. One night, after he had been coming for a few months, I asked, "Henry, how did you come to the Lord?" I just assumed he had already been an active Christian who happened on our Bible study, liked it, and started coming regularly.

"You want to know how I came to the Lord, Brian?" he said. "The first Friday I came here you were teaching out of Ephesians about the old man as opposed to the new man, and it pierced my heart! I knew that's what I needed. I invited Jesus to come into my life and to be that new man in me that very evening."

It blew me away! Henry proved what Paul says in Romans 10:17:

> "So faith comes from hearing, and hearing by the word of Christ."

This junior in high school came in, listened to the Word, believed it, and received it. It worked that sharp, two-edged-sword work in his innermost being, which the Word of God has not only the capability, but the reputation for doing. It's like Peter says in 1 Peter 1:23:

> ... for you have been born again not of seed which is perishable but imperishable, that is, through the living and enduring word of God.

Breaking Bread in Communion

In the New Testament, **"the breaking of bread"** literally refers to "Communion," and I see it as another spiritual bond of unity as represented by those four short bars holding the walls, representing believers, together. Communion in those days was a love feast. It was when brethren gathered and ate together, remembering the body and the blood of the Lord, as they communed. It was a much more casual thing than today's formal "Communion service." Communion was part of their fellowshipping together. It was like they were saying, "As we have a potluck, let's remember the body and blood of our Lord together." Then they would use the elements to do that. It is perfectly acceptable to celebrate Communion together any time a group of believers are together.

Communion is never a private thing. You do not go in the closet and have Communion by yourself. Communion is always set in the context of a body of believers. It does not have to be the whole body; it can be any part of it. You can have brothers and sisters over for dinner together and celebrate Communion, doing it in the context of fellowship.

The breaking of bread represents two things. First, it is a picture of our oneness in Christ. We are all partaking of the same bread, and it represents Him. We are all partaking of Christ. Secondly, the breaking of bread is also a picture of our fellowship together in Christ. This fellowship may be experienced when we get together after church and hang out. If we get together for dinner and prayer, that fellowship will likely bond us together at an even deeper level.

Prayer for All the Saints

A richer fellowship is also found as we come together and pray together, that fourth spiritual bond of unity represented in the four short bars of the tabernacle wall. One vivid example in my own life of how prayer can bond a group together has been the gathering of our church board on a weekly basis to pray. Every Wednesday morning of the month, except one, I meet with the six other board members of our church for the sole purpose of praying, of seeking the Lord's face for Calvary Chapel of Truckee. The one other Wednesday morning we meet each month is a business meeting at which we discuss financial issues related to the administration of the church. I firmly believe that the reason those monthly business meetings go so smoothly, that we don't have to be doing "business" every week, is that such **"a bond of unity"** (Colossians 3:14) has been established between us during those other weeks of prayer. I believe that as a result of our commitment to pray together, the monthly board meetings run smoothly and without contention. You could say that prayer is the true "business" of our group.

Another example in our own church here are the quarterly, round-the-clock, twenty-four-hour prayer vigils that we hold to lift up both praises and supplication to our Lord in prayer for one another. During the week or two prior to the vigil, prayer requests are gathered from the body and people are encouraged to sign up for at least a one-hour block to come pray with a few of their brethren. I say "at least" one hour because, inevitably, people enjoy the bond of unity and fellowship engendered by praying with others, for others, that they often stay longer anyway.

In fact, I believe there is something special, and definitely powerful, in praying for others more than you do for yourself. Paul tells us exactly whom our prayers should focus on primarily, in Ephesians 6:18:

> **With all prayer and petition pray at all times in the Spirit, and with this in view, be on the alert with all perseverance and petition for all the saints …**

We should be praying **"for all the saints."** In other words, we should be praying especially for our brothers and sisters in Christ. Not that you can't pray for others and other things, but this ought to be the heart and the most important aspect of our praying. Why that? Because we all, in one way or another, have been called by God and are involved in His great work to this world in this generation. We need to be praying for each other along that line. Pray for one another. Pray for your brother's walk with Jesus. Pray for your sister's usefulness to Him in the context of her own life. Pray for each other.

The point is, be involved in God's cause and God's work in this world. Be involved in it in an intricate way. Pray! Pray especially for His people. If you pray for a brother, then the fruit that comes forth from his service is also your fruit. That's an investment that you've made in eternity, by just praying for him.

Pray more for others than you do yourself. If every Christian focused on praying for himself, you know how many people would be praying for you at any given time? One! And those would be pretty weak prayers because it seems we can never pray for ourselves with the same faith that we pray for others. But if we're all praying for others, at any particular time you've got many people beseeching the throne of God on your behalf! So, brethren, pray for others.

Your praying is called by God to be a central aspect of your Christian life and your walk with Him.

The Fellowship of "Living Boards"

You may have noticed that I only briefly mentioned "fellowship" as the second spiritual bond of unity. I did that because fellowship, true Christian fellowship, so often is an outgrowth of the three other bonds. So much rich fellowship comes before and after we gather to be taught His Word, to break bread together in Communion, and to pray corporately. Those are the activities that give us the common ground upon which to build further fellowship, one with another, because we truly are the **"living stones"** Peter mentions in 1 Peter 2:5:

> **… you also, as living stones, are being built up as a spiritual house for a holy priesthood, to offer up spiritual sacrifices acceptable to God through Jesus Christ.** (1 Peter 2:5)

The same analogy applies with the tabernacle, only we would be called "living boards." God considers each believer to be a living board in His tabernacle. Just as all the boards were fitted with the gold rings that the bars went through, we have been designed by the Holy Spirit to be bound together in Christ.

> **… and let us consider how to stimulate one another to love and good deeds, not forsaking our own assembling together, as is the habit of some, but encouraging one another; and all the more as you see the day drawing near.** (Hebrews 10:24-25)

You are a vital part of God's work, designed to bring glory to God in this world. If one board were removed from that tabernacle, it would not have been the same. If one stone were removed from the temple, it would have been unsightly. Each of us are one of those stones, one of those boards. There is a particular place and purpose for you in God's design and God's plan for time and eternity.

I cannot wait to get to glory and be there with all the saints of all the ages and see how we fit in, for then we will know even as we are known. We will fully see how you and I fit in perfectly to God's plan of the ages and eternity. We will not sit on a cloud somewhere strumming a harp saying, "Oh, this is so fun." We will be a vital part in the service of the Lord of lords and the King of kings in eternity future. God loves you and wants you to be an integral part of His work. He has designed His eternal plan with you as an essential part. Isn't that glorious?

The Four-Layer Covering

> "Moreover you shall make the tabernacle with ten curtains of fine twisted linen and blue and purple and scarlet material; you shall make them with cherubim, the work of a skillful workman." (Exodus 26:1)

> "You shall make fifty clasps of gold, and join the curtains to one another with the clasps so that the tabernacle will be a unit. Then you shall make curtains of goats' hair for a tent over the tabernacle; you shall make eleven curtains in all." (Exodus 26:6-7)

> "You shall make fifty loops on the edge of the curtain that is outermost in the first set, and fifty loops on the edge of the curtain that is outermost in the second set. You shall make fifty clasps of bronze, and you shall put the clasps into the loops and join the tent together so that it will be a unit." (Exodus 26:10-11)

> "You shall make a covering for the tent of rams' skins dyed red and a covering of porpoise skins above." (Exodus 26:14)

There is so much detail that we could delve into and study at great length, but we will limit our focus here to the covering over the tent. This covering presents to us another incredible picture of Jesus Christ. It is an interesting picture and a blessing to me, because as we walk this wilderness path of life, He is constantly covering us and protecting us. Our walk is in Christ, in the **"shadow"** of His **"wings."** Jesus Christ is all around us. We walk in Him. We cannot walk anywhere that He does not go before us. We are in Christ. This is such an awesome picture.

1. The outer layer of animal skin

The outer layer of the tent covering was a leathery, durable, and waterproof hide of some sort. (The NASB calls it **"porpoise skin."**) The exact meaning of the Hebrew word is not known. Perhaps it was a seal skin of one of the Red Sea variety of seals. It was the layer of covering that was visible to everyone on the outside who would see the tabernacle tent. It was likely the same material used for sandals and the tent coverings of the people in general. In any case, this thick protective covering is all that the common man saw of the tent.

I like that because Jesus became one of us. When natural man looks at the person of Jesus Christ, he only sees another man.

> **For He grew up before Him like a tender shoot,**
> **And like a root out of parched ground;**
> **He has no stately form or majesty**
> **That we should look upon Him,**
> **Nor appearance that we should be attracted to Him.** (Isaiah 53:2)

There was nothing about that seal or porpoise skin to attract any one; it was just functional. To the world, our Lord was just another man. The world may concede that He was a great teacher, religious leader, maybe even a prophet, but the world does not see Him as the Son of the Living God. They do not see His majesty, beauty, and glory.

To those of us who are believers, that outer exterior speaks of His meekness and His lowliness.

> **... who, although He existed in the form of God, did not regard equality with God a thing to be grasped, but emptied Himself, taking the form of a bond-servant, and being made in the likeness of men.** (Philippians 2: 6-7)

That is the seal-skin outer layer of the tent covering, and what it represents to us. To the world, Jesus appears to have been a common man, so they miss the truth of who He was. But to us, God Himself came in the form of a common man. But if we peel back that outer layer, that common **"no stately form or majesty ... that we should be attracted to Him"** (Isaiah 53:2) layer, we come to the next layer, the covering of rams' skins dyed red.

2. The layer of rams' skins (dyed red)

The layer of rams' skins dyed red represents to us why Jesus came to this earth.

Regarding the consecration of the priests, in Leviticus 8:22 we read:

> Then he presented the second ram, the ram of ordination, and Aaron and his sons laid their hands on the head of the ram.

Then the ram was slain. That layer of rams' skins dyed red is a picture of that ram of consecration, or that ram of ordination.

> **Jesus resolutely set out for Jerusalem.** (Luke 9:51b - NIV)

When the time came for Jesus to become the sacrifice for our sins, He was resolutely determined to face the task. The time had come and nothing would deter Him from His fateful trip to Jerusalem.

> "... just as the Son of Man did not come to be served, but to serve, and to give His life a ransom for many." (Matthew 20:28)

His goal and His purpose for coming was to die on the cross for our sins, and is pictured in the rams' skins dyed red.

As we peel back that layer of rams' skins dyed red, we come to the layer of goat's skin and it pictures for us why He *had* to come and be our sacrifice.

3. The layer of goats' skins

The next layer is the goats' skins, or the layer of goat hair. Goats are identified with sin in the Bible. In the parable of the sheep and the goats (Matthew 25), the sheep represent God's chosen children; the goats represent sinners separated from the kingdom of God.

On the Day of Atonement (the one day each year the high priest entered the Holy of Holies), two goats were selected: the scapegoat and the sacrificial goat. The sacrificial goat was designated to represent the sins of the people, and it was slain to pay for the sins of the people. The scapegoat, also representing the sins of the people, was set free in the wilderness a great distance from the camp, so far away that it would never come back—just as our sins have been separated from us as far as the east is from the west, never to be remembered again (Psalm 103:12).

Just as those goats symbolized sinfulness, we are reminded that Jesus became sin for us. So in the layers of the coverings we see that which represents His shed blood, the rams' skins dyed red, completely covering that which represents sin; the "sin of the world" that He bore for us.

Now consider that the two middle layers of the tent covering (the rams' skins dyed red and the goat skin) were hidden from view. These layers were not visible from inside or outside the tent. A priest who went inside the tabernacle saw the inner layer, which we will discuss in a moment. The outer layer was visible from the courtyard, but the two middle layers would not be seen. They were not visible to the human eye. This raises an interesting point.

The layer that represents Jesus dying on the cross is not seen. Mark 15:33-34 tell us that darkness covered the earth from noon to 3 o'clock in the afternoon on the day Jesus was crucified. You might say no one actually *saw* what sin was doing to the Son of God. No one saw the actual sin coming upon Christ as He paid the penalty for our sins.

> **Just as many were astonished at you, My people,**
> **So His appearance was marred more than any man**
> **And His form more than the sons of men.** (Isaiah 52:14)

No one has ever had his appearance and form marred more than Jesus Christ did on the cross. God just darkened the earth so this could not be seen by man.

4. The innermost layer of fine linen

This brings us to the innermost layer of the tent covering, the fine linen embroidered with blue, purple, and scarlet threads, and cherubim. Jesus rose again on the third day. Death could not hold Him down. All the colors of this innermost layer speak of the glory of Jesus Christ, the risen Son of God.

If we could walk inside the tent tabernacle, we would be surrounded by the reality of the risen Jesus Christ. Inside the tabernacle the beauty and the glory of the Lord was visible. Inside the tabernacle were the white, blue, purple, and scarlet colors woven into the linen, representing the purity, deity, majesty, and the sacrifice of Jesus.

In that place which represented the heavenly, the priests were surrounded with the glory of Jesus Christ, the Lord of hosts. The hosts, His angelic army, were represented in the embroidered cherubim. Likewise, we are surrounded by that which represents His majesty, His power, and His glory, including all the angels who are in the service of our Lord, effecting His will, His purpose, protecting His people.

> **The angel of the LORD encamps around those who fear Him ...** (Psalm 34:7)

> **Are they not all ministering spirits, sent out to render service for the sake of those who will inherit salvation?** (Hebrews 1:14)

Inside that tabernacle, the hosts of heaven were visible all around.

As I think of the glory and the might of God pictured in this layer of the tabernacle, I am reminded of the story of Elisha and his servant in the town of Dothan when the Syrian army came and surrounded them (2 Kings 6). As Elisha's servant went out for his morning walk on the wall, he saw the entire Syrian army equipped and ready for battle for the purpose of taking one man, his master, Elisha. The servant was panic stricken, yet Elisha was completely calm. The servant questioned Elisha about this—wasn't the gravity of this situation extremely evident? Elisha prayed that the eyes of his servant would be opened so that he would see what Elisha did not need to see, because he knew in his spirit what was there. As the servant's eyes were opened, he looked back out there and saw that the Syrian army had not changed one iota. Every soldier was right where he was before, equipped with sword, shield, and spear. However, one thing had changed: over and above this army of men, the servant's eyes were opened to see the host of the Lord, in flaming chariots with fiery swords all around this army of soldiers. Suddenly this servant was given a new perspective on the Syrian army. (Can't you just see this servant strutting along the wall thinking, "You can't get me! Ha. Ha. You guys think you are *so* tough. The Lord has a *big* surprise coming for you!")

This beautiful picture is found inside the tabernacle. As you come inside the dwelling place of God, into that place of fellowship with Him, your eyes are suddenly opened to the fact that you are under the protective hand of your Lord. You are surrounded by the hosts of heaven, and the glory of Jesus Christ is all around you. When you live in that place, there is no room for fear. We begin to fear when we are traipsing around in the courtyard or the camp, instead of abiding in the tabernacle, i.e., in the place of fellowship with our Heavenly Father and with Jesus Christ. Through the winged cherubim embroidered on the inner linen covering, God wants us to know how protected we are.

> Let me dwell in Your tent forever;
> Let me take refuge in the shelter of Your wings.
> Selah. (Psalm 61:4)

> Be gracious to me, O God, be gracious to me,
> For my soul takes refuge in You;
> And in the shadow of Your wings I will take refuge
> Until destruction passes by. (Psalm 57:1)

> For You have been my help,
> And in the shadow of Your wings I sing for joy. (Psalm 63:7)

> He will cover you with His pinions,
> And under His wings you may seek refuge;
> His faithfulness is a shield and bulwark. (Psalm 91:4)

That tent tabernacle was the dwelling place of God in the wilderness. But it represents to us as Christians where we actually live with God as our Father. We live in the spiritual reality of that tabernacle with Him. May our eyes be opened to the real spiritual relationship that is available to us.

> I pray that the eyes of your heart may be enlightened, so that you will know what is the hope of His calling, what are the riches of the glory of His inheritance in the saints, and what is the surpassing greatness of His power toward us who believe. These are in accordance with the working of the strength of His might ... (Ephesians 1:18-19)

What an awesome place to live! We dwell in the midst of His glory.

> Have this attitude in yourselves which was also in Christ Jesus, who, although He existed in the form of God, did not regard equality with God a thing to be grasped, but emptied Himself, taking the form of a bond-servant, and being made in the likeness of men. Being found in appearance as a man, He humbled Himself by becoming obedient to the point of death, even death on a cross. For this reason also, God highly exalted Him, and bestowed on Him the name which is above every name, so that at the name of Jesus EVERY KNEE WILL BOW, of those who are in heaven and on earth

and under the earth, and that every tongue will confess that Jesus Christ is Lord, to the glory of God the Father. (Philippians 2:5-11)

Within this one Scripture, we have the four layers of the tent covering represented. Jesus took **"the form of a bond-servant"** and was made in the likeness of men; this was represented in the seal skin cover. He was **"obedient to the point of death,"** which was represented in the rams' skins dyed red. **"Even death on a cross,"** when Jesus hung on the cross and **"became sin for us,"** this was represented by the layer of goat hair. **"Every knee will bow"** represents the fine linen inner part with all the beautiful colors and the angels exalting Jesus Christ.

Right now, in Jesus Christ, you can live in that place and enjoy His glories. God seeks that closeness with you. He wants you to live there with Him in your daily walk. We can live in that place right out there in the world. The beauty of our salvation is that we do not have to go somewhere physically, say, into a tabernacle, to be with God. We live in the reality of His presence with us as we go about our daily lives. We do not have to manufacture any kind of feelings or manipulate any emotions to achieve that place. It is just by faith that we live in that space.

It is when you are in that place where God wants you to dwell, where He wants His children living, that you have something to share with the world. You are His witnesses. If your Christian experience is confined to the courtyard, there is not much to share. But if you live inside that tent in the Holy Place, you will show and share the reality of it in your life. So dwell in that place where God wants you to dwell. Live in that place of joy and peace with Him.

Some people never even make it to the courtyard. Their entire lives are lived out in the "camp," separated from Christ. Others only see the outside of the tent. They have come to Christ for their salvation, but have never progressed past the courtyard in their walk. The only way for anyone to experience this inner tabernacle life, this reality of the presence, power, glory, and holiness of God, is to, first of all, come through the gate and stand at that altar, receiving personally the efficacy of that sacrifice. They must then take advantage of the cleansing at the laver (as I explained in chapter 10) and then, by faith, enter in themselves. A lot of Christians do not abide in the "Holy Place." You probably know some of them because they come to church, but are not living in that place of peace and fellowship with their Lord. If they were honest with themselves, they would have to admit it. For them to come into that special place with God, to experience the fullness of what He has for them, they will have to enter that tent themselves. You cannot do it for them.

Yet there *is* a special point of encouragement for us in our concern for others. We will see as we study the objects that are in the tabernacle and what they represent to us, that the tabernacle represents a very, very effective place of prayer. Battles are won on our knees. An effective prayer life is available to us in there. The best thing you can do for yourself spiritually, and the very best thing you can do for anyone else in your life, is to enter in and abide in that Holy Place yourself.

Chapter Twelve

The Golden Lampstand

"I am the Light of the world; he who follows Me will not walk in the darkness, but will have the Light of life."

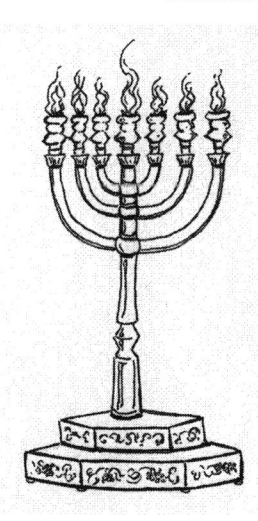

One of the first times I was really confronted and challenged with someone who was living in a genuinely deep walk with the Lord was when I was a student in college. One night, I attended a Christian meeting on campus where there was a young man who shared from his heart about the Lord. I do not think I had ever heard someone talk about a vital, personal relationship with Jesus as he did that night. His testimony really grabbed my attention when he spoke of an incident that had happened to him recently, because I had experienced something similar just the week before. His car had broken down on the freeway yet, with a sparkle in his eyes, he talked about it as "an adventure in Christ." Just the week before, *my* car had broken down on the freeway, but mine was an adventure in total frustration. I viewed having a car broken down on a Los Angeles freeway during rush hour as one of the ugliest experiences of my college career. What a difference in perspective and peace! I was challenged by him. I knew this man had something that was different, that had nothing to do with the basic "church-ianity" I had been raised with. Here was someone who obviously had a relationship with the Lord that was a vital, real, and living thing to him. I had never witnessed that before, firsthand.

You see, I grew up in a church that was very staid. When I say "church," I am not referring to any particular church building or organization—I mean the church in general. Before the incredible Jesus Movement of the 1960s in southern California, from which Calvary Chapel blossomed, I had never seen anyone with that kind of relationship with the Lord.

I remember reading about Andrew Murray when I was in seminary. Andrew Murray was the kind of person who could walk into a room with a presence about him that was noticeably different. A genuine warmth and love exuded from him that was very attractive to people. It was, obviously, his personal relationship with the Lord that captivated people.

I also remember hearing a missionary to India tell about an Indian gentleman who had asked to speak with him. To understand this story, you must know that in India, people would smear oil on their faces to obtain a sheen or a brightness. This gentleman had noticed a brightness in the faces of the Christians he had met, and he wanted to ask this missionary what kind of oil these Christians applied to their faces to get that shine he considered to be unique. At first, the missionary did not know what the gentleman was talking about because the Christians did not put any oil on their faces. But the Indian gentleman kept insisting that there was something they did to get this sheen. He thought the missionary just did not want to tell him what it was. This Indian man complained that his people could not get the special shine and appearance of the Christians from their own oil. He asked the missionary if it was a religious secret. The missionary walked away puzzled until it dawned on him that the man was talking about the presence of Christ in the hearts of the Christian people which was showing in the glow on their faces.

It all comes down to fellowship with God. Fellowship with God has a powerful effect on lives. God said to Abraham, "Walk with Me." Abraham walked with God, and what a dynamic life he lived.

Think about it. Christ came to redeem us to God, not so we would just have a comfortable theology to tuck into our rather mundane lives. He came so that we could walk in fellowship with God on a daily basis. What does it mean to do that? What is it really like?

It is like a priest in the Old Testament who entered the tabernacle. Once inside, he was in a place that was truly exclusive and extremely beautiful. Even then, however, he could not really enter into the fullness that the tabernacle represents to us. He could enjoy the beauty, surrounded by the glitter of pure gold, the fine tapestry, and the reflection of the lighted lamps on the lampstand. It had to be breathtakingly beautiful in there. But the Old Testament priest did not fully comprehend its meaning.

People often move to the mountains where I live, near Lake Tahoe, because it is so beautiful here. Many just want to get away from the city. Once they do get here, though, and live in the midst of this incredible beauty, it almost makes it worse for them because their hearts are still so dark, while what is around them is so beautiful.

I remember playing tennis in Incline Village on a beautiful, warm, sunny morning. Two ladies were playing next to us and as they were walking off the court, one young lady said to the other, "Just another "[expletive]" day in paradise." How sad!

Those priests in the tabernacle could enjoy the beauty around them, but what they saw in the physical sense, we have the privilege of living in the spirit. What we live, in fellowship with Jesus, is the reality. What is seen is simply the picture—and what is not seen is the reality. The world looks at it exactly the other way around.

When the Old Testament priests entered the tabernacle, they left the world behind and they went into a place that literally represented the presence of God. Indeed, as they walked through that entryway into the tent, they were literally 30 feet away from the presence of God; the Shekinah glory of God dwelt just behind the veil. They knew God was with them, that He would take care of them, and that He was watching over them. In that place, they knew God was right there. They entered into a place of nearness to God which was unique in this world.

Standing in that outer room, which was called the Holy Place, they would see the three pieces of furniture which occupied that room. As they walked in, on the left would be the golden lampstand. On the right would be the golden table of the bread of the Presence. Directly in front of them, directly in front of the veil to the Holy of Holies, would be the golden altar of incense.

For a young priest going in for the first time, the thing that would probably grab his attention immediately would be the golden lampstand on the left, because the light of the room would be emanating from there. As we look at that lampstand, by its very design and purpose, it describes the relationship that is ours with the Living God.

The Lampstand

God's instruction for the building of the lampstand is found in Exodus 25:31-40:

> "Then you shall make a lampstand of pure gold. The lampstand and its base and its shaft are to be made of hammered work; its cups, its bulbs and its flowers shall be of one piece with it. Six branches shall go out from its sides; three branches of the lampstand from its one side and three branches of the lampstand from its other side. Three cups shall be shaped like almond blossoms in the one branch, a bulb and a flower, and three cups shaped like almond blossoms in the other branch, a bulb and a flower—so for six branches going out from the lampstand; and in the lampstand four cups shaped like almond blossoms, its bulbs and its flowers. A bulb shall be under the first pair of branches coming out of it, and a bulb under the second pair of branches coming out of it, and a bulb under the third pair of branches coming out of it, for the six branches coming out of the lampstand. Their bulbs and their branches shall be of one piece with it; all of it shall be one piece of hammered work of pure gold. Then you shall make its lamps seven in number; and they shall mount its lamps so as to shed light on the space in front of it. Its snuffers and their trays shall be of pure gold. It shall be made from a talent of pure gold, with all these utensils. See that you make them after the pattern for them, which was shown to you on the mountain."

The golden lampstand provided the light for the tabernacle. God's

Word says some interesting things about God's light.

> Then Jesus again spoke to them, saying, "I am the Light of the world; he who follows Me will not walk in the darkness, but will have the Light of life." (John 8:12)

> "While I am in the world, I am the Light of the world." (John 9:5)

> In Him was life, and the life was the Light of men. (John 1:4)

> There was the true Light which, coming into the world, enlightens every man. (John 1:9)

> "You are the light of the world. Let your light shine before men in such a way that they may see your good works, and glorify your Father who is in heaven." (Jesus in Matthew 5:14a, 16)

> ... so that you will prove yourselves to be blameless and innocent, children of God above reproach in the midst of a crooked and perverse generation, among whom you appear as lights in the world ... (Philippians 2:15)

> ... for you were formerly darkness, but now you are Light in the Lord; walk as children of Light ... (Ephesians 5:8)

With these Scriptures in mind, I would like to make six points about the lampstand, its construction, and what a picture it provides of Him who is truly the light of the world, Jesus Christ.

1) Jesus is the light *of* the world, and we are His lights *in* the world.

When it comes to spiritual light in this world, God's light, Jesus, and He in us, is all there is. There is no other spiritual light in this world.

> For God, who said, "Light shall shine out of darkness," is the One who has shone in our hearts to give the Light of the knowledge of the glory of God in the face of Christ. But we have this treasure in earthen vessels, so that the surpassing greatness of the power will be of God and not from ourselves ..." (2 Corinthians 4:6-7)

We have the Light of the Lord, but it is in earthen vessels, so all the glory will go to God and none of it is to come to us.

> **"Let your light shine before men in such a way that they may see your good works, and glorify your Father who is in heaven.** (Jesus in Matthew 5:16)

Jesus is the Light and we are His lights in the world. With that in mind, when the priests would come and minister in the tabernacle, or worship there, they did it in the light of the lampstand. That was the only light that was in there. So it is, that our service and our worship are futile unless we do as John says:

> "... walk in the Light as He Himself is in the Light ..."
> (1 John 1:7)

There is an admonition here: we believers are to quit milling around in the courtyard, we are to use the laver and get into the tabernacle, into that close relationship with God. That is where His light shines. You see, as long as a Christian is, symbolically speaking, milling around in the courtyard, he cannot be that kind of light in this world. Christ is the light. What matters is not what the Christian can do, what he can produce, how he can live, or what a great and mighty person he can be for God. When he gets into the tabernacle, into that closeness with God, he realizes it is *all* the Lord. It's all by His might and power. Jesus is the light.

Think, for a moment, of the design of the Jewish menorah, which is the lampstand. It is designed like a tree, or a vine. With that in mind, look at Romans 11:16b-18:

> ... and if the root is holy, the branches are too. But if some of the branches were broken off, and you, being a wild olive, were grafted in among them and became partaker with them of the rich root of the olive tree, do not be arrogant toward the branches; but if you are arrogant, remember that it is not you who supports the root, but the root supports you.

We are the branches in this olive tree which belongs to God. Jesus used the analogy of a vine when He said:

> "I am the vine, you are the branches; he who abides in

Me and I in him, he bears much fruit, for apart from Me you can do nothing." (John 15:5)

The branches go forth from the shaft. The vine produces the fruit. The branch simply bears it.

There are seven branches on this lampstand. The central shaft represents Jesus, who is the vine. Six branches come off that shaft. Six is the number of man. The believer who is bound in a personal relationship with Christ, who is living in fellowship with Him, will be shining His light.

When the light is shining, it shows the beauty of the lampstand, as well as the beauty of the inner sanctuary. When His light is shining through us, it will reflect the glory and beauty of the Lord.

As an example, I remember early on in my pastoral ministry, there was a sweet elderly lady in my small church of virtually all elderly people. She was the elderly of the elderly, well into her '80s and not well, physically. Gertrude was a special sister in the Lord. I will never forget Gertrude. She was a sweetheart. She was a skinny, little fireball for the Lord. One day she had a seizure, so she had to be admitted to the hospital. She was not a wealthy lady, so she was put in one of those rooms with ten beds in it, five to a wall. Most of the people in there were on social security or welfare.

On my way to see her, I prayed for the words to encourage dear Gertrude. As I walked down the hall looking for the room, I heard all this raucous activity in one room—it turned out to be coming from Gertrude's room. I walked in to find little Gertrude with her bed right in the center of all these ladies who were just praising the Lord. She was sitting up there in her bed with her bright face and sparkling eyes, and all these ladies were rejoicing right along with her. It was a room of rejoicing in the hospital. I went there to encourage Gertrude; instead, I received encouragement from those ladies. I walked out chuckling that the Lord pulled an "about face" on me. The Lord built *me* up by going to visit "poor, sick Gertrude."

But when a light shines, it shines to the glory of God. That light, when it is shining, shows forth the glory of the lampstand, and the glory of that inner sanctuary. One thing that lampstand tells us is that we have the privilege to live in His light and to be a light for Him. That is a result of entering in and abiding in that Holy Place.

2. It was 60-80 pounds of pure gold.

That lampstand in the tabernacle tent was very costly and valuable. The Scripture tells us that the lampstand was made of a talent of pure gold, which means between sixty and eighty pounds of solid gold. That lampstand on today's gold market would wholesale for more than half a million dollars. It was extremely costly and valuable. It also reminds me of how precious the Son of God is to His Father.

> " ... You are My beloved Son, in You I am well-pleased."
> (Mark 1:11)

Jesus was His only begotten and beloved Son, and yet, the Father gave Him up for *us*.

> As a result of the anguish of His soul,
> He will see it and be satisfied;
> By His knowledge the Righteous One,
> My Servant, will justify the many,
> As He will bear their iniquities.
> Therefore, I will allot Him a portion with the great,
> And He will divide the booty with the strong;
> Because He poured out Himself to death,
> And was numbered with the transgressors;
> Yet He Himself bore the sin of many,
> And interceded for the transgressors. (Isaiah 53:11-12)

Through the **"anguish of His soul"** He justified us that we might become golden branches on the lampstand, which is Christ. Note that the branches were all of equal height. In 1 Corinthians 12, when He talks about the gifts of the Spirit, God says everyone is valuable to Him. The whole purpose of that chapter is to show that one person with one gift is not better, or more important, or more valuable to the body than another person with another gift that may not be as obvious. All the lights shine equally before the Lord.

3. It was all made from one piece of pure gold.

This entire lampstand was one piece of pure gold, just as we, as a body of believers, are one in Christ. That lampstand was not simply a representation of Christ, but also a representation of the *body* of Christ, with Jesus as the centerpiece of that body. The body of Christ emanates from its centerpiece, Jesus. It gets its nourishment and support from Him.

When Paul was confronted by Jesus Christ on the Damascus Road, Jesus said in Acts 22:7, **"Saul, Saul, why are you persecuting Me?"** Paul asked who it was and in the next verse, Jesus said, **"I am Jesus the Nazarene, whom you are persecuting."** That must have been an eye-opener to him because he was persecuting Christians. He did not know he was persecuting "Jesus" Himself!

The lampstand shows us this picture clearly. If someone starts wailing on one of the branches, he is wailing on Jesus. Saul was persecuting Jesus because we are one together with Him. To God, there is no difference. We have been made one with Him.

This lampstand means that we are incredibly valuable and incredibly loved by God. The love the Father has for us and for Jesus Himself cannot be separated.

This is evident in the way that Jesus prayed for His followers in John 17:21-22:

> "… that they may all be one; even as You, Father, are in Me and I in You, that they also may be in Us, so that the world may believe that You sent Me. The glory which You have given Me I have given to them, that they may be one, just as We are one …"

When you look at the lampstand, you see the glory that was given to Jesus was given to us. We are one. The lampstand was one solid piece of gold.

Notice the design of the lampstand. There was one central pre-eminent shaft up the middle of the stand. The branches emanate from it and are one with it. Similarly our new life springs forth from Jesus and is supported by Him. You in Christ, Christ in you. That is the source and the strength of a victorious Christian life. Each individual light is consequently perfectly united with, held up, and held together with the rest of the lamp by Jesus.

Now it is important to note that there is nothing artificially joined in this lampstand. It is one piece of gold, worked into the shape of a lampstand. That pictures how secure we are in Him.

> "My Father, who has given them to Me, is greater than all; and no one is able to snatch them out of the Father's hand." (Jesus in John 10:29)

> **For I am convinced that neither death, nor life, nor angels, nor principalities, nor things present, nor things to come, nor powers, nor height, nor depth, nor any other created thing, will be able to separate us from the love of God, which is in Christ Jesus our Lord.** (Romans 8:38-39)

Nothing can ever separate us from His love. Death can't, and life can't. The angels won't, and all the powers of hell itself cannot keep God's love away. Our fears for today, our worries about tomorrow, or where we are—high above the sky, or in the deepest ocean—nothing will ever be able to separate us from the love of God demonstrated by our Lord Jesus Christ when He died for us.

Lewis Talbot wrote: "Christ is the eternal Son of God. We are sons of God because we believe in Him through salvation. He is the firstborn, we are His brethren. His Father is our Father, His God, our God. He is the head of the body which is His church. We are members of one another. He is the heir of all things, we are joint heirs with Him. He is the second Adam, we are His bride. We have been crucified with Him, buried with Him, arisen with Him, and we are seated with Him in the heavenly places. He is One with the Spirit, our bodies are temples of the Holy Spirit. He is forever glorified, restored to the eternal glory that He had with the Father before the world was. We shall one day behold and share His glory."

Notice there were almond-shaped blossoms. On the shaft, under each one of the branches and going out on the branches there were the almond-shaped blossoms with cups and flowers of gold that made up the branches. It reminds us of Aaron's rod which was an almond rod. When Moses laid it before the Lord in the tabernacle, it sprouted almond blooms and ripe almond fruit by the next morning (Numbers 17:8). In other words, that old dead stick had a resurrection. Consequently, the almond is a symbol of resurrection. It is interesting that the almond is the first to bloom in the spring, as Jesus Christ is the first fruits of a great resurrection of all believers. So this lampstand has resurrection written all over it, up the shaft, and all over the branches.

Also, as illustrated in the almond blossoms on the stem and branches of the lampstand, our new life comes out of His resurrection. In 1 Corinthians 15:12-19, Paul parenthetically said, "If there is no resurrection, I of all people am the most miserable. I have nothing to offer you." Paul also talked about knowing the life-changing power of His resurrection in his own life (Philippians 3:10).

Indeed, when you see the almond blossoms on the lampstand and the light emanating from it, the picture is of the light coming forth through the power of the resurrection. That light shining forth is a manifestation of the power of His resurrection.

As that lampstand pictures that we are one with Christ, bringing forth fruit, it also pictures the light of Jesus shining in you, because you will be living what the menorah represents. You are a branch of His vine.

Just as we are one with Jesus, we are one with one another because all the branches are of the same piece of solid gold.

In John 17:22, Jesus prayed:

> "The glory which You have given Me I have given to them, that they may be one, just as We are one ..."
>
> ... being diligent to preserve the unity of the Spirit in the bond of peace. (Ephesians 4:3)
>
> ... so that there may be no division in the body, but that the members may have the same care for one another. And if one member suffers, all the members suffer with it; if one member is honored, all the members rejoice with it. (1 Corinthians 12:25-26)

Understanding how one we are in Jesus Christ, and in the work He has given us, is vital to the ministry of the Holy Spirit in this world. That lampstand consisted of seven lights shining forth. Seven is the number of completion, the number of perfection. All those lights would shine forth together, as part of one lamp. Similarly, here we are, His lights in the world. But we are just one light in the lamp, which is Christ, shining in this world. We are part of a much larger work of God which involves many others. We are not alone in this work.

It is liberating to me to realize that it is not up to me, personally, to be everything to everyone in this world. No one person's faith, commitment to Christ, growth, or anything else rests exclusively on me. I just have to be that shining light. God has many others who also shine to the glory of His name. He uses many, under His guidance, to bring an individual to Christ and to build spiritual growth in others' lives. I do not have to be everything. I *cannot* be "everything." I am just one light among many that is called to shine for Him, where I am.

That lampstand means it is our privilege to live in that place, and to experience that oneness with Jesus Christ Himself and with one another. But that kind of unity, that kind of fellowship, does not happen until a believer enters into the tabernacle of fellowship with God, until he abides in that space. You will not even have a feel for what that oneness is really like if you are just, spiritually speaking, milling around in the courtyard.

4. It was of "hammered gold."

The lampstand was constructed of hammered gold. It was hammered into shape by a skillful workman. That talent of gold, although extremely valuable and precious, did not typify Jesus Christ and His church until it was *hammered* into a thing of beauty.

Again, quoting Lewis Talbot, "He was from all eternity beloved of His Father, co-equal and co-eternal with Him, but not until He was wounded for our transgressions and bruised for our iniquities was the church formed from His wounded side."

Without the hammering, you do not have a golden lampstand. Without the cross, you do not have a living church. So the hammering is a picture of what Jesus endured on the cross to create this lampstand. In a very real sense, but to a far lesser degree, we (the branches) share in enduring the hammering.

In Philippians 3:10, Paul said that he desired to know two things: the fellowship of His suffering and the power of His resurrection. You may be amazed that Paul wanted to know the fellowship of His sufferings. But you do not have to worry about wanting it, or not wanting it. You will, in one way or another, know of the fellowship of His suffering. That is part of Christian life and Christian growth.

In "The Hiding Place," by Corrie Ten Boom, Corrie wrote about her sister, Betsy, and of her own experiences in a Nazi concentration camp. These very staid, prim, and proper middle-aged ladies were forced to strip down to total nudity in front of the gawking guards to be laughed at, mocked, lusted after, and ridiculed. We cannot imagine how utterly humiliating it would have been for those ladies to endure. Corrie was in absolute agony; but Betsy, who was right behind her, said, "Corrie, Corrie, this is glorious. Jesus, our Savior, was stripped for us, and was made a public humiliation for us. Now we get to be humiliated for Him." What an attitude! What a heart to know the fellowship of His suffering. Betsy had tuned into it.

> "Blessed are those who have been persecuted for the sake of righteousness, for theirs is the kingdom of heaven. Blessed are you when people insult you and persecute you, and falsely say all kinds of evil against you because of Me. Rejoice and be glad, for your reward in heaven is great; for in the same way they persecuted the prophets who were before you." (Jesus in Matthew 5:10-12)

When we are called to endure suffering, in whatever form it comes, we are sharing in the suffering of Christ. We have something very special in common with the saints of the ages, and with Jesus Christ Himself, although we will never know the extent of what He suffered for us. The beauty of our Lord is that He identifies with any suffering for Him. There is a bond that is inseparable. This is seen in the lampstand which was purposefully hammered into its unique and beautiful shape.

A goldsmith once pointed out to me that hammering gold makes it stronger. As we are hammered into objects of usefulness and beauty, we are strengthened in Him. So that lampstand also pictures the "cross-bearing" of the believer.

5. The light was never to go out.

The light of the lampstand was to burn continually.

> Then the LORD spoke to Moses, saying, "Command the sons of Israel that they bring to you clear oil from beaten olives for the light, to make a lamp burn continually. Outside the veil of testimony in the tent of meeting, Aaron shall keep it in order from evening to morning before the LORD continually; it shall be a perpetual statute throughout your generations. He shall keep the lamps in order on the pure gold lampstand before the LORD continually." (Leviticus 24:1-4)

There are times in this life when it seems like the darkness is overcoming the light, the darkness seems to be prevailing. God is telling us, through this lampstand, that His light will never go out. His light will always shine. It is with that same spirit that He tells us the gates of hell will not prevail against His church (Matthew 16:18). It may look like the church is losing ground. It may appear that the forces of darkness are winning, but they will never prevail against His church. The Lord is so faithful that way. Our perception is often askew, and we do not see things the way they really are.

Take, for example, the church in the Sudan. Evangelical missions entered that part of Africa just before the turn of the twentieth century, in the late 1800s. They were ministering in the Sudan for fifty or sixty years before World War II broke out. In that period of time, being a hard country to minister in, as it is to this day, there were an estimated 200 evangelical Christians in the entire country. At the beginning of World War II, the Italians invaded the Sudan, took it over, and all evangelical missionaries had to leave. There was a period of five years in which there was no outside contact with those 200 evangelical believing Christians in the Sudan. The church in the world beyond the Sudan was very concerned. It was such a little church to begin with, and so fragile. They wondered if they would even find a church when they were able to return. Five years later when the war was won and the missionaries were able to get in to see what happened to that little group of 200, it had grown in five years from 200 to 200,000!

It is interesting that missionaries got the gospel started in China before the Communist take-over and for the fifty years or so that they were ministering there, it was a struggle. When the Communists took over, the missionaries were kicked out. Since then, however, there has been phenomenal growth. It just shows that God promised His light would not go out, and when everything humanly possible might make us think it has been snuffed out for sure, the light still continues to shine. It will *not* go out.

Consider that the gospel of Jesus Christ has to be completely reborn in every generation. It is the born-again experience in the life of the believer that is at the heart of the living church. We can pass on forms and rituals, but we cannot pass on the life. God has been faithful to rebirth His gospel through every generation. God has no grandchildren.

We are all His children, **"... sons of God through faith in Christ Jesus"** (Galatians 3:26). That light is always shining. That light shines through each of our lives, and each one meaningfully counts for God in an eternal way.

6. That light was to shine "before the Lord."

God made it very clear that the light of the lampstand was to burn before the Lord. It was to be lit and kept burning **"before the Lord."** The lampstand burned for Him.

There are times when no one sees the light burning except the Lord Himself. There were many times when no one was in the tabernacle to enjoy that light, but it would continue to burn before the Lord Himself.

Likewise, the primary purpose of our lives is to shine before the Lord. Sadly, there are those who shine before men, and not before the Lord.

In Genesis 17:1, the Lord told Abram to, **"Walk before Me, and be blameless."** That is what we are called to do. We have one Master. There will be times when you do things that no one seems to appreciate. But your Lord will, because you are doing it for Him. Live your life before Him. Do not be concerned about anyone else and what he or she might think.

As a fellow was walking down a busy street in Atlanta, Georgia, there was a group of people gathered around watching something on the sidewalk which had captivated their attention. So he walked over and looked through the crowd to see what was so fascinating. There was a dog, a mutt, doing incredible tricks in the middle of the circle. What was amazing was that there was no one there to give commands. By all appearance, this dog was doing these tricks all by himself. This fellow knew *someone* had to be there giving the dog its commands, but could not see anyone doing so at first. This fellow started to watch where the dog was looking most frequently. Finally he noticed a little boy along the side of the crowd acting very nonchalant. However, this little kid was giving ever-so-slight commands, just small hand motions to the dog that would cause the dog to respond in incredible ways.

When it was all over and everyone else went their way, this fellow went up to the kid and asked how much money he would want in exchange for the dog. The kid told him he would not sell the dog for all the money in the world. As this Christian gentleman walked away, he considered what an example that was for us to follow. We only have one Person to watch and follow. We live for the One who died for us. If a crowd is blessed, great. But we do not do it for the crowd. We do it for Him.

The light of that lampstand was to shine before God, whether anyone was in the sanctuary or not. The light was to stay on, shining before God. Whatever we do, we do for Him.

Similarly, we are not to stand in judgment regarding another's light. We are not to judge another's servant. As we serve the Lord, He is the judge of our service.

We are here to be a blessing to God, not necessarily to man. Our analysis of how good we are doing, is never ultimately to be gauged by our popularity, or how appreciated we are by people. We are to live purely, ultimately, and finally for Him and in that place of fellowship with Him.

Two Necessary Requirements

There are two very necessary requirements for that lampstand to keep shining for the Lord: a continual supply of pure olive oil and regular trimming of the wick.

1. A Continual Supply of Oil

Aaron had to go in and make sure the lampstand was full of oil twice a day, morning and night. It had to have a continual supply of oil.

This paints such a beautiful picture for us. The reason the light of the gospel will continue to burn is because God has guaranteed a constant and ample supply of oil, in the Holy Spirit.

> "… but you will receive power when the Holy Spirit has come upon you; and you shall be My witnesses both in Jerusalem, and in all Judea and Samaria, and even to the remotest part of the earth." (Jesus in Acts 1:8)

Jesus guaranteed His disciples that a supply of oil (the Holy Spirit) would be there all the time, constantly available.

> "I will ask the Father, and He will give you another Helper, that He may be with you forever; that is the Spirit of truth, whom the world cannot receive, because

> it does not see Him or know Him, but you know Him because He abides with you and will be in you. I will not leave you as orphans; I will come to you." (Jesus in John 14:16-18)

There is a constant supply of the Spirit. There is never a situation where the Holy Spirit is not there to help, to guide, to comfort, to direct, and to empower the believer.

> "... and lo, I am with you always, even to the end of the age." (Jesus in Matthew 28:20b)

So the supply of the Holy Spirit is there. The obvious admonition here is to make sure you are getting the oil as needed to remain full. It is as simple as this: no oil, no light.

It is like the parable of the ten virgins in Matthew 25:1-13. Five of them ran out of oil and there was no light for them.

Jesus received the Holy Spirit and He was ready for ministry. The oil that filled the central shaft of the lampstand was the same oil that was used for all the branches.

Peter, who had previously denied Jesus three times before mere servants, after being filled with the Holy Spirit stood before the same group that had orchestrated the crucifixion of Jesus and said, **"We must obey God rather than men"** (Acts 5:29). Wow, what a difference a little oil can make!

The disciples who fled the night Jesus was crucified were the same disciples who rejoiced in the book of Acts that they were counted worthy to suffer and to bear shame for His Name (Acts 5:40-41).

The same group of guys who could not exorcise a demon-possessed boy would be the guys who would proclaim the gospel, bringing thousands to Jesus Christ. Tabitha would be raised from the dead, and people would be healed and delivered from bondage by the ministry of these same men. The whole difference was the oil, the Holy Spirit of God.

> **And do not get drunk with wine, for that is dissipation, but be filled with the Spirit ...** (Ephesians 5:18)

Be filled with the Holy Spirit. There is plenty of oil. The admonition is to be continually being filled with the Holy Spirit. The supply is ample and always there when we are abiding in Him in the tabernacle, in that place of fellowship with Him.

With that in mind, remember this old chorus:

"Fill my cup, Lord.
I lift it up, Lord.
Come and quench this thirsting in my soul."

When I would sing that chorus, I used to picture the cup as a goblet. Fill my cup, Lord. But in relation to the lampstand, we can think of those cups which would hold the oil and it gives a deeper understanding of the place of the Holy Spirit in our lives and service. Keep the cup filled with the Holy Spirit of God.

The Lord's command was for this light to always be shining. The oil must be supplied on a regular basis to keep it burning.

> **This is the confidence which we have before Him, that, if we ask anything according to His will, He hears us. And if we know that He hears us in whatever we ask, we know that we have the requests which we have asked from Him.** (1 John 5:14-15)

Do you know it is His will for you to be filled with His Spirit? First, because He commands it. Secondly, because He said that light is to be kept burning and that light can be kept burning only if there is an ample supply of oil. As you ask the Lord to fill you with His Spirit, you can know that you have what you ask of Him, because it is His will.

2. Trim the lamp.

Those lamps needed to be regularly trimmed. When Aaron went in to supply the oil twice a day, he would also trim the wicks. The high priest had this job; he alone would trim the wicks with the golden tongs so it might burn more brightly.

> **"Every branch in Me that does not bear fruit, He takes away; and every branch that bears fruit, He prunes it so that it may bear more fruit."** (Jesus in John 15:2)

Every branch that bears fruit, He prunes that it might bear more fruit. That is represented in the trimming of the wick.

I heard a fellow once describe to me a couple of neighbors he had as he was growing up. They both had rose bushes in their front yard. One neighbor really went out at the right time of year and pruned his rose bushes almost back to the ground, and they looked miserable when he was done pruning them. There was almost nothing left. It seemed cruel. The other neighbor let his rose bushes go unpruned, and branches were hanging all over the place. When it came time for the roses to bloom, the ones which had been trimmed produced big, beautiful, fragrant roses. The ones which had not been trimmed produced only a few little flowers. That is exactly what Jesus is saying here. He prunes His branches so that they will bear more fruit. The branch is cut back so the fruit will be more plentiful. That is exactly what God does in our lives.

> **Consider it all joy, my brethren, when you encounter various trials, knowing that the testing of your faith produces endurance. And let endurance have its perfect result, so that you may be perfect and complete, lacking in nothing.** (James 1:2-4)

Nothing is by accident or chance. Everything that comes into our lives as a believer can be counted as joy. God is not letting the devil get a machete out and come after us. He, Himself, is doing the pruning, and He is doing it that we might bear more fruit. He is cutting limbs back so that we might have more fruit eternally, that our treasure in heaven might be all the greater. So to any trial that comes along, we can truly say, "Thank you, Lord." We as Christians generally don't, but we could—and we really *should*. God is either trimming us for greater fruit, a brighter light, or He wouldn't allow the trial.

With the Old Testament lampstand, it was the high priest himself who did the trimming. Similarly, Jesus is the only one that does the pruning in our lives. So when any trial or tribulation comes into our lives, in whatever form it takes, it is governed by the hand of Jesus Christ Himself. He has one purpose in mind, to effect such a wonderful good in your life and through your life that when you stand before Him someday you will give abundant praise and thanksgiving for what He produced with it.

> Blessed is a man who perseveres under trial; for once he has been approved, he will receive the crown of life which the Lord has promised to those who love Him. (James 1:12)

It is comforting that the high priest trimmed the wick and refilled the oil at the same time. Jesus never trims your wick without pouring the comfort, strength, guidance, and sustenance of the Holy Spirit upon you at the same time. He provides abundant grace for the need.

> "These things I have spoken to you, so that in Me you may have peace. In the world you have tribulation, but take courage; I have overcome the world." (Jesus in John 16:33)

Everything the lampstand stands for, spiritually, is found and experienced in the tabernacle, not the courtyard. So it behooves us to understand and appropriate to ourselves the full benefits of the cross, to use the laver, and to enter into that place by faith and abide in the presence of our Heavenly Father. Practice living in His Presence. Live tight with Him. He wants that for you. It is done by faith. Then you become a representative of His, shining His light, being an instrument of His Spirit in this world.

The Old Testament priests had to go to the tabernacle, physically, to experience the benefits of the lampstand, but it was not a spiritual reality in their lives. We can take the spiritual reality of the lampstand wherever we go, and we can experience the presence of God in our lives. That was what Jesus was saying when He spoke to the woman at the well in Samaria, when she inquired as to the true place to worship.

> "But an hour is coming, and now is, when the true worshipers will worship the Father in spirit and truth; for such people the Father seeks to be His worshipers. God is spirit, and those who worship Him must worship in spirit and truth. (John 4:23-24)

What a joy! What a privilege! There is no reason for any of us not to live in that place of communion with God.

Chapter Thirteen

The Golden Table of the Bread of the Presence

"I am the bread of life; he who comes to Me shall not hunger, and he who believes in Me shall never thirst."

Jesus in John 6:35

Recall for a moment the story in John chapter 4 when Jesus ministered to the woman at the well in Samaria. His disciples had gone into town to get food. Standing at the well waiting for them to return, Jesus asked the Samaritan woman to draw some water for Him. She asked why He, being a Jew, would ask *her* for water. Jews did not generally talk to Samaritans, *especially* Samaritan women. Jesus told her that if she really knew who He was, she would ask and He would give *her* living water, water that would spring unto eternal life in her heart. Then Jesus told her to go get her husband. When she admitted that she had no husband, He told this woman, whom had never seen Him before in her life, that she was right in saying that she did not have a husband, that she had been married five times and the fellow she was currently living with was not her husband. Amazed, she perceived He must be a prophet, and ran into town to bring everyone she knew back to see Him.

While she was gone, the disciples came back with some food. As they sat down to eat, Jesus did not join them. When they inquired as to why He was not eating, He told them He had food to eat that they knew nothing about. Totally missing the point, as usual, the disciples thought someone must have given Him food to eat while they were gone. They did not understand that He was referring to the spiritual nourishment that He had received while ministering to that Samaritan woman. He was talking about something far beyond physical bread. He had spiritual food that the world knew nothing about.

I believe that what He was talking about was the essence of that life which was lost in the Garden of Eden.

> **The Lord God commanded the man, saying, "From any tree of the garden you may eat freely; but from the tree of the knowledge of good and evil you shall not eat, for in the day that you eat from it you will surely die."** (Genesis 2:16-17)

We all know that Adam lived physically 930 years after the day that the Lord promised he would **"surely die."** But what *did* happen was that he died spiritually on the very day that he disobeyed God's only commandment to him. He lost a major dynamic in his life. He was a shadow, a shell, of what he had been before. Adam and Eve knew it because they experienced the difference. Because we were born in this fallen condition, it is hard for us to fully understand what was lost. But that spiritual dynamic is revived in a life that has been restored to God through Jesus Christ.

One of the most tragic things in the world is when a person becomes a "Christian," (at least in name), and does not enter into the abundant life in Christ. What that life is like, the spiritual essence of it, God has patterned for us in the tabernacle. He wanted us to know what that life is like, so He drew a picture of it. It is illustrated for us by what was on the inside of the tabernacle.

As we looked inside that tent in the last chapter, we saw the menorah, the golden lampstand, on the left side of the first of two rooms, the Holy Place. The lampstand pointed to a new light in a born-again believer's life, the light of Jesus Christ Himself. In other words, a believer possesses spiritual understanding and enlightenment which he did not have before. There is a guiding direction that is of God, and there is the power of a witness for Jesus Christ.

On the right side of that room called the Holy Place was another piece of furniture. It was a table called the table of the bread of the Presence and we read about that in Exodus 25:23-30:

> "You shall make a table of acacia wood, two cubits long and one cubit wide and one and a half cubits high. You shall overlay it with pure gold and make a gold border around it. You shall make for it a rim of a handbreadth around it; and you shall make a gold border for the rim around it. You shall make four gold rings for it and put rings on the four corners which are on its four feet. The rings shall be close to the rim as holders for the poles to carry the table. You shall make the poles of acacia wood and overlay them with gold, so that with them the table may be carried. You shall set the bread of the Presence on the table before Me at all times."

There God made a very special provision for his priests, who picture New Testament believers. In the place of fellowship with Him, He has food for us to eat. In the tabernacle it was called **"the bread of the Presence."**

> "For the bread of God is that which comes down out of heaven, and gives life to the world." Then they said to Him, "Lord, always give us this bread." Jesus said to

them, "I am the bread of life; he who comes to Me will not hunger, and he who believes in Me will never thirst." (John 6:33-35)

Let's look at the bread of God in the tabernacle and in the New Testament and consider the interrelation and connection. As we examine the **"bread of the Presence,"** we will begin to find connections in the Word which are unbelievably rich.

This bread of the Presence was placed on a table in the outer room, the Holy Place. The only place you could taste this bread was in His presence. This bread was not found out in the camp. This bread was not even available in the courtyard. To taste this bread, you had to come inside the tent and abide in the presence of God.

Spiritually, as a believer, this bread cannot be tasted and enjoyed while your head is in the world, or while you are living a life of compromise. It is for those who have been consecrated as priests unto God, who, by faith, have entered into the tabernacle. In other words, this bread is for that believer who knows why he is here and is going about the ministry that God has given him in life, regardless of what his job is in the world. He is someone who has used the laver, and he is by faith abiding in the presence of his God.

> **For thus the Lord GOD, the Holy One of Israel, has said, "In repentance and rest you will be saved, in quietness and trust is your strength."** (Isaiah 30:15a)

"In repentance and rest you will be saved." There is a real rest in your spirit, your soul, and even your body when you enter into fellowship with your Maker.

> **If we say that we have no sin, we are deceiving ourselves and the truth is not in us. If we confess our sins, He is faithful and righteous to forgive us our sins and to cleanse us from all unrighteousness.** (1 John 1:8-9)

If you go around thinking you are actually a good person, you are deceiving yourself. But **"if we confess our sins, He is faithful and righteous to forgive us our sins and to cleanse us from all unrighteousness."** That confession is represented by the laver. You just go to that spiritual laver, and honestly and sincerely take those things before the Lord which need to be cleansed from you, confessing them as sin. Then you do in your life what is necessary to make that repentance, that restitution, right. You straighten things out, and you do it before the Lord. That is the place of repentance. From there, by faith, you simply enter into the tabernacle, that special place of communion and fellowship with God which has been provided for you in Christ, and you have entered the place of rest. **"In repentance and rest you will be saved."**

God seeks after the person who will come to that place and be in that place of fellowship, of worship, of obedience in service before the Lord. You may be going to the store to get a loaf of bread, you may be busy about your job, but you are available to the Lord as His servant. Spiritually, you are abiding in the tabernacle with Him. This **"bread of life"** is tasted there. When Jesus told His disciples in John 4:32, **"I have food to eat that you do not know about,"** that is what He was describing to them.

Two Christians can be working in a warehouse loading shelves. One person can be living in the tabernacle, in the presence of the Lord, tasting the bread. The other is just doing a job, not even aware that he is missing spiritual nourishment.

Where was the bread of the Presence kept? It was stacked on the table in the tabernacle. By now it should be pretty obvious Who the table represents. The table was made of acacia wood (symbolizing humanity) covered with gold (symbolizing deity). Obviously, it represents Jesus Christ.

Jesus said to them, "I am the bread of life ... " (John 6:35)

The bread was for the priests to eat. It was food for them. They could pick it up and eat it. Jesus said:

> **"I am the vine, you are the branches; he who abides in Me and I in him, he bears much fruit, for apart from Me you can do nothing."** (John 15:5)

Our spiritual bread comes from a personal living relationship with Jesus Christ. This spiritual bread is His provision from Him to you. He gives it to you. There are times when all we need, more than anything else, is just a taste of that good bread. When we live in a relationship with Jesus, He gives it to us, sometimes when we are not even expecting it. You may be totally alone and receive that spiritual nourishment in an unexpected time or way, because He gives it to you. It comes from Him to you.

This bread is to your spirit the very same that basic physical food is to your body. It is just as important, just as nourishing, and just as necessary. It is that which produces abundant life in us. It is the source of our abundant life.

When Jesus, who had not eaten in forty days, was being tempted by Satan to turn the stones into bread to eat, Jesus responded by saying:

> " ... It is written, 'MAN SHALL NOT LIVE ON BREAD ALONE, BUT ON EVERY WORD THAT PROCEEDS OUT OF THE MOUTH OF GOD.'" (Matthew 4:4)

There is food available that is more necessary to life than physical bread after forty days and forty nights of fasting. This spiritual bread is still more important.

> ... like newborn babies, long for the pure milk of the word, so that by it you may grow in respect to salvation ... (1 Peter 2:2)

One of the avenues through which this special nourishment comes to you is through the Word of God. It is experienced by enjoying the Word of God, receiving the Word of God, letting the Word of God do its cleansing and nourishing work in your life. God desires that His Word would be inner, meaningful sustenance to you. He wants His Word to be nourishment to you. Consequently, this nourishment comes by reading the Word. It comes by hearing the Word. It comes by meditating on the Word, taking the time to ponder what God has to say to you.

"Selah" is a word in the Psalms which has not been definitely defined. Since no one really knows what it means, all attempts to define it are conjecture. My humble opinion is that it is a musical term meaning "pause" or "rest." So as I teach through the Psalms, every time we come to **"selah,"** we pause for a minute, take a rest, and consider what is being said in the Word. That is a form of meditating on the Word. Take a minute before you go on to the next stanza, take a break and think about it. That is a part of allowing God's Word to be that nourishment to you.

It is not a matter of reading through the Bible in a year. "Okay,

I'm going to read about three chapters a day and in a year I'm done." So what? It is more important to let God's Word speak to you and nourish you than to speed read and miss what God wants to say to you personally.

Jesus gives you this bread. Very early on when I was a youth pastor, I had a little youth group in southern California. My wife's sister and her husband, Gary, attended the same church as my wife and I. One time, Gary was asked to deliver the Sunday evening message, which he did, and his message was truly anointed. Instead of being happy for my brother-in-law, though, I sat in the rear of the church wrestling with jealousy. I was the youth pastor of the church and Gary wasn't even on staff, yet he was sharing a wing-dinger of a message. People were getting blessed while I was sitting in the back row being jealous. After it was over, all kinds of people said to me, "What a message! Wasn't that great?" I agreed, with this plastic smile on my face, "Yeah, it sure was!" But inside I was depressed.

I gave myself a double whammy that night. A double whammy is when you know the way you are feeling is wrong, and then you feel guilty because you feel that way. Not only are you in the wrong space, but you are lacerating yourself with guilt. So I was one miserable basket-case that night. I called myself a man of God, and I was trying to lead kids into a closer relationship with the Lord, but my flesh, my jealous feelings, were coming out all over the place and I felt so unworthy. The enemy was using that to wag his finger in my face all night long.

I could not sleep that night and I had to go into another room and be alone. When Joyce and I were first married, we had no furniture. We had a little radio that sat on the floor because we had nothing to put it on. So I got down on the floor, stretched out, and listened to the radio which was tuned to a Christian station. During the early '70s, there was a preacher out of Chicago who had a program which came on late at night. He always talked in a soft, monotone voice. I was lying on the floor, feeling like a creep, with my face a few inches from the radio so I wouldn't awaken Joyce.

Right away it was apparent that the Lord was talking directly to me through this man in Chicago. He began to minister the Word of God to me, saying exactly what I needed to hear. I was lying there being bathed in the Word of God. It was a cleansing experience, but it was a **"bread of**

the Presence" experience for me, too. About half an hour later, the Lord, through this broadcast, just lifted me up, cleansed me, and renewed me. I had partaken of the food that the world knows nothing about. I went to bed and slept like a baby.

I was a seminary student at the time, so I got up the next morning, got in my car for the Monday morning commute to seminary through the L.A. freeways, and turned on the radio. Another Christian program was on through which the Lord spoke directly to me again. It applied specifically to my situation. It was like the Lord was just feeding me more bread. All the way to seminary the Lord was ministering to my spirit through the teaching on the radio.

When I arrived at seminary and went to morning chapel, everything the chapel speaker said spoke to me. I received my third serving of the bread during chapel. That is how awesome our Lord is, to abundantly cleanse and nourish someone who clearly didn't deserve it.

The truly amazing thing to me is when the Lord uses me and my teaching ministry to serve that bread of the Presence to someone else. I'll give you just two simple examples. As I was teaching through Daniel one Sunday morning, two ladies started talking excitedly to each other, nearly distracting the service. Afterward, they left a note for me, and the next week they came up and apologized to me for being such a distraction. For two weeks they had heard from other sources a reference to God as "El Elyon," and did not know what it meant. They had been wanting to ask me about the meaning. During my sermon, I used that term and explained what it meant, so it blew them away. To them it was a miracle that I would speak on "El Elyon" when I did.

The second incident happened when another lady came up and shared a rare experience she had with the Lord. One Saturday evening, after she put her children to bed, this woman opened up the Word. All of a sudden the words came to life for her like never before. God started sharing things with her spirit that were rich and deep. It was an incredible Saturday night for her, but what was more incredible was that in the morning, during the Sunday service, everything I talked about was exactly what God had been sharing with her the night before. God was giving her a double portion of the bread of the Presence.

That is the food that the world knows nothing about. You will know what I mean when you have eaten that bread. You are fed when you abide in the spiritual tabernacle of His presence. Jesus gives that food. So that bread is found in that "Holy Place" of fellowship with Him, and is often served up through His living Word.

I remember reading some time ago about an incident at the end of World War II when our troops took the island of Okinawa. Okinawa was a Japanese island, and although the Okinawans did not consider themselves necessarily Japanese, the Japanese controlled Okinawa long before the war. The United States took Okinawa from Japan near the end of the war to build an air strip so that mainland Japan could be bombed more easily and readily.

Clarence Hall was a war correspondent at the time who shared a story of some troops who were going to the various villages, securing them, and telling the people who were in charge now that they were "liberating them." (I do not know how liberating the Okinawans thought this was.) But the troops came to one interesting village that was totally unique from all the other villages they had seen. Two little old men walked out and bowed low before the first American troops to reach their village. Through an interpreter they said, "We are Christians, and we greet you as fellow Christians." The American soldiers got a chaplain who came and talked to these two men.

The chaplain learned that thirty years before, around 1915, an American missionary on his way to Japan had stopped in Okinawa and talked to these same two men. He had shared the Lord with them. He gave them a Japanese Bible and left. These guys took that Bible and absorbed it. They had received just enough grounding from the missionary to get the idea and they took it from there with the help of that one Bible. One guy became the village's spiritual head and the other was the teacher of the Word. The people of that village openheartedly accepted the Lord and His Word.

When Clarence Hall got there, he drove a jeep around, looking at the village with an old crusty Marine Corps sergeant. This village was totally different from the others on the island. The people were gentle, kind, and friendly. The village was immaculate. It was not like the other dirty, rancid villages filled with miserable people that the troops and correspondents had seen. This was totally different. The old Marine Corps sergeant said to Clarence Hall, "You know, maybe we've been trying to make this world over with the wrong kind of weapons. Look what happened here with a couple of old guys, one Bible, and people who want to be like Jesus!"

That **"bread of the Presence"** transformed that Okinawan village. That's powerful nourishment!

A Fresh Supply

> **"Every sabbath day he shall set it in order before the LORD continually; it is an everlasting covenant for the sons of Israel.** (Leviticus 24:8)

Notice that this bread was placed out fresh each week, and it was there for the priests to eat. That makes me think about our old Christian tradition of weekly gatherings. From the very beginning the church has gathered weekly, on Sunday, Resurrection Day, to worship the Lord, sing His praises, and hear His Word spoken.

I heard about a man who wrote a letter to the editor of his local paper in which he complained about what little good is accomplished by attending church. To prove his point, he said that he had gone to church many, many times over the years, but he could not remember one sermon he ever heard. So, he asked, "What's the point?"

The following week someone else in town replied to the newspaper's editor: "You know, I've been married for thirty years. My wife has faithfully fixed me dinner almost every evening for those thirty years, yet I can't actually remember the specifics of any one meal she fixed for me. But somehow I feel if I hadn't eaten them, I wouldn't be here." His point was that whether or not you remember the essence and the points of a sermon, when the Word of God is proclaimed, there is nourishment. Being in the Word is not going to be electrifying every time, but it *will* be nourishing every time.

There was an elder in our church who has since moved away who spends time in the Word every morning and every evening, seven days a week. He and I used to get together about once a week to have breakfast and share together. During one of our meetings, he mentioned that he had been reading in a part of the Bible which lists genealogy after genealogy. He made this comment to me, "I'm reading through those genealogies with the Lord. I don't know why God put them in there, and I don't know why I should have to read them. But I do know God put them in there for a reason, and I know it will be good for me to read them. So *I am* going to read them." There is nourishment there.

If you have children, you know that, if they could, every night they would eat ice cream for dinner. Purely for "health reasons," they might add chocolate syrup, whipped cream, and nuts. But we as parents know that what they really need are things like salads, veggies, fruit, and meat. We know what those little bodies need. Likewise, God knows what that spirit of yours needs, so He gave you His Word. Nourish yourself on it! Sometimes it might feel like you are eating spinach, but it truly is good for you. It is good for the soul. God inspired each little jot and tittle for you. The Word of God is a big part of that bread represented in the tabernacle.

God said to keep the bread fresh, replace it on a regular basis. The Word of God is always fresh. Consider this fact. You can take any other piece of literature on the face of the earth, and if you spend enough time in it you will get bored with it, it will lose its fascination, and you will soon find discrepancies in it. The Bible is exactly the opposite. I have been studying the Bible for more than thirty years now, seriously studying it. Believe me, it is fresher to me now than it was thirty-plus years ago when I started. Far from having discrepancies, it proves itself over and over for its inspiration, accuracy, and truth. It is a phenomenal book; it is our bread.

Nourishing Service

Jesus made another point about spiritual food to His disciples in John chapter 4.

> **Jesus said to them, "My food is to do the will of Him who sent Me and to accomplish His work."** (John 4:34)

Another aspect of that food is being available to be used by God in service. That also is food, nourishment, bread. As important as receiving the Word of God for yourself, is the nourishment received by giving it away. It involves saying, "Here I am, Lord, use me." This is so exciting because God can use any one of us so dynamically, any time, any way. You do not have to be a Bible scholar to be usable in incredible ways by Him.

Many years ago, A.B. Simpson wrote an excellent two-volume work on the Holy Spirit. In this work, Simpson describes his own desperate desire to be filled with the Holy Spirit as a young man in Bible College. One day he entered his apartment and spoke to the Lord. He said, "Lord, I'm going to fast, pray, and stay in this room until you endow me with power from on high. Until you fill me with the Holy Spirit, I am not going anywhere. I'm not eating anything. I'm waiting on you. Fill me with the Holy Spirit." He was determined to receive the fullness of the Holy Spirit.

An hour later there was a knock on the door. (In our day, his cell phone would have vibrated.) He did not even want to open the door. He explained through the door that he was having a quiet time before the Lord and he asked who it was. It was a friend from Bible College. He asked what the visitor wanted and the visitor explained that there was a mutual friend who lived on the next block who was really in need of help. He needed someone to come visit him. This person standing at Simpson's door felt A.B. should be the one to see him. Simpson explained that this was not a good time, and that he could not go see this friend in need. The visitor at the door reminded him that he had made a commitment to serve the Lord; for that reason, the visitor thought A.B. should reconsider and do this service for his friend. A.B. prayed about it and felt he should go. So A.B. put on his coat and left to minister to his friend.

It was a divine appointment. As he shared with his hurting friend, and as they prayed together, A.B. said he felt such an endowment from the Holy Spirit. He realized that right there, as he stepped out in faith to help his friend, God answered the prayer of his heart. He did not need to stay in his room and wait for the Lord. In fact, it wasn't until he stepped out in faith to be a servant of God that he was endowed with that power from on high.

Jesus said that the food He had was doing the will of the One who sent Him.

I cannot tell you the number of times, particularly before the mid-week service, when I have felt tired, exhausted, and empty. Each time that has happened, I have had to go to mid-week service and teach the Word. I was studied up, but I was dry. But I did not have the option of staying home. Unlike most, I could not say, "I don't feel like going tonight, I think I'll just veg at home instead. What I *really* need tonight is TV." Not only did I *have* to go, but I had to *teach*. Invariably, I will go to church with this attitude, "Here I am, Lord. I do not feel like I have anything to offer, but here I am." I have made myself available and inevitably have been blown away with the way He faithfully ministers to the body *and* feeds *me* the bread of life.

What Paul says in 2 Corinthians 12:10 is so true, **"... for when I am weak, then I am strong."** We theoretically believe that, but, at times we do not believe it in our hearts. We question it when we should be experiencing it. This is hard to understand until you are literally in the place to experience His strength in your weakness.

As a pastor, there have been times when I have been too weak to even psych myself up. At times, I have felt wiped out, tired, and alone. There have been times in my life when I did not even feel like God could be with me. Each and every time I have felt that weak, He has been there, working through me in His strength. That is why it is so important to just be available to be an instrument for His Word, no matter where you are, no matter how tired or unspiritual you may feel. Just be available. At the most unusual times you will find yourself being filled with that provision. I walk away from each mid-week service thinking, "I have a food to eat that the world knows nothing about." I have feasted. I am so thankful that I *had* to go!

Years ago, when I was first married, I would do the laundry, before we got a washing machine. I would take a load of wash to the laundromat and read a book. One day, as I was doing our laundry, I noticed a lady who was also reading a book while her laundry was in the wash. Anytime I see someone reading a book, I am curious about what it is, but I don't want to be obtrusive. As I was putting my load in the washer, I glanced over and noticed this girl was engrossed in a Christian book. So I asked if she was a Christian, and she became excited. She said she was a Christian and she asked me if I was. She started sharing about her life, and we visited until she was ready to go. She said our conversation was so neat because she had prayed before she came to the laundromat that she could be used today. She was thrilled that as she was doing laundry she got to talk about the Lord. I thought at the time that was kind of funny because I was the one who initiated the conversation, but God had definitely used her because it was an uplifting time for me also. She was just being available to the Lord at the laundromat and in a sense, we "broke bread," the bread of the Presence, together.

Your service to God is part of that spiritual food that the world does not understand. Your spirit can actually sense the nourishment and the overflowing. Jesus said there is food to eat that the world does not know or have any part of. It is not hotdogs or Subway sandwiches. It is in the bread of His Presence, set on the table in the Holy Place. It is the bread of life.

The key here, of course, is Jesus Himself. The table is Jesus, because He gives it to you. But He Himself is also the bread of life.

Remember what Jesus said to the church in Ephesus in Revelation 2: 1-7. Ephesus was a church doing all the right stuff. They were busy doing good things. It was working, energetic, alive, accomplishing things, and it probably had a lot of great programs happening. It was a full-service church doing great things. Jesus said, **"But I have this against you, that you have left your first love."** You can be so busy doing good and right things that you neglect the most important thing, your relationship with Jesus. Jesus told them to repent. He did not say "adjust." He said to **"repent,"** and return to that love relationship.

During the Jesus Movement, in the late '60s and early '70s, Calvary Chapel was a phenomenal ministry in southern California. It was unique in the world. It was even covered in Time Magazine. Around that time, Chuck Smith was asked by reporters what his goals were for Calvary Chapel. His goal was simple, "Just to know Jesus better."

Jesus bought that relationship with you at the cross. That is where the bread was broken. In partaking of His bread, you realize that He is available to you in a personal way. Practice, by faith, this communion with Him. He is your constant companion, best friend, and personal confidant.

Remember what Jesus said to the church at Laodicia in Revelation 3:14-22.

> **"Behold, I stand at the door and knock; if anyone hears My voice and opens the door, I will come in to him and will dine with him, and he with Me."** (Revelation 3:20)

He was saying He would break bread with us so we can partake together. He wants in. He wants that kind of intimate communion. It is in that sweet communion with Him that we know the Lord is with us in our lives. We know that He is with us because He tells us that in His Word. We believe it, and we consequently experience it as we go through the day, His presence, His bread of life.

I remember putting this experience to the test one time when I was in seminary. I woke up one morning and I told the Lord I was going to go through that day, all day, consciously with Him. Every little thing was consciously shared with Him. I was a chatterbox to the Lord all day long. I talked to Him about every little minute detail. As I took my shower, I thanked Him for the warm running water. When I went to the kitchen, I even thanked Him for my cold cereal. "Thank you, Lord, for Cheerios!" I found myself sincerely thanking God for everything. I was filled with abundant gratitude for things I had previously taken for granted. There was a car in the driveway—amazing! "Thank you, Lord!" Then it started—that was even *more* amazing (especially if you knew what I was driving). "Thank you, Lord!" Everything was His. It was such a neat day.

Why don't we all do that more often? We should have that constant sense of living in His presence, of living in the Holy Place with Him. We can enjoy basking in the light of Jesus Christ and tasting the bread the world does not comprehend. Why don't we stay in that place with Jesus instead of mindlessly running back into the "saved but not fellowshipping" courtyard?

A Secure Provision

The table of the bread of the Presence represents another truth to us: our provision is securely there for us.

> "You shall make for it a rim of a handbreadth around it; and you shall make a gold border for the rim around it."
> (Exodus 25:25)

There is a gold rim around the table. That bread in the jostling journey through the wilderness was not going to slide off the table. It was secure. The rim was gold, representing the Lordship of Jesus Christ.

This reminds me of His promise to the believer in Psalm 23.

> **The LORD is my shepherd,**
> **I shall not want.**

> He makes me lie down in green pastures;
> He leads me beside quiet waters.
> He restores my soul;
> He guides me in the paths of righteousness
> For His name's sake.
> Even though I walk through the valley of the shadow of death,
> I fear no evil, for You are with me;
> Your rod and Your staff, they comfort me.
> You prepare a table before me in the presence of my enemies;
> You have anointed my head with oil;
> My cup overflows.
> Surely goodness and lovingkindness will follow me all the days of my life,
> And I will dwell in the house of the Lord forever.

It is probably kind of silly, but sometimes I like to picture **"goodness and mercy"** (KJV), as these two little angels who follow me around wherever I go, taking care of me. They are God's goodness and God's mercy, and they follow me.

That bread is not going anywhere, it is secure.

Christian author Neil Anderson publishes a list similar to the one below in his book "Victory Over Darkness." Each statement is followed by the scriptural reference that supports it and is meant to encourage believers regarding our identity in, and relationship with God as believers:

"I am a Son of God. God is my spiritual Father. I am a joint heir with Christ, sharing His inheritance (Romans 8:16-17). I am a new creation today. Every day for the rest of my life I am a new creation, the old things have passed away (2 Corinthians 5:17). I am a temple, the dwelling place of God. His Spirit and His Light dwell in me (1 Corinthians 6:19). I am God's workmanship, His handiwork, born anew in Christ to do His work (Ephesians 2:10). I am chosen of God, holy and dearly loved (Colossians 3:12). I am a citizen of heaven. I am a fellow citizen with the rest of God's family (Ephesians 2:19). I am chosen and appointed by Christ to bear His fruit (John 15:16). I am a son of light, not darkness. I am a member of a chosen race, a royal priesthood, a holy nation, a people for God's own possession (1 Peter 2:9). I am an alien and a stranger in this world in which I temporarily live (1 Peter 2:11). I am an enemy of the devil. I am born of God. The evil one, the devil, cannot touch me (1 John 5:18). I am united to the Lord and am in one spirit with Him (1 Corinthians 6:17)."

We can feed on these things. There is nourishment, a special provision, for us there.

Enough for Everyone

There is one final point I would like to make about this table. It is an ample supply that the Lord has provided for us. The twelve loaves of bread obviously represent the twelve tribes of Israel, and I believe this means the bread is a special provision for *all* of us.

> "Then you shall take fine flour and bake twelve cakes with it; two-tenths of an ephah shall be in each cake. You shall set them in two rows, six to a row, on the pure gold table before the LORD." (Leviticus 24:5-6)

There were some tribes of Israel that seemed to be almost in disfavor with God, Dan being one of them. It is interesting to do a study of the tribe of Dan because you discover that he was a rascal, and it's almost like God gave him the leftovers. For example, in the marching order, Dan was in the rear. The tribe of Dan ate the dust of all the other tribes marching through the wilderness. Also notice that in Revelation, in setting apart the 144,000 when God puts an anointing on 12,000 from each tribe, the tribe of Dan is mysteriously absent. In the end of Genesis, when God lists the name for "Dan," He uses a Hebrew word which can almost be translated "and that other guy." Yet the bread is for all twelve tribes. They are all included, including Dan.

The bread is for everyone in the body of Christ, not just a chosen elite. It is not just for pastors. It is for the body, for everyone. Each loaf was two-tenths of an ephah of bread. That is twice as much as a person needed for his daily ration.

This says two things to me. First, there is an ample supply there and, secondly, there is an overflow effect resulting from that abundance.

There is never a day when His provision and His grace are not more than equal to the need. It is not just enough for the need, it is more than is needed.

In the aftermath of World War II, there was a widow with two small children. She had been made a widow by the war and she was extremely poor. She did not know where her next meal was coming from and she had to feed her children. But she was a Christian and as she committed this problem to the Lord, He brought to mind the verse in Philippians 4:19, where Paul promises, **"And my God will supply all your needs according to His riches in glory in Christ Jesus."**

She wrote this verse down on a blank piece of paper and took it with her as she went out the door to the market with her little children. The owner of the market was behind the counter, so she walked up to him and handed him this piece of paper. He read it as she asked, "Can you help us? We have no food." His attitude was, "Oh, brother." Standing behind the scales on the counter, he taunted her saying, "Let's see how much this is *really* worth." In an effort to humiliate her, he put the piece of paper on one side of the scales and a loaf of bread on the other side. The scales did not move. By this time other people were walking into the market and they became fascinated. He put some milk on the scales, but they still did not move. He put on more bread and a few apples on the scale. With all this food on one side and this little piece of paper on the other side, the scales did not move.

This poor widow rejoiced and the other shoppers chuckled. Finally, the owner grabbed the bag, handed it to her and told her to be gone. She walked out exclaiming, "Thank you, thank you! Oh, bless the Lord!" She was thrilled to death and *he* was humiliated. After he had helped his customers, he examined the scale and, sure enough, it had jammed. There was a logical explanation as to why the scale did not move, but the point is that it jammed at just the right time … in God's timing.

That is just one small example of the ample supply of the Lord that can come in the most unusual times and ways. Here's another.

A pastor and his wife, Joe and Pat, from Calvary Chapel of Gardnerville were good friends with my wife and I years ago. We had gone to Israel together for the first time in 1981 with Chuck Smith. My wife and I hit it off with them because they were the nearest Calvary Chapel to us at the time, and they had six children, just like us. One day Joe was killed in a mudslide on Slide Mountain, which was appropriately named. As he was helping a brother in his church build a house in the canyon, there was an unexpected rush of mud that came down. Everyone got to safety but him. When he died, Pat called my house and said, "Brian, Joe's gone. The Lord took him." She told me what happened.

So there was Pat with six kids to raise alone. We went down to see her and performed the funeral a few days later during which Pat was just radiant in the Lord. She sat there with those six little children in the front row at this memorial service, and she glowed. After the service her friends started sharing with us that they were amazed at her strength, but they all believed her life would soon come crashing down around her. They encouraged us to be prepared to be there for her when that happened. I knew to be prepared, in case she did become emotionally devastated, but I really didn't think that it would happen to her. And it did not. She was strong in the Lord all the way through. She knew the Lord would supply all her needs and He did. He supplied, because Pat was one of those Christians who daily lived in fellowship with her Lord, "in the tent," so to speak.

The other thing that two-tenths of flour, that over-abundance, means is that when we partake of that provision, there is an overflowing effect. It overflows from our lives. If you eat of that bread, it will bear influence in other people's lives. There is bread for them, too. The best thing you can do to see your loved ones come to Jesus is to partake of that bread yourself. Preaching to those you love, or hog-tying them and dragging them to church, may not work. But if you eat of the bread, if you live in an intimate relationship with Jesus, it will overflow from your life.

I heard a story of a fellow who was a recovering alcoholic. He had come to Christ and he was delivered from alcoholism, but he knew the temptation of alcohol. Just the smell of it could trigger the desire for it in him. He went to a party one night, not knowing if there were going to be any Christians at the party. There was a lot of alcohol flowing freely at the party of some friends and business associates and he was right at that point where he was ready to have a drink. His defenses were going down, and just as he was ready to give in and take a glass, a lady nearby was offered something to drink and she just politely said, "No, thank you." He recognized this woman from his church. Her "No, thank you" allowed him the strength to also say, "No, thanks."

He started to play a little game. He decided to watch her, and if she took a drink, he would take a drink. But if she did not take a drink, he would not. This lady had no idea this was going on. She had no idea God was using her. She never took a drink. So all evening when people would come up and offer this man something to drink, he would say, "No, thank you," all evening long. He went up to her as she left the party and thanked her, explaining how she had unknowingly helped him resist temptation.

This same thing is happening in our lives. When we are living in that "Holy Place" of the tabernacle, we are affecting people in ways we do not even know. You will not be aware of how until you get to glory, and then you will be amazed at the way God was using you when you were oblivious to His working through your life. If you have been thinking, "God can't use me," you are wrong.

These effects come from living in that Holy Place of communion with Jesus. If you are inclined to think that you are not much influence, or that your presence has little influence, think of this:

> **And a woman who has an unbelieving husband, and he consents to live with her, she must not send her husband away. For the unbelieving husband is sanctified through his wife, and the unbelieving wife is sanctified through her believing husband; for otherwise your children are unclean, but now they are holy.** (1 Corinthians 7:13-14)

The presence of a believer in Jesus Christ, in a house, in a community, in any environment, has a powerful spiritual effect on that place.

> **"Do not work for the food which perishes, but for the food which endures to eternal life, which the Son of Man will give to you, for on Him the Father, God, has set His seal." Therefore they said to Him, "What shall we do, so that we may work the works of God?" Jesus answered and said to them, "This is the work of God, that you believe in Him whom He has sent."** (John 6: 27-29)

Trust Him with that situation that your life is in right now. Trust Him completely, all the way through it. He has a provision there for you as you look to Him and fellowship with Him, and trust in Him.

Chapter Fourteen

The Golden Altar of Incense

Therefore He is able also to save forever those who draw near to God through Him, since He always lives to make intercession for them.

Hebrews 7:25

"Moreover, you shall make an altar as a place for burning incense; you shall make it of acacia wood. Its length shall be a cubit, and its width a cubit, it shall be square, and its height shall be two cubits; its horns shall be of one piece with it. Aaron shall burn fragrant incense on it; he shall burn it every morning when he trims the lamps. When Aaron trims the lamps at twilight, he shall burn incense. There shall be perpetual incense before the Lord throughout your generations. You shall not offer any strange incense on this altar, or burnt offering or meal offering; and you shall not pour out a drink offering on it. Aaron shall make atonement on its horns once a year; he shall make atonement on it with the blood of the sin offering of atonement once a year throughout your generations. It is most holy to the Lord." (Exodus 30:1-3, 7-10)

There was one other piece of furniture in the outer room, the "Holy Place," of the tabernacle. A small golden altar of incense stood directly in the center, right before the veil. On the other side of the veil was the Holy of Holies which contained the fabled ark of the covenant. This small altar was an altar for burning fragrant incense, and it was constantly burning. When the priests would step into that room, on the left was that beautiful menorah made of solid gold which provided light to the room. The gold would sparkle, and he would smell the fragrant aroma which emanated from the altar of incense. The altar would glow softly as the incense continually burned.

With that golden altar of incense and that fragrant aroma, we learn of a third vital aspect of our fellowship with our Lord, as His chosen children. This aspect of our walk is realized when we are abiding in the tabernacle. It is not appreciated, understood, or truly experienced outside the tent tabernacle.

That golden altar of incense pictures two things for us as believers: the ongoing intercession of Jesus Christ for us, and of the power and authority of the prayers of the believers.

The Intercession of Jesus

Aaron, the high priest, was the one who burned the incense on that altar. It was his job to keep the incense burning on that altar. As high priest, Aaron is, of course, a picture of Jesus Christ. What we have is a beautiful picture of the intercession of Jesus Christ for us.

We learn from the New Testament that Jesus is in heaven at the right hand of the Father. If you were to ask what He is doing there now, bodily, there is one clear answer to that. The answer is Hebrews 7:25:

> **Therefore He is able also to save forever those who draw near to God through Him, since He always lives to make intercession for them.**

Jesus is interceding on our behalf with the Father. To appreciate that is to get a grip on the forgiveness of God and how we live in His forgiveness. Just as that Old Testament altar was always burning, so Jesus Christ is constantly interceding for you and me.

If anyone could have been haunted by his past as a believer, it would have been the Apostle Paul, who persecuted the church so violently. Yet

Paul lived in the joy of the Lord and the fullness of the forgiveness of God. He understood how forgiving God was, and he thrived in the knowledge and assurance of that forgiveness.

When you abide in the tabernacle, you also live in that realm of forgiveness. You can rest in that forgiveness. You cannot help but be resting in the Lord when you are spiritually dwelling in the tabernacle. You may do a lot of spiritual and emotional yo-yo-ing when you are in the courtyard, but when you are in the tabernacle you experience the peace of His continual forgiveness.

When Wycliff translators were translating the Bible into an Eskimo dialect, they tried to find an Eskimo word for "forgiveness." The best Eskimo word that they could come up with for that was "issumagijouju-ngnainermik." The word literally means "not being able to think about it anymore." That pictures so beautifully, the forgiveness of God. Within ourselves we do not have the capability of forgiving that way. But God does! When He forgives, He forgets! (Isaiah 43:25). It is like we had never sinned in the first place.

I was reading about a fellow who was waiting in the pastor's study to meet with his pastor. When the pastor heard a loud "Yahoo!" from the study, he rushed into the room. This man had been looking at some of the pastor's books and he flipped through a book that said the deepest parts of the ocean are over seven miles deep. He was thrilled. The pastor looked at him with an expression of, "So what?" Then the fellow explained that the Bible said our sins have been buried in the deepest sea. "That is so deep," he said, "no way are those sins ever going to come up again!" That was an exciting thing for him to contemplate and he was rejoicing. God actually forgets our sin because of the finished work of Jesus on the cross.

> **"I, even I, am the one who wipes out your transgressions for My own sake, and I will not remember your sins.**
> (Isaiah 43:25)

When we are humbly and honestly in that space where we confess our sins before the Lord, when we wash at the laver in the tabernacle courtyard, and then if we go back to the Lord and say, "Lord, you know that sin . . ." the Lord says, "What sin? I don't know what you are talking about." When a sin is confessed, it is forgiven and forgotten.

But living in that space in the tabernacle is not a license for freedom in sinful living. You may try to play those games in the courtyard, but you never play those games in the tabernacle.

God wants you to be able to bounce right back and walk with Him. You do not have to go through some religious process to regain your intimate fellowship with Him again. To be able to walk with Him, you do not have to sit there and say, "Oh, I've just had an awful thought! What do I need to do now? Oh, I'd better do this, and then this, and then this . . . and I hope by next Sunday I'll be able to be with You, Lord."

It is simply a matter of, "Oh, Lord, thank You! I reject that dumb thought, and the blood of Jesus Christ has already cleansed me from that, and I am in fellowship with You and walking with You." At that very moment, you are forgiven, because Jesus is at the throne and He **"always lives to make intercession"** for us (Hebrews 7:25).

God told Aaron to keep that altar of incense burning in the tabernacle because, at any time, you or I may need the benefit of the forgiveness of God that it represents to us through Jesus.

> **If we confess our sins, He is faithful and righteous to forgive us our sins and to cleanse us from all unrighteousness.** (1 John 1:9)

When you are in the tabernacle, you are safe and secure in Jesus. When you understand the intercession of Jesus on your behalf, you begin to realize how protected you are in Him.

> **He will not allow your foot to slip;**
> **He who keeps you will not slumber.**
> **Behold, He who keeps Israel**
> **Will neither slumber nor sleep.**
> **The Lord is your keeper;**
> **The Lord is your shade on your right hand.**
> **The sun will not smite you by day,**
> **Nor the moon by night.**
> **The Lord will protect you from all evil;**
> **He will keep your soul.**
> **The Lord will guard your going out and your coming in**
> **From this time forth and forever.** (Psalm 121:3-8)

Our Lord neither slumbers nor sleeps. He guards our going out and our coming in, all the time. We are protected by Him.

This reminds me of the story of a little grandma during World War II. When the air-raid sirens would go off in London and the whole family would go racing downstairs to the basement, Grandma would not go. She just slept in her bed. The grandchildren would say, "Come on, Grandma, we've got to go down to the basement." Grandma would say, "Leave me alone, I'm sleeping." One day her little grandson came to her and asked, "Grandma, how come you don't go down to the basement with us when the air-raid siren sounds?" And Grandma said, "Well, son, it's like this. My Bible tells me that my Lord neither slumbers nor sleeps in watching over me, so I figure there's no reason two of us should lose sleep over this thing."

> **The angel of the LORD encamps around those who fear Him, and rescues them. (Psalm 34:7)**

I remember reading about a senator back in 1845. Senator Thomas Benton was a cantankerous, tough senator. He had fights and arguments with a lot of men in the Senate. He had been invited, along with the Secretary of the Navy and the Secretary of State, and other dignitaries and senators to a ride on the latest American battleship, the USS Princeton. It had the biggest cannon in the world at the time, which they called "the peacemaker." They were preparing to fire the cannon to impress the dignitaries with the power of this weapon. As the dignitaries gathered behind this huge cannon on deck, Benton had a nice front row position to watch this event. But just as they were preparing to fire the cannon, someone behind him tapped his shoulder to speak with him. As he leaned over to talk, Gilmore, the Secretary of the Navy, took the opportunity to elbow his way around Benton and get right in front of him, just before the cannon was fired. This agitated Benton. However, as the cannon went off, it exploded, and Gilmore was killed instantly, as were many others, including the Secretary of State. It was a tragic event, but Benton came out unscathed.

If Gilmore had not elbowed his way in front of Benton, Benton would have been dead. As a result, Benton's whole outlook changed and he then and there devoted his life to the Lord. He wrote letters to those whom he had feuded with in the senate, Daniel Webster being one of them. He asked their forgiveness and said he was a new man walking with the Lord. He spent the rest of his life being there in service to the

Lord. His entire perspective changed because the providential hand of God had protected him.

Jesus' intercession for us has that power and works in that way, not just interceding for us because of our sin, but interceding in terms of guidance, direction, and protection.

Jesus told Peter in Luke 22:31-32:

> "Simon, Simon, behold, Satan has demanded permission to sift you like wheat; but I have prayed for you …"

Jesus was right there at the golden altar in the Spirit praying for Peter.

> "… that your faith may not fail; and you, when once you have turned again, strengthen your brothers."

Jesus is before the throne of God on our behalf, in that place of intercession, all the time. When we are abiding in that tabernacle, when we are spiritually abiding in that Holy Place, we realize He is continually interceding for us. We know we are safe. We know we are secure, regardless of what is going on around us. That's one of the blessings of abiding in that place of fellowship with Him.

> … but if we walk in the Light as He Himself is in the Light, we have fellowship with one another, and the blood of Jesus His Son cleanses us from all sin. (1 John 1:7)

Because of the light, we can have fellowship with one another, "koinonia." There is a realization, a knowledge, an understanding, a rest, a spiritual peace that the blood of Jesus Christ is cleansing you from all sin. That is a present-tense thing. The blood cleanses, and keeps cleansing from all sin. You realize that, when you are abiding in the tabernacle. Outside, in the courtyard, you do not have that assurance. We do not deserve that place before the Lord, and yet, it is ours to enjoy through Jesus Christ.

The fire for the golden altar of incense came from a very interesting source. It only came from the big bronze altar out in the courtyard. The place which pictures the cross where sin was judged and paid for was the source of fire for the golden altar of incense. This speaks of the effectiveness of the intercession of Jesus on our behalf, in that it is based on His finished work on the cross.

Remember the story in Leviticus chapter 10 of Nadab and Abihu who jumped the gun a bit? God lit the fire at the big bronze altar and He commanded them to take the coals from that fire to light the golden altar of incense. These two boys jumped in and they tried to use **"strange fire"** to light the golden altar of incense. They died right then and there. That may seem like God was being unreasonable, but it is a very clear picture for us. We have no standing before God apart from the cross. It is the cross and the cross alone that gives us our standing before God and makes Jesus' intercession for us completely effective.

What was that strange fire? It was fire from any source other than the big bronze altar. Any other source than that which God commanded would be strange fire in God's eyes. God insisted the fire for the altar of incense had to come from the bronze altar because that was where sin was judged and dealt with completely.

That example pictures for us the intercession of the Lord on our behalf. We do not deserve His intercession. His intercession for us is purely by His grace, but it is effective because of the cross. Our standing before God is in the finished work of Jesus on the cross. It is in Jesus Christ alone and there is no other way I can be justified before God, except by Him, through the cross. At the end of the Sermon on the Mount, Jesus said something very interesting:

> **"Not everyone who says to Me, 'Lord, Lord,' will enter the kingdom of heaven, but he who does the will of My Father who is in heaven will enter. Many will say to Me on that day, 'Lord, Lord, did we not prophesy in Your name, and in Your name cast out demons, and in Your name perform many miracles?' And then I will declare to them, 'I never knew you; DEPART FROM ME, YOU WHO PRACTICE LAWLESSNESS.'"** (Jesus in Matthew 7:21-23)

Those are pretty heavy words. Jesus told us what the will of the Lord is in John 6:28-29:

> **Therefore they said to Him, "What shall we do, so that we may work the works of God?" Jesus answered and said to them, "This is the work of God, that you believe in Him whom He has sent."**

We must have faith that Jesus was sent by the Father on our behalf. We must have faith in the new covenant, established at the cross. It is a marvelous thing, at times difficult to grasp, but it is very simple. We must trust 100 percent in what Jesus accomplished at the cross for our standing with God. If we take 1 percent of that and put it on us, we will end up being a basket case. We will experience "yo-yo" Christianity. We will feel really good about ourselves in a self-righteous way one minute, and like a miserable failure the next. But when we base our faith and salvation 100 percent on the finished work of Jesus on the cross, and have no confidence in our own flesh, then we are in a space of faith and our standing with Him is completely settled in our own hearts.

As we read of that altar of incense burning, and that incense and fragrant aroma filling the air twenty-four hours a day, it is a reminder to us that Jesus Christ is indeed our friend, advocate, supporter, helper, intercessor, and protector. It is the Holy Spirit that makes us absolutely aware of that as we dwell with Him in that **"tent of meeting."**

It is in this spirit of presenting ourselves to the Lord and knowing that He is the One in charge, that we know we are safely kept in His peace. God is not requiring sinless perfection every moment of our lives. We are to just rest in His finished work on Calvary.

So the issue is not, "How much did you sin today?" The issue is "How available were you to be of use to the Holy Spirit today?" Because the sin issue was taken care of on the cross, live in the realm of God's forgiveness, knowing the blood of Jesus Christ cleanses you from all sin, and abide in fellowship with Him.

So, one thing that golden altar of incense pictures is Christ constantly interceding before the throne on our behalf.

Power in Prayer

The altar of incense also represents the prayers of the saints, and the power and authority of those prayers offered to God.

> **When He had taken the book, the four living creatures and the twenty-four elders fell down before the Lamb, each one holding a harp and golden bowls full of incense, which are the prayers of the saints. (Revelation 5:8)**
>
> **Another angel came and stood at the altar, holding a**

> golden censer; and much incense was given to him, so that he might add it to the prayers of all the saints on the golden altar which was before the throne. (Revelation 8:3)

In both of these Scriptures from Revelation, we see a heavenly **"golden altar of incense"** right there before the throne of God and the incense represents the prayers of the saints, which are a sweet aroma to our Heavenly Father.

Therefore, not only is the golden altar of incense recognition of Christ as our intercessor and all that means to us in our walk with Him, but it is a place, in the tabernacle, of power and authority before the throne of God in prayer. With that in mind, look at what Jesus says in John 15:7:

> **"If you abide in Me, and My words abide in you, ask whatever you wish, and it will be done for you."**

There is power in prayer.

> **"You did not choose Me but I chose you, and appointed you that you would go and bear fruit, and that your fruit would remain, so that whatever you ask of the Father in My name He may give to you."** (Jesus in John 15:16)

What does it mean to ask the Father **"in My name?"** It means to represent Christ before the throne of God, to represent His concerns, His will, His purpose, His work, and His cause. If you do that, you are praying in His name. You are going before the Father on His behalf.

When you are abiding in the tabernacle, you are one of those little lights on the lampstand representing Him. You are being nourished by the bread of His Presence because you are living in fellowship with Him, and you have power in prayer because you are in Jesus Christ and He is in you, in a very special experiential way.

There were horns on the corners of that little altar of incense. In the Bible, horns symbolize power and authority. (For example, in the book of Daniel, the horns on the beast represent kings and their power and authority.)

We do not really appreciate and realize the influence we have with God in prayer when He owns our heart, when we are living, by faith, in fellowship with Him. We do not realize the power and influence we bear before God in prayer. Add to that reality the fact that for us, as New Testament believers, the veil separating the Holy Place from the Holy of Holies is gone because of the cross. When we bow in prayer in the spirit, we are directly before the throne of God, there is no barrier, no separation, no veil. No wonder we are admonished in the Word to pray! No wonder the enemy works so hard to discourage us, to divert our attention and detour us when it comes to prayer! We have open access to the throne and power before God in prayer. Our prayers are a fragrant aroma to our Heavenly Father, in the very tabernacle of heaven. The incense is the prayers of the saints before the Father.

With this in mind, when you think about your prayer life, be reminded of the golden altar of incense. God planted it there in the tabernacle to impress upon you the place you have before the throne in prayer.

> **Be anxious for nothing, but in everything by prayer and supplication with thanksgiving let your requests be made known to God. And the peace of God, which surpasses all comprehension, will guard your hearts and your minds in Christ Jesus.** (Philippians 4:6-7)

George Mueller was a man of prayer. In reading his autobiography, it is apparent that his whole life was lived in full dependence on God's provision, God's leading, and God's miracle-working power all the time because he was totally a man of prayer. A man of prayer in the Bible was Daniel. He really believed in prayer. These men had childlike faith to just ask God to help in any situation, and to believe that He would answer them.

It is interesting that when you go to that Holy Place in the tabernacle, everything there is God's provision for you. It is not a place where you are told to go out and do great things for God. In that place of rest, God provides for you. Through the altar of incense, symbolizing prayer, He offers us direct access to His throne so we *can* live our lives that way.

George Mueller once said: "I spend hours in prayer every day, but I live in the spirit of prayer." I really like that. It is important to spend special time in prayer, alone with God. Daniel did that three times a day: morning, midday, and evening. That quiet time with God is an important part of your Christian walk. If you do not establish time to pray, your prayer life will likely go by the wayside. I am not telling you that you are required to spend hours in prayer. But it is important to set aside your special time with the Lord, to have that relationship and that time of communion with Him each day.

Occasionally during a mid-week service I set aside time just to answer questions that are presented to me during the week. One evening the question came up regarding the issue of tithing. The question was: Is tithing something that is commanded in the New Testament? No, it is not. Tithing is not commanded in the New Testament. But I shared that the Old Testament was a tutor for New Testament believers; it gives us guidance and direction, even though we are not bound to those laws. Tithing is a good rule of thumb. Tithing is a good place to start in your giving. It is wonderful to give 10 percent off the top to the Lord, because we tend to be such tightwads, we need something like that to put us in the mode of being givers. To me tithing is a joy. It is my favorite check to write and I give it joyfully because it is a definite step of faith in His provision, and act of worship—I feel it is the least I can do. Then there is giving that can take place beyond that. There is no command to tithe, but it is a good rule of thumb.

Similarly, in the area of praying, when you take time during the day to pray, you make time for God. There is no law that requires us to pray morning, noon, and night. God does not make that requirement. We are absolutely free in the area of prayer. It is like any other area of our Christian walk. We do not have to walk in condemnation because we did not take time to pray today. But, just like tithing does something to put you in the giving mode, it is a good idea to make up your mind to pray morning, noon, and night. It puts you in the habit of praying regularly throughout the day. Take that time out to pray. Make that time. Then from that place, you go out in the spirit of prayer. Be like Mueller: live in the spirit of prayer.

In my own walk, when I have that quality time with the Lord in morning prayer, that tunes me in for the day. I have made contact, then, as I go through the day, I am living in contact with my Heavenly Father. I have established that communication first thing in the morning by spending some time in prayer.

As Mueller said, "I pray as I walk and as I lie down. I pray when I awake. The answers are always coming. Thousands of times have my prayers been answered. When I am persuaded that a thing is right, I go on praying until the answer comes. I never give up. I have been praying every day for fifty-two years for two men, sons of a friend of my youth. They are not converted yet, but they will be. How can it be otherwise when we have the unchanging promises of God?" Now that is praying in the Spirit. As a matter of fact, one of those men came to Christ just before Mueller died, and the other, just after. Both were saved.

In talking with people who are sharing concerns, I will ask if they have prayed about the particular issue in question. Some may say, "I've prayed, and I'm hoping . . ." That is one very common attitude.

But how different it is when you ask if someone has prayed about a problem, and they say, "Yes, you watch. God is going to deal with it."

Now which attitude edifies you the most? Which one of those encourages you? Which one makes you really start to think about those prayers you offer? It is so edifying when someone prays who believes in his God to answer him!

So where are you living in your prayer life? What is your response when people ask if you have prayed about something? Take that before the Lord. God tells us to trust in Him, to believe in Him. When I hear someone say, "My God is going to come through," that builds me up, encourages me, comforts me, and edifies me. But if someone waffles, "Well, I hope so . . ." I just think, "Oh dear."

Look at the nature of these admonitions to pray in Scripture:

> **Enter His gates with thanksgiving**
> **And His courts with praise.**
> **Give thanks to Him, bless His name.** (Psalm 100:4)

Come into that tent of meeting, come into that inner sanctuary with your Lord, with thanksgiving and praise and blessing His Name.

> **Through Him then, let us continually offer up a sacrifice of praise to God, that is, the fruit of lips that give thanks to His name.** (Hebrews 13:15)

How do I offer up a sacrifice of praise to God? It is the fruit of your lips, giving thanks to His name. Praise His name. Come into His presence with praise.

When we look at Daniel's prayer life we see this very thing. Daniel was a man who praised God in his prayer life. In his prayers, even when he had a burden on his heart and he needed to pray about a need, he praised God. He began his prayers in praise. He entered in with a spirit of praise (Daniel 9).

> **Be anxious for nothing, but in everything by prayer and supplication with thanksgiving let your requests be made known to God.** (Philippians 4:6)

Paul tells us to come to God with thanksgiving, even in those times when we are deeply troubled. Do you ever feel like you do not have anything to be thankful for in a particular situation? Well, you can always be thankful that the situation is not out of your God's control. You can always be thankful that God promises that all things work together for good for those who love Him and are called according to His purpose (Romans 8:28). You can always be thankful that even though you walk through the valley of the shadow of death, He will be with you. His rod and His staff will comfort you. He will prepare a table of feasting before you in the presence of your enemies. Goodness and mercy will follow you wherever you go until you enter into the house of the Lord (Psalm 23). You can always be thankful that He is there, watching you, helping you, shepherding you. You have abundant reasons to offer praise and thanksgiving to your God—always.

In Acts chapter 4, a prayer meeting was held just after some of the brethren had their lives threatened. They were told not to proclaim the gospel publicly, or die. Their very lives were in danger. That is not a little thing! Today, we live in a society in which we might get a hand slapped for being bold for Christ. Back then they died an agonizing torturous death. It was not just a lethal injection. It was torturous. Yet Jesus' commandment to them (and to us) was to go into all the world and proclaim the gospel to all creation. There was nothing arbitrary about the command. Go and proclaim. So there they were, in a real dilemma. Read the prayer of Acts chapter 4. In their prayer they declare: "You are the Lord. You are God. You are in control. You laugh at the governments of the world that try to put you down or stop your work. You laugh in heaven at that. Lord, we know You have put a commission on us. Give us boldness to proclaim Your Word with signs and wonders following."

If it were me, I might have said, "Let's drop the signs and wonders part because that's what got us in trouble in the first place. Surely we don't *need* signs and wonders. It was when Peter and John healed this guy that the trouble started. Those signs and wonders caused the big stir that got us the big threat. So maybe we could just share and leave the signs and wonders out, and we could stay out of trouble."

But they said, "Lord, give us boldness, with signs and wonders following." It was like they were going to Herod and the Sanhedrin saying, "In your face," and doing it anyway. If it meant dying for the cause, then so be it. After all, He died for us.

Oh that we might have a church that would not look at the threats of governments and men as something to prevent Christians from sharing the gospel!

Prayer gives us an awesome place of power before the throne. Pray to be everything God would have you be, in the spirit of thanksgiving. Praying with that spirit of thanksgiving will do wonders for your prayer life. Paul tells us in the Word to never make a request from the Lord without including praise and thanksgiving. That is what he is saying. Do not go before God without having a mantle of thanksgiving around you. Keep that spirit of praise and thanksgiving alive in your prayer life.

The Intercession of Believers

Prayer is also a place of intercession. Jesus gives us that example. The golden altar of incense represents to us that Jesus is at the throne of God making intercession on our behalf. He is our intercessor. That golden altar of incense represents that place of intercession in our prayers. When we look at the Bible we see that the bulk of prayer is intercessory prayer, standing in the gap for others.

Harry Ironside was asked the question: "If you have been praying for someone for years and they die with no apparent indication whatsoever that they were saved, does that weaken your confidence in prayer and your resolve to pray?" In response to that question, he told this story.

A mother had prayed for her wayward son who had gone away and joined the merchant marines. She had prayed all his life that he would come to know Jesus, but he was out there living life totally in the world. One night, she woke up with the burden to pray for her son. She got down on her knees and prayed. Several weeks later, her son came to her door and said, "Mom, I'm born again." Rejoicing, she asked what had happened. The son shared his testimony with her.

He had been in an awful storm a few weeks before. The waves were towering over the ship. There was real concern for the safety of the ship because the storm was so intense. As they were working on deck and making sure things were properly tied down, the ship suddenly lurched and he was swept into the sea. As he was going down, he realized he was not saved and he cried out with all of his heart to Jesus. Then he lost consciousness.

The next morning when the storm had abated, and the crew came out to clean up the debris on the deck, they found his half-dead body plastered against the bulkhead. Some wave must have crashed onto that ship with him in it. When he revived, he was a born-again believer.

You can pray for someone right up to their death with no indication that anything has happened. Because you do not know what is going on inside that soul and spirit, though, you just can't say. If that young man had died, his mother would have thought he died in unbelief.

There is power in intercession symbolized in the tabernacle by the golden altar of incense; you have the power of intercession before the throne of God.

Abraham interceded before the Lord for Lot. Lot was in Sodom, when Abraham interceded on his behalf. But the next thing Abraham knew was that there was smoke going up from Sodom. The smoke was like a giant stovepipe, and Sodom had obviously been destroyed. There is no record that Abraham had any contact with Lot or knew anything about Lot after that. All Abraham knew was that Sodom had burned. It would have been easy for Abraham to think that his intercession did not help. He might have believed that Lot was lost, burned in the city. Abraham may never have known that angels went to Lot in the city of Sodom and told Lot, "Lot, we cannot destroy this place until you and your family are out of this city." They literally picked him up and ushered him out of that city. I am sure Abraham's intercession was a major part of that.

> "I searched for a man among them who would build up the wall and stand in the gap before Me for the land, so that I would not destroy it; but I found no one. (Ezekiel 22:30)

God looked for someone to stand in the gap, someone to intercede in prayer for Jerusalem in the days of Ezekiel, but there was no one. He is still seeking those who will "stand in the gap" today.

That leads me to one of my favorite stories along this line. It has to do with a missionary and his family in modern Indonesia. There was a housewife in Alabama whose family helped support that missionary family. One day, she woke up and began doing her normal daily routine when out of the blue, she had this impression that she should pray for this family. She called a couple of sisters in the church, asked them to come over and pray. They prayed fervently for that family, had a cup of coffee together, and then parted.

A few months later that missionary family was on furlough to the United States and they visited this lady's church. As they were sharing about their mission, they told of a hair-raising experience they had had.

They were in the back country of Indonesia with their three small children, traveling by dugout canoe from their mission station down to where there was more civilization so they could fly out. The river was terribly swollen from the rains and the canoe was moving very rapidly. Their canoe hit a root just under the surface of the river and it flipped over. The husband, wife, and three small children were dumped into the turbulent, rushing river.

As the husband was getting pummeled down the river, he grabbed a branch that he was able to hold on to, and frantically looked for his family. At first, he saw no one. Suddenly, he saw his wife who had grabbed hold of something along the riverbank, but the children were nowhere in sight. Just then, as he felt something hit his leg, he reached down and pulled up one of his children. No sooner had he gotten the first one set than a second child hit his leg. As soon as he had rescued that one, the third child bumped into his leg. They had hit his legs far enough apart that he could get them secured. He testified that it was a miracle of God.

After the meeting the women went up and asked what day, exactly, that had happened. When they compared notes, they discovered it had happened on the very same day, and at the same time of day that those ladies were praying for them.

God has put a golden altar of incense in the tabernacle to tell you there is a place, a central place, in your walk for prayer. In that place of fellowship with our Heavenly Father there is a standing invitation to pray. Pray always about everything. Abide in Him, remain in that tabernacle and take advantage of the altar of incense. In other words, believer, pray! *Pray!*

Chapter Fifteen

The Ark of the Covenant

"Do not think that I came to abolish the Law or the Prophets; I did not come to abolish but to fulfill."

Jesus in Matthew 5:17

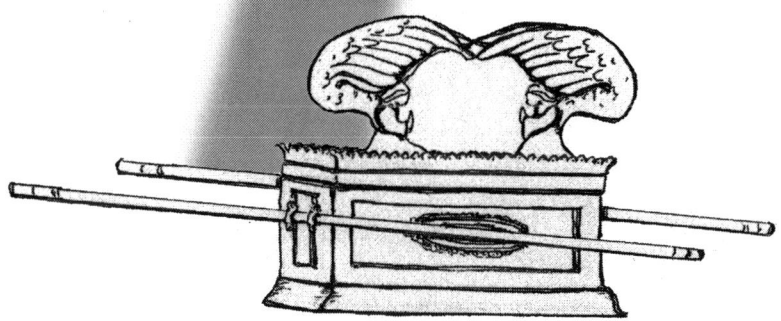

Since we entered the tent during our spiritual tour of the Old Testament tabernacle in the wilderness, we have looked closely at the three pieces of furniture which were in the outer room. There, in that room known as the Holy Place, God showed us how ample His provision is for us, for life, for ministry, and for service. We basked in the light of the menorah which pictures for us the spiritual light of the Lord's guidance in our lives, and the witness of a believer empowered by the Holy Spirit. We tasted of the bread of His Presence which represented the strength, nourishment, and refreshment in the Spirit that comes through Jesus Christ to us, a food that the world knows nothing about. Then we saw the golden altar of incense, that little altar located directly before the veil which separated this room from the inner room, the Holy of Holies. That altar prefigured the ongoing intercession of Jesus Christ for us, and the power of our intercession in prayer for others.

Now, we will venture right through the veil into the Holy of Holies, the very dwelling place of God in that camp. As we've seen, only the high priest could enter that room and only once a year, on the Day of Atonement. No one else could go in there for any reason, at any time. In fact, they would tie a rope around the high priest's ankle to drag his body out, should he die while he was in there. Otherwise, they'd have to wait a year until the new high priest could enter to get him out of there. That's how exclusive that room was in that day.

In spiritual reality, however, we, as believer-priests, have open access to the real Holy of Holies at any time. So, how is it that we can just boldly enter into the very throne room of heaven of which the Holy of Holies was simply a shadow, a picture? As believer-priests, why aren't we also limited to the Holy Place, that outer room where the tabernacle priests served? It is for the same reason that we can boldly enter into the throne room of God today in prayer, because of the finished work of Jesus Christ on the cross. Not only is Jesus Christ our sacrifice for sin, but He is also our High Priest who took His own precious blood into the true Holy of Holies, to God Himself in heaven. The moment that Jesus died on the cross, the veil of the temple, which separated the Holy Place from the Holy of Holies (just as it did in the tabernacle), was torn in two, from top to bottom. That was God's dramatic way of saying the way is now open to every believer in Jesus to enter into the very presence of God. Unlike the tabernacle high priest who did his work of sprinkling the blood of the sacrifice on the mercy seat of the ark, and then left, not to return for another year, believers are invited to come boldly into the presence of God, and to abide there, as it were, in the Holy of Holies.

The Holy of Holies was radiant with the Shekinah glory of God. The rest of the tabernacle was built around this room. Indeed, the cloud by day and the pillar of fire by night rested over this room. Within this room was housed just one piece of tabernacle furniture, albeit, the most important one: the ark of the covenant. In that ark, we see the source of that awesome provision experienced in the Holy Place. It is all summed up in the ark of the covenant.

The Ark of the Covenant

When God told Moses that He wanted them to build a tabernacle, He began with the ark of the covenant because the tabernacle was built around it. The first instructions given were those regarding the ark, the box which held the Ten Commandments.

> "They shall construct an ark of acacia wood two and a half cubits long, and one and a half cubits wide, and one and a half cubits high. You shall overlay it with pure gold, inside and out you shall overlay it, and you shall make a gold molding around it. You shall cast four gold rings for it and fasten them on its four feet, and two rings shall be on one side of it and two rings on the other side of it. You shall make poles of acacia wood and overlay them with gold. You shall put the poles into the rings on the sides of the ark, to carry the ark with them. The poles shall remain in the rings of the ark; they shall not be removed from it. You shall put into the ark the testimony which I shall give you.
>
> "You shall make a mercy seat of pure gold, two and a half cubits long and one and a half cubits wide. You shall make two cherubim of gold, make them of hammered work at the two ends of the mercy seat. Make one cherub at one end and one cherub at the other end; you shall make the cherubim of one piece with the mercy seat at its two ends. The cherubim shall have their wings spread upward, covering the mercy seat with their wings and facing one another; the faces of the cherubim are to be turned toward the mercy seat. You shall put the mercy seat on top of the ark, and in the ark you shall put the testimony which I will give to you. There I will meet with you; and from above the mercy seat, from between the two cherubim which are upon the ark of the testimony, I will speak to you about all that I will give you in commandment for the sons of Israel." (Exodus 25:10-22)

On the Day of Atonement, the one day each year that he was commanded to enter that inner room, the high priest was literally walking into the very presence of God, where His glory dwelt. It is like the Lord was saying, "When you come into the tabernacle, and into the Holy of Holies, You are really coming to Me."

As believers, we do not go into the spiritual tabernacle of His presence just to get the goodies God has to pass out. We go into the tabernacle to come to Him. Notice what He said in Exodus 25:22.

> "There I will meet with you; and from above the mercy seat, from between the two cherubim which are upon the ark of the testimony, I will speak to you ..."

The Holy of Holies was the meeting place between God and man. The glory and wonder of it is, as explained by the very design of the tabernacle, that Jesus has opened the way for us to freely enter that place at any time.

Now, consider the ark itself. The ark was two and a half cubits long, one and a half cubits wide, and one and a half cubits high. It was approximately 3.5 feet long, 2 feet high, and 2 feet wide. Like other pieces in the tabernacle, it was made of acacia wood, that old desert scrub tree, and was completely covered with pure gold. The lid was simply called "the mercy seat." The ark had two cherubim (angels) on it, one on each end of the lid. The cherubim and the lid were made of one piece of hammered gold, and the cherubim were facing toward the mercy seat with their wings outstretched over it. It was there that God told the Israelites He would dwell in their midst.

Virtually everything about the ark represents Jesus Christ and what he means to us. To go to the very throne of God is to see Jesus.

The ark itself, made of acacia wood covered with gold, as we have seen before, is clearly and simply Jesus Christ, wholly God (the gold) who became a man (the wood) for us. What was in the ark, under the mercy seat, is very enlightening. Three items were kept in the ark: the original Ten Commandments on tablets of stone, a golden jar of manna, and Aaron's rod that had budded.

The Law Fulfilled

Exodus 25:16 tells us that the stone tablets of the Ten Commandments were placed in the ark, which represents Jesus. That means those Ten Commandments, the law of God, are now hidden in Christ. Jesus Christ has fulfilled the law for us.

Jesus acknowledged that in Matthew 5:17, when He said:

> "Do not think that I came to abolish the Law or the Prophets; I did not come to abolish but to fulfill."

The law could not do anything for us but point out our guiltiness before God. To paraphrase Romans chapter 7 we could say, you know the law is good. You know the law is right. You know the law is righteous. There is nothing wrong with the law. The problem is in me, because the law points the finger right at me and nails me every time. The law looks at me and tells me I am dead, but Jesus has stepped in on my behalf. Jesus died for me.

Paul says in Galatians 3:13:

> **Christ redeemed us from the curse of the Law, having become a curse for us—for it is written, "Cursed is everyone who hangs on a tree"—**

Jesus took our place, so, consequently, the righteous demands of the law have been fulfilled in Christ for us. That is the key. When Jesus said, "I did not come to abolish the law, but to fulfill it," He did not just mean He would live a perfect life in perfect obedience to the law, and thus fulfill the demands of the law in His own life. He also meant that in His death He would fulfill the demands of the law for us. He would take our death penalty upon Himself, and the requirements of the law would be fulfilled and satisfied on our behalf in Jesus Christ. He came and took our place.

To nail that point down, once a year the high priest would go in to the Holy of Holies with the blood from the sacrifice and sprinkle it on the mercy seat. The blood was shed for the sins of many. This will become evident in the next chapter as we look at Yom Kippur, the Day of Atonement.

So the law of God, the only thing that can condemn, is hidden in Christ under the blood. We are safe and secure in Him.

This reminds me of a story of Martin Luther. He was having a tough day. The enemy was needling him for all his shortcomings, his weaknesses, his sinfulness, and the sins which so easily beset him. He was feeling miserable. So, finally, he sat down at his table with pen in hand and said (and I paraphrase), "Okay, Satan, lay it on me. What is wrong with me?" As things started coming to his mind, he wrote them down until he had a list of every sin that he could think of. He looked at it, not believing the list to be complete yet, so he said, "Come on. Surely there must be more!" Sure enough, more sins started coming to his mind, so he added those to his lengthy list of sins. Finally, he couldn't think of any more ways that he had failed, of any more character flaws or other shortcomings in his life and walk. So, at that point, he wrote right over that list, "The blood of Jesus Christ cleanses me from all sin." He was free.

Consequently, the law has no more authority over us. In Christ, we are free from the requirements and demands of the law. It holds no more authority over believers, at all.

In Romans chapter 7, Paul likens the authority of the law to being married to a husband. As long as that husband is alive you are under his authority. But when he is dead, you are free from that authority. You are free to marry another husband. He says that we were married to and under the authority of the law, but in Jesus Christ the law died to us, and now you are free to be married to Jesus. You are free from the demands of the law.

> **Therefore, my brethren, you also were made to die to the Law through the body of Christ, so that you might be joined to another, to Him who was raised from the dead, in order that we might bear fruit for God.** (Romans 7:4)

> **But now we have been released from the Law, having died to that by which we were bound, so that we serve in newness of the Spirit and not in oldness of the letter.** (Romans 7:6)

Believers are free. The old stone Ten Commandments were inside the ark of the covenant, under the mercy seat, and the blood was sprinkled on the mercy seat for its coup de grace. We are free from the law. Christ in me is the fulfillment of all the righteous demands of the law in me.

> **Therefore there is now no condemnation for those who are in Christ Jesus.** (Romans 8:1)

> **Therefore no one is to act as your judge in regard to food or drink or in respect to a festival or a new moon or a Sabbath day—things which are a mere shadow of what is to come; but the substance belongs to Christ.** (Colossians 2:16-17)

Paul tells us in Colossians not to let anyone judge us in relation to anything regarding the law, because we have been set free from it. Those laws were simply the shadow of things to come. Jesus, Himself, is the fulfillment of that law. If you have a relationship with Jesus today, do not give up the freedom of that relationship to be bound to the laws and ordinances of man, including the Old Testament law of God. Jesus has completely fulfilled and satisfied all the demands and requirements of the law for us. It is forever tucked away under the mercy seat, satisfied in Jesus Christ.

Manna From Heaven

Hebrews 9:4 tells us of the other items which were kept in the ark:

> ... and the ark of the covenant covered on all sides with gold, in which was a golden jar holding the manna, and Aaron's rod which budded, and the tables of the covenant ... (Hebrews 9:4)

This jar of manna symbolically is a similarity to, yet is different from, the bread which was out on the table in the Holy Place. In the book of John, Jesus told the people around Him and His disciples that the manna was actually a picture of Him.

> So they said to Him, "What then do You do for a sign, so that we may see, and believe You? What work do You perform? Our fathers ate the manna in the wilderness; as it is written, 'HE GAVE THEM BREAD OUT OF HEAVEN TO EAT.' " Jesus then said to them, "Truly, truly, I say to you, it is not Moses who has given you the bread out of heaven, but it is My Father who gives you the true bread out of heaven. For the bread of God is that which comes down out of heaven, and gives life to the world." Then they said to Him, "Lord, always give us this bread." Jesus said to them, "I am the bread of life; he who comes to Me will not hunger, and he who believes in Me will never thirst. (John 6:30-35)

> "I am the bread of life." (John 6:48)

> "Your fathers ate the manna in the wilderness, and they died. This is the bread which comes down out of heaven, so that one may eat of it and not die. I am the living bread that came down out of heaven; if anyone

> eats of this bread, he will live forever; and the bread also which I will give for the life of the world is My flesh."
> (John 6:49-51)

It is at the ark that we discover that fullness of life does not come just from what Jesus provides for us, but that He Himself is our provision.

Years ago, when I was pastoring a different church, the children would sit in the service with the adults until I gave a children's talk. Afterward, we would dismiss the children to go to their Sunday School classes and then I would give a sermon to the adults. One story I told the kids was a story called "The Gully."

"The Gully" story was about a little six-year-old boy named Johnny who lived in Scotland. His parents lived on a farm, a long way from his school. In fact, his home was so far from school that he would walk to the school on Sunday afternoon, spend the week at the boarding school, and then walk home on Friday afternoon. His parents had walked to school with this little boy so he knew how to get there. One day, the time had come for him to go off to school for the week on his own. His mom and dad told him they would really miss him while he was gone for the week, as they handed him the things his mom had packed for him to take to school. His dad said to little Johnny, "Now, we want you to come home *right* after school on Friday. Don't wait until Saturday morning to come back, as some of the other children may do. Come home directly after school dismisses on Friday, Johnny."

Johnny did not *want* to come home Friday afternoon because of a place known as "the gully," which was right between school and his house. Every little kid in that area knew that at night when it got dark, "the gully" was haunted. They just knew there were monsters in that gully that came out at night. Johnny knew that, rush as he might, he would probably hit the gully around dusk, maybe even a little after dark, and he did *not* want to go through that gully alone when it was shadowy, much less dark. So he asked if he could please come home on Saturday morning instead. But his parents insisted he had to come home Friday afternoon.

Johnny worried about the gully all week long. In fact, it was difficult to think of much else. So, Friday afternoon, as soon as school was over, he gathered his stuff and raced for home, hoping against hope that he would hit the gully while it was still light. Even though he was traveling as fast as his little legs would carry him, the sun was going down fast, and by the time he came to the edge of the gully there was hardly any light left in the sky. He looked down into that dark place and it looked like a thousand midnights. It was black down there as he stood on the edge of the gully building up the nerve to go through it; fear was gripping his heart. Suddenly, the worst of his fears began to be realized. He heard a noise in the gully. "Maybe I just *thought* it was a noise," Johnny thought. "Maybe I imagined it." Still, he waited to find out, frozen where he stood. There it was again, only louder this time! It was real, all right! There was *something* in that gully and he could tell by the sound, it was *big*. He didn't know what to do. He was too afraid to go forward or backward, to even move at all. He just stood there at the edge of the gully, frozen in utter terror.

Again he noticed movement, heard more noise, and then . . . "Johnny, is that you?"

It was his dad. Phew! His father walked up to him and said, "Come on, I wanted to walk the rest of the way home with you."

"Oh, thanks, dad!" He took his father's arm, and marched through that gully with no more fear. He almost dared any monster to try to come out because he was with dad.

That is the way God goes through life with us. He is there for us. He is our provision, if we would only realize it. The light, the bread, and the golden altar of incense are all encompassed in what He has for you, but what He has for you is not the heart of it. The heart of it is He Himself.

The first church I pastored was in Los Angeles. It was a small congregation made up primarily of great-grandparents, about forty elderly people, and only two young couples. One fellow, Dave, who was in his early thirties, had a little boy named Todd who was about four years old.

The bathroom in the church was upstairs. In the men's room, there was an outer door, a space, and then an inner door. There were separate light switches at each door, one for the entry space to the bathroom and one for the bathroom itself. One day, Dave had to take his son, Todd, to the men's room. When they got into that little space between the hall and the bathroom, he flipped off the light. There were no windows in that little space, so it became pitch black. Then Dave started making wailing sounds to try to scare his son. But Todd didn't make a peep; he just stood there silently. So, Dave asked, "Todd, are you there?"

"Yes, Daddy."

"Are you scared?"

"No, Daddy."

"Why not?"

"Because you're here, Daddy." It was an honest answer from a son who trusted his father completely.

That is exactly the way your God wants you to feel as you go through the dark valleys of life. It is okay. As David said in Psalm 23:4:

> **Even though I walk through the valley of the shadow of death, I fear no evil, for You are with me; Your rod and Your staff, they comfort me.**

That golden jar of manna is that picture of the sustenance of God's presence. He is our provision. And what a perfect provision that manna was.

> **When they measured it with an omer, he who had gathered much had no excess, and he who had gathered little had no lack; every man gathered as much as he should eat.** (Exodus 16:18)

That manna was always sufficient. The provision was not based on their ability to gather manna, but it was based on the graciousness of God to supply it. It was always a sufficient and satisfying provision.

> **The house of Israel named it manna, and it was like coriander seed, white, and its taste was like wafers with honey.** (Exodus 16:31)

Manna was like coriander seed. It was white and tasted like wafers with honey. It was pleasing to the taste. Just as the provision of Jesus Himself to us is not only sufficient and sustaining, but He is, at the same time, very satisfying.

> **O taste and see that the LORD is good.** (Psalm 34:8)

> **The sons of Israel ate the manna forty years, until they came to an inhabited land; they ate the manna until they**

came to the border of the land of Canaan. (Exodus 16: 35)

Throughout the forty years in the wilderness, the manna was faithfully there for the Israelites. Similarly, Jesus is with us, every single moment of every single day through our earthly sojourn, right until the moment we are ushered into His glorious presence. There is manna for the journey in Him. Indeed, He *is* our manna.

The manna in the ark was kept in a golden jar. Gold, of course, is a symbol of the deity of God. This provision comes through the Holy Spirit, through God Himself. Paul spoke of this in Romans 14:17:

> ... for the kingdom of God is not eating and drinking, but righteousness and peace and joy in the Holy Spirit.

The manna was in the golden jar. It represented that righteousness, peace, and joy that is in the Holy Spirit. Who is our righteousness? Jesus Christ. Whose peace and joy have we been promised? The supernatural, unfailing peace and joy of Jesus Christ.

> "Peace I leave with you; My peace I give to you; not as the world gives do I give to you. Do not let your heart be troubled, nor let it be fearful." (Jesus in John 14:27)

> "These things I have spoken to you so that My joy may be in you, and that your joy may be made full." (Jesus in John 15:11)

Everything we need for the journey is found in Jesus and is available to us through the Holy Spirit who has been "given to us" (Romans 5:5).

Aaron's Rod

The third item in the ark was Aaron's rod that had budded. In Numbers chapter 17, we have recounted for us the story of Aaron's rod. Korah and his men rebelled against Moses and Aaron. They questioned why Moses should lead the people and why Aaron should be the high priest. Korah and his men felt they were just as qualified to lead as Moses and Aaron.

The longer I am in the ministry, the more I believe there may have been an element of truth in what they said, strictly from a worldly perspective, that is. Maybe Korah was more eloquent than Moses, who knows. But I can look around me and wonder why the Lord called *me* to be the pastor of Calvary Chapel of Truckee. There are men in my church who are every bit as capable in so many ways. Why am I the pastor of this church? It is simply the appointment of God.

In the same way, I can look at God blessing another person's ministry and wonder why God is blessing their ministry that way and He is not blessing mine in the same way. Compare, compare, compare. To ask this question is to have the heart of Korah, a heart of rebellion. Why not me, Lord? Why them?

My point is that God puts us all in a different place, on a different walk. When things happen to us, we may look around and wonder why God is blessing someone else one way when He is not blessing us in that same way. When we are committed to following Him and bad things are happening to us and not to someone else, it's easy to ask why.

I have six children, all of whom are now grown and living life apart from mom and dad. My two youngest children, Tim and Dave, both knew the Lord from an early age. But I always called Tim "my spirit-filled son." Of all my kids, he has had such a heart for the Lord since earliest childhood. He is just unique in that way. I long suspected that he would end up in full-time ministry someday, and I'm proud to say that he is serving as my assistant pastor here in Truckee. God has a special anointing on that man to teach the Word of God which started to show itself at a very early age. His heart has always been tender toward the Lord.

While he was growing up, though, Tim was also a strong, buff young man, and he was a very good athlete. Everyone in our family was sure that of all the kids, Tim would be the athlete. His brother Dave, who is three years younger than Tim, was more interested in bugs and snakes when Tim started playing ball. Tim played sports all the way through school: basketball, football, baseball, and soccer—and he was outstanding at all of them. Football was probably his best sport. As a sophomore in high school, he was starting running back on the offense, and safety on the defense. He was on the kickoff team, the kick receiving team, the punting team, and the punt return team. He was in what they called the "iron man" position.

Hopes were high for Tim to be the star of the local team, which has long enjoyed a winning tradition, often taking the Nevada State Championship (even though we live in California, our school is in the Nevada league). In fact, Tim was featured in the local newspaper pre-season; our town was told to keep an eye on Tim Larson.

In the first scrimmage of the season, he took a handoff. That very first time he got his hands on the ball, he ran for about 30 yards, was tackled, and his arm was broken in half. He looked down to see his arm going off in a different direction. He said he heard it pop on his way down. It felt to him like he had lost his arm. He thought if he could look back down the field, he might see his arm lying on the 20-yard line. After the players peeled off of him, Tim set his arm back into place, sort of. The team's most promising player was out for the season.

After a year of recuperating, he went back to school during his junior year ready to pick up where he left off. He had been in training and he was looking forward to a great season, with much of the same team returning that had won the state championship the year before. The coach was really excited to see him return.

During the summer, the team did a seven-on-seven competition in preparation for football season. It was a touch game, no tackling. Even so, the first time he got his hands on the ball he blew out the ACL in his knee, and he was again out for the entire season. I got to the scrimmage just shortly after it started. I looked around the field for Tim, only to find him sitting on the sideline with ice on his knee. He cried as I drove him home, but he also started singing a praise song. He was singing softly to himself a song of thanksgiving to the Lord for all the things He brings into our lives. I was amazed to hear it, knowing that his season had ended before it began, again.

During his senior year, Tim went back to play football again, back to the scene of the crime, if you will. This time, during a pre-season game, he did not get injured *too* badly. He was playing defense when he blocked a pass, fell down, and crunched his hand. It was swollen to the point where he could hardly use it. He was injured, but it certainly didn't mean he couldn't return soon and play.

But the next thing I knew, Tim told me he was not going to play football at all that year, his senior year. When I asked him why he decided not to play, he told me he had said a prayer on the way down to play in that pre-season competition. He had prayed, "Lord, if You really don't want me to play football, You don't need to give me a season-ending injury this year. Just a little injury will tell me You don't want me to play football." And that is exactly what happened. His injury was a little one, but it was big enough that he took it as a sign from God, and he left sports. He could not understand why God did not want him to play football, but he trusted that God had something else for him.

Now David, our youngest child, who at first was more interested in bugs than sports, has turned out to be quite an athlete himself. He is even better than Tim. He ripped up every sport in high school, ending his senior season as first-team All-State Nevada on offense and defense and playing on the state-championship-winning football team. He was an exceptional high school basketball and baseball player as well, winning MVP honors in both sports, and is now preparing to play football in college in southern California.

I often think about how easy it would have been for Tim, who has had such a heart for the Lord, to look at David and say, "God, why is this happening?" David is MVP this, MVP that, makes the All Stars, bats in the clean up position, all that kind of stuff. It would have been so easy for Tim to wonder what was going on. But all I have ever seen from Tim is support for his little brother. It amazes me.

As a believer, do not start thinking that someone else is succeeding in an area that you think you should be because that person is living a more righteous or better life. Don't start thinking that someone else's ministry for God is being blessed more abundantly because he must be more "in tune with God." If you are sincere in your faith in Jesus Christ, endeavoring to walk by faith in Him, that is simply not true. Brethren, all fruit is born of grace, not merit. It is all about grace.

God has you on the path you are on right now because there is something He wants to do in your life and in eternity for which He is preparing you. God has plans for you for eternity. Believe it or not, the path He has you on now is preparing you for that. That is such an awesome thought! You are not just living for right now. Maybe you are living through something that will benefit you 10,000 years down the road, earth time.

You may look at someone who seems to be floating through life on a bed of roses. Believe me, if he is a Christian, God has got His own way of dealing with him, and He is doing what He needs to do in his life to prepare him for his own place in eternity.

It is like Jesus told Peter, when Peter looked at John and asked, "What about him?" Jesus told Peter, "If I want him to hang around until I come back, that's not your business. You feed my sheep" (John 21:15-22).

God called me into the ministry, raised me up to proclaim His gospel, and stuck me, of all places, in Truckee, California. I was from the Los Angeles area, where all the "action" is, where the greatest needs are because that is where the most people are in this corner of the world. Yet God plucked me up and put me in a little mountain resort town of about 10,000 people. At first I thought I might be here about five years, but I have been in snowy little Truckee for about thirty years now, proclaiming the gospel to a group of people that comes and goes. I lovingly refer to our church as Calvary Chapel of the Revolving Doors. People come in, say "hi," get tired of the snow (this *is* where the Donner Party was stranded in the nineteenth century, after all), and then they leave.

Now I could sit here and try to figure that one out until I am blue in the face. I could tell myself that I must really be a bad pastor because God had to put me someplace where He knew I would stay out of trouble. But that is not my concern. Jesus has said to me in many different ways, "What is that to you? If I want to raise up Chuck Smith and bless his ministry, that is not your concern. Brian, you just feed my sheep."

Back to the rod. I was telling you the story of Aaron's rod, which happened when Korah and his buddies believed they were just as good as Moses and Aaron, and that they could lead the people instead. But, as we've seen, our ministry has nothing to do with our merit, but the sovereign appointment of God. The wisest thing Korah and his guys could have done was to respect God's choice, as my son Tim did, and just be what God called them to be.

To deal with this situation, Moses did what he was in the wise habit of doing when there was trouble in the camp. He went crying to God. He would go flat on his face before God and ask, "What should I do? *Help!*" That was the perfect thing to do because God did tell him. The Lord told Moses that the elder of each tribe should bring to Moses his own rod and let God show them, through the rods, whom He had chosen. So Moses took the twelve rods, one from the elder of each tribe, Aaron being the elder of the tribe of Levi, and set them before the Lord in the tabernacle. The next day Moses went into the tabernacle, picked up the rods, and brought them out to the elders. Each elder knew his own rod. All of the rods remained the same, nothing more than long, dead sticks, except for Aaron's rod. His rod, which was an almond branch, had leafed, budded, blossomed, and there were ripe almonds hanging on it (Numbers 17:1-10). Aaron's rod was placed inside the ark of the covenant as a reminder of this event.

What exactly happened to that rod? First, it was resurrected from the dead. This is the primary reason why, in the Bible, the almond pictures resurrection. The rod is also a symbol of the guiding of the Lord. **"Your rod and Your staff, they comfort me"** (Psalm 23:4). The rod symbolizes the shepherd's guidance. So this rod of Aaron's was simply a picture of our risen Lord, our risen living Savior, who is our faithful guide. He guides us, not only through life, but through the porthole of death into eternity. He has gone there before us. He is the perfectly trustworthy One. He knows the way. Indeed, He made the way for us, past death into fullness of life. He will lead us from here with His faithful, guiding hand. We will experience it in its fullness as we go through that place we call physical death into His eternal presence. He is our faithful guide.

I remember hearing a story about a missionary who was being led by a native guide into the back country of Africa. They came to a huge, seemingly impassable marshy bog. The missionary figured they would have to take an extra day to go around it, but the guide said, "It is okay. I know the way across." It was marshy, but there were clumps of grass all over it. The guide told the missionary, just before they crossed, to follow *exactly* in his steps, to step *only* on the clumps that he stepped on. For the next couple of hours, they followed a circuitous route from clump to clump across this big marshy area, but this missionary did exactly what his guide said. He stepped exactly where the guide stepped and they crossed without incident. When they got across, the missionary asked why he had to step just where the guide stepped. The guide explained that most of the clumps had no roots to them, they were not attached to the ground, they were just floating on quicksand. One step on the wrong clump would have been disastrous. It was impossible for the missionary to tell the difference with a casual glance, but the guide knew exactly which ones were solid.

Such is life. We have so many different options and opportunities. But Jesus knows the way. He is the way. There may be another way that looks okay to natural man, but, as Proverbs puts it, it is the way of death (Proverbs 14:12). If you follow Jesus, He will lead you safely through this life. David calls it **"the way everlasting"** (Psalm 139:24, KJV).

So what we have in Christ, as represented in the ark of the covenant, is the absolute assurance in Him that when we have Jesus, we know the law of God has been satisfied in every way for us. It is a settled issue. We have union with Him. He is our provision. Everything else is simply icing on the cake. To top it off, I have an absolutely faithful guide, right now and into eternity future.

These three items, the Ten Commandments, the golden jar of manna, and Aaron's rod were right under the mercy seat. They represent what Jesus Christ means to us. And He is faithfully all of these things, as a loving extension of His mercy to us.

> **Therefore there is now no condemnation for those who are in Christ Jesus.** (Romans 8:1)

> **Therefore let us draw near with confidence to the throne of grace, so that we may receive mercy and find grace to help in time of need.** (Hebrews 4:16)

We find help when we come to Him. We often have a tendency, however, when we need His help the most, to cower away from Him in a sense of unworthiness. That is sort of like Adam and Eve when they had fallen. They went and hid in the garden. Instead of running to Him, they ran away from Him.

But the Lord says, by everything on the ark, and everything in it, that this is the place of help. It is the seat of mercy and it is the place of grace. Mercy is the passive aspect, and grace is the active aspect of God's lovingkindness to you. God does not strike you with lightning. He does not come and fry you. That is mercy. He is there to help you, guide you, and direct you into fullness of life. That is grace.

So when you come to Him, you are not going to get what you really deserve. (I *never* pray for God to give me what I deserve, do you?) You can bank on His mercy. In addition, you *will* get what you *do not* deserve. That is His grace.

Those times when I have felt the most unworthy, God has often used me the most powerfully. Then, sometimes when I feel like I am clean and ready to be used, I will have a spiritually flat experience. That is because all that He has for us is under that mercy seat. It is His mercy and His grace that create my usefulness—it has nothing to do with my merit.

In the Holy Place, in that place of fellowship with the Lord, we see that marvelous provision from the Lord: that supernatural light, the golden menorah; that supernatural provision, the bread on the golden table; and that place of power in prayer, the golden altar of incense. We do not deserve it, so it is easy to worry that His provision might not last. We wonder if what He has for us will be there when we really need it. We wonder how we can even expect His grace and His mercy because we feel so unworthy.

When that happens to you, simply enter into the Holy of Holies of His very presence, and see the ark of the covenant. There, at the mercy seat, you will hear the Lord assure you that, "Yes, I will always be there, every day, every moment, regardless."

> "... and lo, I am with you always, even to the end of the age." (Matthew 28:20b)

> "I will never desert you, nor will I ever forsake you." (Hebrews 13:5b)

If, on occasion, you feel a little separated from God, like you are languishing in the courtyard rather than fellowshipping in the "tent of meeting," just use the laver. Confess your sin, accept His forgiveness, and then come on back inside the tent. March right into the Holy Place, which now includes the Holy of Holies because the veil separating them is gone.

As we see from the pictures given to us in the tabernacle, our sinfulness is no longer the central issue in our relationship with God. We have been set free from the law of sin and death. The main focus of the tabernacle is to know Him and to abide with Him by faith in His grace to us. The tabernacle cries out that God is inviting us to rest in His presence as His beloved, to accept His provision as a free gift of His grace. That is exactly what we do as we abide day by day, moment by moment, in the spiritual Holy of Holies—the very throne room of God (Ephesians 1:3).

Chapter Sixteen

The Day of Atonement

But when Christ appeared as a high priest of the good things to come, He entered through the greater and more perfect tabernacle, not made with hands, that is to say, not of this creation; and not through the blood of goats and calves, but through His own blood, He entered the holy place once for all, having obtained eternal redemption.

Hebrews 9:11-12

The most holy day for ancient Israel was Yom Kippur, the Day of Atonement. On that day, everything the tabernacle symbolizes in pictures was acted out before the people. The purpose, the meaning, and the victory that was won at the cross was prophetically acted out on the Day of Atonement. There is also a life application for believers pictured for us in the events of that special day.

The enemy, Satan, with all his might, all his power, and all his weapons cannot destroy a believer. Do you realize that? The best he can do is to attempt to nullify a believer's effectiveness. I think one of the primary weapons in his arsenal is encapsulated in that old word we call "discouragement."

Many times I have counseled with a Christian and discovered that the crux of that believer's problem was not a result of anything going on in his life, nor was it caused by anyone else. The problem was that believer's own attitude. He was just discouraged, depressed, downhearted.

Years ago, a team of four horses were hitched to a sled to pull logs which had been cut down in the forest. The loggers put so many logs on this one load that it was too heavy for the horses to pull. They coaxed the horses and whipped them, but they could not get them to budge that load of logs. They lightened the load by taking a log or two off, and the horses strained but they just could not budge it. Finally, they took half the load off, which should have made it an easy load for the horses to pull. But the horses would not move the load, or anything else for that matter. They literally had to unhitch the horses and remove them entirely from the load. The horses had been overwhelmed. They had been, in their own way, discouraged trying to pull that load, and had completely given up.

We as believers can be so like that. When things come to attack our lives and our sense of well being we can get so discouraged that we end up putting ourselves on the shelf and we will not attempt something for the Lord simply because of that discouragement. I am convinced that is one of the enemy's primary weapons against the body of Christ.

Now, look at the tabernacle with that in mind. The tabernacle is about your relationship with the Lord, a victorious relationship in the Lord. There was absolutely nothing within that tabernacle that addressed your personal abilities. It was entirely about Jesus Christ. Every part of it echoes Christ.

Donald Barnhouse put why God uses us this way: "It is not because there is good in us, but because there was grace in Him."

I have heard Chuck Smith tell about his experiences pastoring in Arizona before moving to Costa Mesa to pastor Calvary Chapel. Often he would spend two or three days in prayer and fasting in the desert, beseeching God to bless his ministry. On his return, although tired and weary, he would expect marvelous things to happen; however, they were worse than they were before he fasted and prayed. His error was in thinking that because he was being "good," because he would bask in prayer for days before the Lord, everything would improve; yet the ministry would seem worse than it had been before. The message that God was pressing into him was that it was not in any way by his efforts or his holiness, but it was purely and solely by the grace of God that God would bless him and work through him.

That is the cry of the tabernacle. May God reveal to us how much that occasional debilitating discouragement is caused by simply not resting in the fact that all good things come purely and solely by the grace of God. It is so important that we understand that as believers. The tabernacle in the Old Testament was designed so that point could be driven home to us.

> **For by grace you have been saved through faith; and that not of yourselves, it is the gift of God; not as a result of works, so that no one may boast.** (Ephesians 2:8-9)

God's grace is what the tabernacle was all about. Every detail of the tabernacle in the wilderness cries out that truth. On the Day of Atonement, God put it all together in one annual solemn event which the Jews call Yom Kippur. God used this most holy of holidays to remind us of the basis of our standing with God. In so doing he drew a prophetic picture for Israel, because this was the national Day of Atonement for sin, the day God declared His love and acceptance of Israel as a nation.

We find this information in Leviticus 16. The Day of Atonement was the day that the high priest entered into the Holy of Holies with the blood of the sacrifice to bring it before the throne of God to make atonement for the sins of the nation. Now, as we study this, remember the high priest is a picture of Jesus Christ, our great High Priest. The

Holy of Holies is a picture of the throne room in the very presence of God.

As we look at this day, we will focus on certain highlights of things that took place on the Day of Atonement to get an overall view from this passage of what was done and what it means to us spiritually.

1. Aaron laid aside his beautiful high priestly garments to become a servant for His people.

> The LORD said to Moses: "Tell your brother Aaron that he shall not enter at any time into the holy place inside the veil, before the mercy seat which is on the ark, or he will die; for I will appear in the cloud over the mercy seat. Aaron shall enter the holy place with this: with a bull for a sin offering and a ram for a burnt offering. He shall put on the holy linen tunic, and the linen undergarments shall be next to his body, and he shall be girded with the linen sash and attired with the linen turban (these are holy garments). Then he shall bathe his body in water and put them on. (Leviticus 16:2-4)

Aaron, as the high priest, could not just go tripping into the Holy of Holies at any time. No one was allowed into the Holy of Holies, with one exception: once a year, as high priest, Aaron was required to go into the Holy of Holies for a specific purpose.

On this particular day, in order to do this particular task, he laid aside those special garments of the high priest: the blue robe, the ephod, the breastplate, the gold crown, and all he wore was the white linen tunic. That is interesting because in Philippians 2:6-7 we are told regarding our Lord:

> ... who, although He existed in the form of God, did not regard equality with God a thing to be grasped, but emptied Himself, taking the form of a bond-servant, and being made in the likeness of men. (Philippians 2: 6-7)

Jesus set aside His heavenly beauty and glory and came as a man and He came to be a servant. That whole picture of service is so evident in what the high priest wore on the Day of Atonement.

The high priest was dressed in all white, which symbolized the purity of Jesus, who was still holy and still righteous with that perfect sinless nature.

> **For we do not have a high priest who cannot sympathize with our weaknesses, but One who has been tempted in all things as we are, yet without sin.** (Hebrews 4:15)

But in coming to earth to bring atonement for sin, Jesus laid aside the beautiful garments of his heavenly glory to become a servant for His people.

2. Aaron did his job completely alone.
Leviticus 16:17 says:

> **When he goes in to make atonement in the holy place, no one shall be in the tent of meeting until he comes out, that he may make atonement for himself and for his household and for all the assembly of Israel.**

The high priest did his job completely alone. What a picture of our Lord Jesus who told His disciples on the night before the crucifixion, that even they would flee from Him. This was a suffering that He would have to bear all by Himself. The sacrifice for sin was made utterly alone. We cannot even comprehend that aspect of it. As He was taken prisoner, those men, who were His dearest earthly friends, deserted Him. Of course, He was in perfect oneness with His Heavenly Father, but then, as He hung on the cross to bear the sin of the world, He cried out in Matthew 27:46: **"My God, My God, why have You forsaken Me?"** The emphasis is on **"You."** Why have *You* forsaken Me? There, suspended between heaven and earth, on a Roman cross, bearing the sin of the world, He was fully alone. And because of that sacrifice, we will never ever have to be alone.

On the Day of Atonement, the people watched and waited. The solemn duty of the high priest was to go in alone. This was the day he would go into the Holy of Holies, to bring the blood of the atonement into the presence of God. The people waited because the forgiveness of God, their acceptance and their standing before Him was going to be made on that day through this man, or they would not have it at all. That is why they liked their high priest so much, because he was their hope before God. In fact, he was their only hope. He was the one that would go in on that day to square the account with God for the people, just as Jesus did, all alone, at Calvary for us.

3. As far as the people were concerned, their atonement centered around two goats. How the high priest squared their account with God on that day is very unique and beautiful.

> He shall take from the congregation of the sons of Israel two male goats for a sin offering and one ram for a burnt offering. Then Aaron shall offer the bull for the sin offering which is for himself, that he may make atonement for himself and for his household. He shall take the two goats and present them before the Lord at the doorway of the tent of meeting. Aaron shall cast lots for the two goats, one lot for the Lord and the other lot for the scapegoat. (Leviticus 16:5-8)

There were the two goats, plus a ram for the burnt offering, and the bull for his offering. (The burnt offering and the bull for his offering were standard procedure, not specifically reserved for the Day of Atonement.) The two goats were especially for this occasion. They spoke directly to what was happening for the nation of Israel. Lots were cast. One goat would be killed as a sacrifice; the other would become the **"scapegoat."**

> Then Aaron shall offer the goat on which the lot for the Lord fell, and make it a sin offering. (Leviticus 16:9)

> Then he shall slaughter the goat of the sin offering which is for the people, and bring its blood inside the veil and do with its blood as he did with the blood of the bull, and sprinkle it on the mercy seat and in front of the mercy seat. (Leviticus 16:15)

The blood of the bull had already been applied to cover the sins of the high priest. Then, the high priest took the blood of the sacrificial goat into the Holy of Holies, and there he sprinkled the blood seven times before and on the mercy seat for the atonement for the sins of the people of the nation. So the high priest was acting as an intermediary at that point for all the people.

The blood was sprinkled seven times. That is the number of perfection, the number of absolute and total completion. This reminds me of a story that will give you an appreciation of the number seven. About a hundred years ago, there was quite an accomplished mathematician named Ivan Panin. He was a Harvard professor of mathematics and a devoted Christian. He knew that in Bible times, even in the times of the New Testament, they had not developed or put in use numbers as we know them today. Roman numerals were just coming out, but the Hebrews and Greeks were not privy to Roman numerals at that point. Of course, in the Old Testament, they did not have any numbers at all.

So how did they do basic math? They did them with letters. Each letter had a numeric value. There were twenty-four letters in the Hebrew alphabet, so the first letter had the numeric value of one. The twenty-fourth letter has the numeric value of twenty-four. That is the way they did their math. The context of the letter determined if it was being used to refer to a number or to the letter of a word. The numbers in your Bible used that numeric code. The Greeks did the same thing. They applied numeric value to their letters in the same way.

Realizing this, Dr. Panin began to play around with the numeric value of the letters in the Bible. After playing around a little bit he was astounded to discover that there was a beautiful numeric design to the Bible as a whole. Every book was perfectly numerically complete. This is what he discovered: the key number was seven. He found it was possible to add up all the numeric values of all the letters in each book of the Bible and the total number was divisible by seven. If the numeric value of all the proper names were totaled, the sum would be divisible by seven. The total of the numeric value of all the places were divisible by seven. The numeric value of sections of the book was divisible by seven. The same exact design applied to the New Testament.

He did not have time to go through the whole Bible and do this, but he spot-checked all over the Bible and he found it to be perfect in every case. This book has an incredible design. Realizing that, he confirmed for himself that this book was supernaturally designed by God. If one jot or tittle of the book were removed, it would throw the design off. That is what Jesus said. Not one jot or tittle will pass away from the law until it was completely fulfilled. Every stroke of the pen is there by the inspiration and design of God.

This is interesting because when Panin worked on the last part of Mark, the part that some modern versions say should not be there, it fits perfectly into the numeric design of the Bible. To remove that section of Mark would throw off the whole design. This is only one aspect of research that points out the incredible design and inspiration of this book. In Scripture, seven is the number which stands for that which is perfect or complete. Panin discovered the more he got into the numeric design of the Bible the deeper it went.

So when Aaron sprinkled the blood seven times, it meant the sin issue was completely and perfectly satisfied. The righteous and holy God was satisfied perfectly. So when Jesus cried out from the cross, **"It is finished,"** that was the heart of what He was saying. The mission was accomplished. The sin of the world had been atoned for perfectly.

The high priest was separate from all the people until this task was finished. This was the job he had to do and everyone stood outside the tabernacle compound, gathered around, waiting for the high priest. No one could be in the tent of meeting, he had to do this alone.

This reminds me of when Jesus appeared to Mary and told her not to cling to Him or to touch Him because he had to go to His Father and her Father (John 20:17). It is possible that He was taking the fruit of that atonement, the blood of atonement, into the presence of God and presenting it to Him for the atonement of the world. He could not have contact with her. He had to be alone to finish that job which was completed on the day of the resurrection—just as the high priest could have no contact with anyone until His ministry of presenting the blood of the sacrifice before the ark in the Holy of Holies was completed.

So one goat was slain and the blood was taken into the Holy of Holies, which satisfied the sin issue. Now we have the other goat which was called the scapegoat.

> **But the goat on which the lot for the scapegoat fell shall be presented alive before the LORD, to make atonement upon it, to send it into the wilderness as the scapegoat.** (Leviticus 16:10)

> **When he finishes atoning for the holy place and the tent of meeting and the altar, he shall offer the live goat.**

> Then Aaron shall lay both of his hands on the head of the live goat, and confess over it all the iniquities of the sons of Israel and all their transgressions in regard to all their sins; and he shall lay them on the head of the goat and send it away into the wilderness by the hand of a man who stands in readiness. The goat shall bear on itself all their iniquities to a solitary land; and he shall release the goat in the wilderness. (Leviticus 16:20-22)

As the high priest laid his hands on this goat, confessing the sins of the nation in total, all the sins of the nation were transferred to that goat. That goat was then taken away, far out into the wilderness. It was released in a solitary place out in the desert, so far away that the goat would never find its way back. They did not want the scapegoat, which was bearing all their sins, coming back into camp after a while. He was forever gone. What a beautiful picture of the way the Lord has removed our sins from us. Jesus' atonement for our sins was so complete and so perfect, and the justice and holiness of God were so perfectly satisfied, that our sin, every bit of it, has been removed from us forever.

> **As far as the east is from the west, so far has He removed our transgressions from us.** (Psalm 103:12)

Not only is the sin issue completely covered, but my sins have been removed, so far away that they can never to be remembered again. I am so delivered from sin that it will probably take me the rest of my life to begin to get a feel and an idea of how free from sin I truly am. It was all accomplished by the work of Jesus at Calvary when He cried out, **"It is finished."** And then He went into the Holy of Holies, before the throne of God, and made that great atonement once and for all, and forever.

4. The high priest also burned incense before the ark.

> He shall take a firepan full of coals of fire from upon the altar before the LORD and two handfuls of finely ground sweet incense, and bring it inside the veil. He shall put the incense on the fire before the LORD, that the cloud of incense may cover the mercy seat that is on the ark of the testimony, otherwise he will die. (Leviticus 16:12-13)

Between the offering of the bull for his family's sin and the offering of the goat as the sin offering for the people, Aaron would take coals from the bronze altar in a handheld firepan, and two handfuls of incense and burn the incense on those coals in the Holy of Holies before the mercy seat on the ark. The smoke and sweet aroma would fill that room and "cover" the mercy seat.

The fragrant aroma burning on those coals picture the intercession of Jesus Christ Himself. It symbolizes, first and foremost, His intercession for us. It pictures His ultimate act of intercession, His shed blood on Calvary for the remission of our sins.

So in between the high priest's presentation of the blood, he burned the incense that produced a sweet smelling aroma before God. The burned incense was accepted as a sweet aroma to God as it symbolizes that ultimate act of intercession which Jesus accomplished at Calvary. The smoke "covered" and obscured the mercy seat as darkness covered and obscured man's view of Christ's sacrifice on Calvary.

So Jesus is now seated at the right hand of God at the throne (Ephesians 1:20). He is seated, that means the work is done, the effectiveness of that intercession is settled forever.

5. The high priest came out of the Holy of Holies in glory.

> **Then Aaron shall come into the tent of meeting and take off the linen garments which he put on when he went into the holy place, and shall leave them there. He shall bathe his body with water in a holy place and put on his clothes, and come forth and offer his burnt offering and the burnt offering of the people and make atonement for himself and for the people.** (Leviticus 16: 23-24)

So the high priest took off the linen garments, washed at the laver, and then he put on those special high priestly garments that were his to wear, the garments that were **"for beauty and for glory."** And he came back out to the people and made atonement at that time, again, for the people. Although it was accomplished in the Holy of Holies, he came back out to make another sacrifice for the people, in the spirit of "I'm back with you now."

Before the high priest reappeared before the people, he would set aside the garments of beauty and glory, wearing only the linen garments of white and went about his work. When they saw him again, after he finished his work, he came forth from that holy place dressed in those beautiful garments of glory.

I think this is a beautiful picture of the second coming of Christ. He has gone into the presence of the Lord and is now seated there, and the next time we see Him, He will be in His full glory. When He appears at the Second Coming, He is going to intercede based on Calvary, forgive, and extend atonement for the sins of Israel.

> **"And in that day I will set about to destroy all the nations that come against Jerusalem. I will pour out on the house of David and on the inhabitants of Jerusalem, the Spirit of grace and of supplication, so that they will look on Me whom they have pierced; and they will mourn for Him, as one mourns for an only son, and they will weep bitterly over Him like the bitter weeping over a firstborn."** (Zechariah 12:9-10)

When Jesus makes His appearance, Israel is going to look upon Him *whom they have pierced*, the crucified Christ, and they will wail and mourn in repentance and remorse over what they have done. They will mourn as for an only son. Who is Jesus? He is the only begotten Son of God (John 3:16). They will mourn as over a firstborn. And who is Jesus? He is the **"firstborn"** (in preeminence) over all creation (Colossians 1:15). They will look upon Jesus whom they have pierced. They will mourn for Him, the Christ, their Messiah, the Living God. And so there, in brokenness and repentance, they will realize that the Jesus those Christians always talked about is really their Messiah. On that day, the day of His return, it will hit them, as a nation, in the face.

> **"In that day a fountain will be opened for the house of David and for the inhabitants of Jerusalem, for sin and for impurity."** (Zechariah 13:1)

> And so all Israel will be saved; just as it is written,
> "The Deliverer will come from Zion,
> HE WILL REMOVE UNGODLINESS FROM JACOB." (Romans 11:26)

The Lord will immediately bring cleansing and forgiveness to them because of their repentance and because of their remorse for Him. It is just like Aaron, who came out in his holy garments and made atonement for Israel, right on the spot.

It's important to note that on the Day of Atonement, as the high priest fared, so fared Israel. If God accepted the high priest and the sacrifice the high priest brought into the Holy of Holies, God accepted Israel.

> **But when Christ appeared as a high priest of the good things to come, He entered through the greater and more perfect tabernacle, not made with hands, that is to say, not of this creation; and not through the blood of goats and calves, but through His own blood, He entered the holy place once for all, having obtained eternal redemption. For if the blood of goats and bulls and the ashes of a heifer sprinkling those who have been defiled sanctify for the cleansing of the flesh, how much more will the blood of Christ, who through the eternal Spirit offered Himself without blemish to God, cleanse your conscience from dead works to serve the living God?** (Hebrews 9:11-14)

The point is, as God accepts Jesus Christ, His only begotten Son, God accepts you. That is literally what it means. God accepts Jesus and He accepts you, because Jesus atoned for you.

I had a part-time job for a couple of years to help out the family income in addition to my pastoring. It was just a little one-day-a-week front-desk job at a motel at Lake Tahoe. There was a girl there who worked as a maid. She did not know the Lord, but when she found out I was a pastor, she made it a point to talk to me. Her life had been such a mess, and she wanted to know Jesus so badly. But she had a deep sense of unworthiness. I shared the principle with her that if God accepts Jesus, He accepts you. That is how much He loves you and He took your place for you. It is not a matter of your worthiness. It is a matter of His love and grace for you. I saw the light go on and Gina gave her heart to the Lord.

What a Lord we serve! What a beautiful Lord. We are never to forget that Jesus is the basis of our standing before God. With that in mind, do you realize, that there is no place, ever, in God's plan for your life, for discouragement? That has been dealt with. When you are discouraged, you are believing the lie of the enemy, every time. In Jesus Christ there is no place for discouragement.

> **Therefore if anyone is in Christ, he is a new creature;**

> the old things passed away; behold, new things have come. (2 Corinthians 5:17)

That verse right there summarizes what the Day of Atonement meant to Israel. So when that high priest would come out of that place in his holy garments, a cheer in Israel would go up. "Hallelujah! Glory to God! We have been cleansed before the Lord, forgiven before God."

Similarly, our standing with God is fresh, new, and alive. All the garbage of our lives is history. God has cleaned the slate. As we humbly and openly walk with Him by faith, our relationship with God is continually fresh and new. Anyone who is in Christ is a new creation. Every day, every single day, we are cleansed. It is not a matter of you once having been a new creation when you accepted the Lord, but now getting all messed up again. You are a new creation this moment. The old things, just like on the Day of Atonement, have passed away. New things have come, and that goes for today.

When I counsel someone who has gone down into the pit of despair after knowing the Lord, I can tell them that in Jesus they are a new creation. Through humble confession and repentance, the old is washed away, and there is a brand new person.

Granted there are consequences for the things we do. Do not get me wrong—I do not deny that; but we can face those consequences with the guiding hand and the power, sufficiency, and provision of our Lord Jesus Himself.

Darrell is a brother who is very involved in prison ministry. He told me about a man who recently went to court and was sentenced to four years in prison. At one of their prison ministry meetings, the guy just raised his hands up before the Lord and said, "I'm doing my time with Jesus." You can take any situation into His presence, be guided by His hand, and it can be used to bring glory to God.

You are a new person, old things are passed away. New things have come. That is the Day of Atonement. That is what God is crying out on that day. Their experience once a year is your moment-by-moment experience in Jesus Christ.

6. It was a day of rest.

> **This shall be a permanent statute for you: in the seventh**

> month, on the tenth day of the month, you shall humble your souls and not do any work, whether the native, or the alien who sojourns among you; for it is on this day that atonement shall be made for you to cleanse you; you will be clean from all your sins before the Lord. It is to be a sabbath of solemn rest for you, that you may humble your souls; it is a permanent statute. (Leviticus 16:29-31)

The Day of Atonement was a day of rest. It was a day in which they simply witnessed the grace of God. The high priest did the work. The people rested in God. In the New Testament we read:

> So there remains a Sabbath rest for the people of God. For the one who has entered His rest has himself also rested from his works, as God did from His. Therefore let us be diligent to enter that rest, so that no one will fall, through following the same example of disobedience. (Hebrews 4:9-11)

The Israelites in the wilderness were disobedient to God and did not enter into that rest of faith. On this day, the Day of Atonement, God told the people to rest. They were to rest in what God was doing, in what God and the high priest were accomplishing on their behalf. Again, in the New Testament we read:

> So then, my beloved, just as you have always obeyed, not as in my presence only, but now much more in my absence, work out your salvation with fear and trembling; for it is God who is at work in you, both to will and to work for His good pleasure. (Philippians 2:12-13)

"Work out your salvation" means resting by faith in God doing His work for you and through you in accomplishing the fullness of your salvation. You are saved, so let your salvation manifest itself and become evident in your life. We do that by resting in the work of God. If you are not resting in Him, you are working too hard, and it is futile work, absolutely futile. This is a gloriously liberating truth.

> So we see that they were not able to enter because of unbelief. Therefore, let us fear if, while a promise remains of entering His rest, any one of you may seem

> **to have come short of it.** (Hebrews 3:19 - 4:1)

A Christian can understand the basis of his relationship in the Lord and yet miss its meaningful effect in his daily life. So there is a definite life application to the believer as we look at the Day of Atonement. The Christian's standing before God is permanent. The veil of the temple was forever rent. So enter into that rest and abide in the Holy of Holies. Live and walk in the full reality and the blessing of His presence, power, and provision. It is a gift from Him to you.

> **The Lord your God is in your midst, a victorious warrior. He will exult over you with joy,**
> **He will be quiet in His love, He will rejoice over you with shouts of joy.** (Zephaniah 3:17)

That was where Peter was living when he was sentenced to death. He was to be executed the next day at the command of the king, Herod Agrippa. But when the angel came to rescue him from prison, the angel had to smite him to wake him up. I cannot fathom sleeping soundly the night before my scheduled execution.

The first recorded Christian concert in history consisted of Paul and Silas in the Philippian jail singing praises in the hearing of all the other prisoners and the jailer. They were singing praises to God after they had been scourged with whips, and then shackled in the inner chamber of that prison. Nevertheless, in the Spirit, they were dwelling in the Holy of Holies.

God is inviting you into the Holy of Holies, regardless of your circumstances. When the storms are raging around you, you can live in the place where people may come around, even Christians, and tell you that you are apparently not appreciating the gravity of the situation. They may tell you that you are too heavenly minded to be of any earthly good, just because you happen to be abiding in the Holy of Holies. You can rest, knowing that your God will guide, provide, lead, protect, and work out His glorious plan. We all have the privilege of just resting in Him. Near the end of his life and ministry, Paul wrote to Timothy:

> **For I am already being poured out as a drink offering, and the time of my departure has come. I have fought the good fight, I have finished the course, I have kept the faith; in the future there is laid up for me the crown**

> of righteousness, which the Lord, the righteous Judge, will award to me on that day; and not only to me, but also to all who have loved His appearing. (2 Timothy 4: 6-8)

Paul knew it was time for him to go. He had fought the good fight of faith. Fighting that good fight meant keeping himself in that place of rest, that place of faith in the Lord, without being jarred from it, whether by circumstances, by temptations, or lies of the enemy (however they come to you).

It is sad that, in being involved in a fellowship of believers, a lot of "jarring" comes from our own brothers and sisters in Christ. I am amazed how much we Christians can abuse each other. Even well-intentioned words, often shared in the guise of "telling the truth in love," can be so harmful when they are carelessly spoken by someone who does not understand how to abide with Jesus.

Paul said he fought the good fight, he had finished the course. He kept the faith. Henceforth there was a crown of righteousness waiting for him from Jesus. The crown was attained simply by steadfast faith.

Our tendency is to base our faith on our circumstances. If our circumstances are looking really good, then we must be blessed. If our circumstances are bad, then we go around saying, "I'm under spiritual attack, man." Or we just feel we are in an awful place and we cannot abide in the Holy of Holies because we are on the battle line, facing a big fight. However, circumstances should have nothing to do with our faith.

Peter could sleep the night before he was supposed to be executed. Though bloody and bruised, with open wounds, Paul and Silas could sing from a prison cell. It was from a prison in Rome that Paul wrote:

> **Rejoice in the Lord always; again I will say, rejoice!"**
> (Philippians 4:4)

Jesus has established and secured our place with Him. We can always go to God, whatever the situation. We all have trials and struggles. It is those very things God uses to teach us how to live in that place of rest in Him. You will not learn how to live there except by those trials and tribulation, so He governs them and only allows what will be ultimately beneficial to you to get you resting in Him.

I have not, by any sense of the word, "arrived" in my walk with the Lord. I can be just as crabby about something as the next person. But I have seen the faithfulness of God in some incredible ways.

One of the tough things about being a pastor is when the "sheep" bite you. You want to tend the sheep, but sometimes they bite, and it really hurts.

One Sunday we had a glorious service, but afterward this guy came up to me who was really hurting. He laid in to me and he raked me over the coals. He was in my face. I was a little concerned, because even though it was after the service, and a lot of people had taken off, there were still many people standing around talking and fellowshipping, and he was raising his voice. I was afraid this was going to become a "scene" in about one minute. But it was such a blessing to me to realize that, as he was in my face, I was not even upset. I had a peace, and because of that I could minister to him. I could help him. In fact, I reached out and gave him a hug. I could share openly with him from the Lord because I was not in the way, defending myself or being offended. It was glorious.

I recalled times in my past when something like that would happen and it would just fillet me. I would walk out of church wounded, licking my wounds, wanting to go home and find a quiet corner to just dress my wounds for a while. This was altogether different. God showed me right there that His work was being accomplished. God was helping me understand that I was dwelling with Him in the Holy of Holies, while this guy was ranting and raving in my face. It was a neat place to be, but it is through those kinds of situations that the Lord teaches us.

I tell people experiencing difficult times, "You do not have to be a super saint." All you have to do at that point is just survive, because God will work in you those qualities. We have a faithful Lord who is so good!

That brings up our final point.

7. The people were to humble their souls.

> **This shall be a permanent statute for you: in the seventh month, on the tenth day of the month, you shall humble your souls and not do any work, whether the native, or the alien who sojourns among you ...** (Leviticus 16:29)

On the Day of Atonement the people were to humble their souls. This was a **"permanent statute"** for them. He talks about the same thing in Leviticus chapter 23. Speaking of the Day of Atonement, He says:

> **On exactly the tenth day of this seventh month is the day of atonement; it shall be a holy convocation for you, and you shall humble your souls and present an offering by fire to the Lord.** (Leviticus 23:27)

Any person who would not humble himself on this same day was to be cut off from his people (Leviticus 23:29).

The humbling of the soul was and is very important to God. The King James Version uses the term **"afflict your souls."** The NIV says, **"deny yourselves."** But it all carries the same idea and the same principle. To not be humbled was to be cut off from the people, to be banished and possibly even sentenced to death. So that humbling was an extremely important aspect of that day and is to us also.

James does a great job of describing what this means to a believer.

> **Draw near to God and He will draw near to you. Cleanse your hands, you sinners; and purify your hearts, you double-minded. Be miserable and mourn and weep; let your laughter be turned into mourning and your joy to gloom. Humble yourselves in the presence of the Lord, and He will exalt you.** (James 4:8-10)

This passage explains pretty well what God is calling for on the Day of Atonement: brokenness and humility before the Lord. Apart from that you will not experience the fellowship of the saints or fellowship with your God. This will include "cleansing your hands and purifying your hearts." Hands refer to what we are doing, our actions. In Psalms we are told to:

> **Trust in the Lord and do good. ...** (Psalm 37:3a)

Doing good is the outcome of trusting in the Lord. How often we might like to simply trust in faith and know the situation is going to be fine. But maybe we are afraid that just having simple, child-like faith will not be enough.

Are you willing to tell the Lord that faith in Him will not work?

When Peter and Jesus needed some tax money, Jesus told Peter to put a line in the water. When he did, the first fish that came up had a coin in its mouth which covered the tax for both of them. Our God is able in any situation!

You can decide right now, from this moment forward, to begin to live your life by faith in God, humbly trusting and resting in His way and His will for your life. He is able to lead you, and He will honor His promises.

> **I have been young and now I am old, yet I have not seen the righteous forsaken or his descendants begging bread.** (Psalm 37:25)

David made a statement we can really cling to here. He had experienced a long and challenging life, but he saw God come through every time for those who were His. What a comfort!

When James says to **"purify your hearts"** (James 4:8), he means your attitude, your thinking. It is one thing to say you trust God and believe in Him, and it is quite another thing to really believe He will be faithful, whatever the circumstance.

Too often people say they believe in God and believe in Jesus, and they say they trust Him, but then they live like He really does not exist. They act as though He is not really going to do for them what He says He will do in His word.

I like what Dwight L. Moody said on one occasion about doubts. Someone came to him and said, "Mr. Moody, don't you ever have any doubts?"

Here was his reply: "I don't have time to doubt. Some people are full of doubts because they have nothing else to do. They have doubts at morning, at noon, and at night. They think doubts, doubts, doubts all the time. If you get busy in the Lord's work, you begin seeing Him answer your prayers and away go your doubts. How is one going to doubt when he sees a man delivered from the pit of sin, standing firmly secure in the grace of God for five, ten, or twenty years? And people say they can't help but doubt. My friend, you can get rid of doubts if you'll follow God's way. First, believe on Christ with your heart. Second, confess Him. Third, don't be ashamed of Him. Fourth, get to work for Him. It's that simple."

So, when James says, **"Be miserable, mourn, weep; let your laughter be turned into mourning and your joy to gloom,"** do it. Humble yourself before God! Get serious about it. Sin is a serious thing to God. It's what destroys lives; it is what sent Jesus to the cross; but, hallelujah, if you will **"Humble yourself in the presence of the Lord ... He will exalt you"** (James 4:10). That is a sure promise of God.

Like someone once put it, "It is through the valley of humility that leads the path to exaltation."

It comes down to God's desire that you live in His presence, despite the circumstances of life. Despite how brilliant you think you are or how lackluster you may feel. Live in that place and let Him do it all. He made you for a purpose; let Him use you, His way. That source of discouragement we face is actually God's avenue to exaltation.

Believe in the faithfulness of God. Entrust Him with everything in your life. Have real faith in your Heavenly Father. Live in that holy place of fellowship with your Creator. Abide with Christ in the tabernacle of His presence. He has made the way for you to do that.

You see, that's what the tabernacle in the wilderness is telling you. It's a shadow in the desert of the real thing, which is you abiding in Christ and enjoying His love and fellowship; always, forever.